Pentaho 5.0 Reporting By Example Beginner's Guide

Create high-quality, professional, standard reports using today's most popular open source reporting tool

Mariano García Mattío

Dario R. Bernabeu

BIRMINGHAM - MUMBAI

Pentaho 5.0 Reporting By Example Beginner's Guide

First published: August 2013

Production Reference: 2210813

Published by Packt Publishing Ltd.Livery Place
35 Livery Street
Birmingham B3 2PB, UK.

ISBN 978-1-78216-224-7

www.packtpub.com

Cover Image by Emilce Riot (emilceriot@yahoo.com)

Credits

Authors
Mariano García Mattío
Dario R. Bernabeu

Reviewers
Dan Keeley
Diethard Steiner

Acquisition Editor
Edward Gordon

Commissioning Editor
Llewellyn Rozario

Lead Technical Editor
Anila Vincent

Technical Editors
Vrinda Nitesh Bhosale
Jalasha D'costa
Mausam Kothari
Dominic Pereira
Sonali S. Vernekar
Anita Nayak

Copy Editors
Gladson Monteiro
Insiya Morbiwala
Aditya Nair
Adithi Shetty
Laxmi Subramanian

Project Coordinator
Rahul Dixit

Proofreaders
Faye Coulman
Jonathan Todd

Indexer
Rekha Nair

Graphics
Ronak Dhruv

Production Coordinator
Pooja Chiplunkar

Cover Work
Pooja Chiplunkar

About the Authors

Mariano García Mattío is a systems engineer for the IUA and specialist in distributed systems and services for the Facultad de Matemática Astronomía y Física (Faculty of Mathematics Astronomy and Physics) FaMAF UNC. He is an associate professor of: databases 1, databases 2, and advance database systems at the IUA, school of engineering; database engines at the IUA, school of administration; object-oriented programming paradigm, and distributed systems at the IUA's master in embedded systems. He is the teacher in charge of assignments for applied databases at the UCC. Also, Mariano is the co-director of the research project on new information and communication technologies at the UCC and co-director of the research project on networks monitoring and communication systems at the IUA. He is also a member of the Virtual Laboratories research project at the IUA and co-founder of eGluBI. He is the coordinator of the social network Open BI Network. He specializes in Java SE and Java EE technologies, node.js, administration and design of databases, and OSBI. His blog site is `http://jmagm.blogspot.com/`.

Dario R. Bernabeu is a systems engineer at the Instituto Universitario Aeronáutico (University Aeronautic Institute) IUA. He is the Cofounder of eGluBI (`www.eglubi.com.ar`). He specializes in development and implementation of OSBI solutions (Open Source Business Intelligence), project management, analysis of requirements/needs, deployment and configuration of BI solutions, design of data integration processes, data warehouse modelling, design of multidimensional cubes and business models, development of ad hoc reports, advanced reports, interactive analysis, dashboards, and so on. A teacher, researcher, geek, and open source software enthusiast, his most notable publication is "Data Warehousing: Research and Concept Systematization – HEFESTO: Methodology for the Construction of a DW". Being the coordinator of the social network Open BI Network (`www.redopenbi.com`), he makes many contributions to various forums, wikis, blogs, and so on. His blog site is: `http://tgx-hefesto.blogspot.com/`.

About the Reviewers

Dan Keeley is a computer science graduate who started his career in open source BI tools at the very beginning. He has full experience of the entire Pentaho stack and many successful implementations under his belt. He is a well-known Pentaho community member and founder of the Pentaho London Usergroup.

Diethard Steiner, currently working as an independent senior consultant in London, U.K., has been specialized in the field of open source business intelligence solutions for many years. He has been very passionate about his work, regularly publishing tutorials on his blog, *Diethard Steiner on Business Intelligence* (`http://diethardsteiner.blogspot.co.uk/`), which over the years has gained a loyal following. He has been implementing end-to-end solutions (from data integration to reporting and dashboards) for several clients and projects and has gained a deep understanding of the requirements and challenges of such solutions.

www.PacktPub.com

Support files, eBooks, discount offers and more

You might want to visit www.PacktPub.com for support files and downloads related to your book.

Did you know that Packt offers eBook versions of every book published, with PDF and ePub files available? You can upgrade to the eBook version at www.PacktPub.com and as a print book customer, you are entitled to a discount on the eBook copy. Get in touch with us at service@packtpub.com for more details.

At www.PacktPub.com, you can also read a collection of free technical articles, sign up for a range of free newsletters and receive exclusive discounts and offers on Packt books and eBooks.

http://PacktLib.PacktPub.com

Do you need instant solutions to your IT questions? PacktLib is Packt's online digital book library. Here, you can access, read and search across Packt's entire library of books.

Why Subscribe?

- Fully searchable across every book published by Packt
- Copy and paste, print and bookmark content
- On demand and accessible via web browser

Free Access for Packt account holders

If you have an account with Packt at www.PacktPub.com, you can use this to access PacktLib today and view nine entirely free books. Simply use your login credentials for immediate access.

Table of Contents

Preface

Pentaho 5.0 Reporting By Example Beginner's Guide is a practical book that clearly presents the concepts that form the foundation of what is to be learned and then puts those concepts into practice through step-by-step visual guides. This book, in addition to giving the what and the how, specifies the why. It also encourages the reader to create his or her own reports. You will feel confident about creating your own professional reports with graphics, formulas, subreports, and so on.

What this book covers

Chapter 1, What is Pentaho Report Designer?, provides a quick overview of Pentaho Report Designer (PRD), its engine, its common uses, its main features, and its evolution.

Chapter 2, Installation and Configuration, explains how to download, install, and configure PRD 5.0. It also describes how to configure system requirements in PRD and explains database use in the book.

Chapter 3, Start PRD and the User Interface (UI) Layout, explains how to start PRD in different operating systems, explains its layout, and explains each area of its user interface.

Chapter 4, Instant Gratification – Creating Your First Report with PRD, explains how to create your first report, how to define its data sets, how to configure the report's sections, how to add and set insertable objects and functions, and how to preview and export your report.

Chapter 5, Adding a Relational Data Source, explains how to download the JDBC driver of MySQL, how to create JDBC-type data sets, aggregation functions, and also how to modify the charset.

Chapter 6, Adding Groups, explains how to generate groups in the report and how to configure the behavior of the sections.

Chapter 7, Adding Parameters, explains how to create simple parameters and nested parameters, how to make a Parameter obtain its values through a data set, and how to dynamically construct SQL queries according to the values of Parameters.

Chapter 8, Using Formulas in Our Reports, explains how to create and use formulas.

Chapter 9, Adding Charts, explains a chart's functions, the good and bad practices of using charts, each type of chart, and how to create and configure your own charts.

Chapter 10, Adding Subreports, explains how to add and configure subreports and how to set its internal Parameters.

Chapter 11, Publishing and Running Reports in Pentaho BA Server, explains about Pentaho BA Server and how to publish, display, and work with your reports in the Pentaho User Console.

Chapter 12, Making a Difference – Reports with Hyperlinks and Sparklines, explains how to create, configure, and use Hyperlinks and Sparklines in your reports.

Chapter 13, Environment, Stylesheets, and Crosstabs, explains how to use, add, and configure environment variables, stylesheets, and crosstabs.

Chapter 14, PRD Reports Embedded in Web Applications, explains how to embed and run PRD reports in your web applications.

Appendix, Sakila DB Data Dictionary, , explains each table's data dictionary, as well as a small sample of the data.

What you need for this book

In order to use this book, you need a computer that is less than four years old with at least 1 GB of RAM memory and a good Internet connection.

When we started writing this book, stable versions of Pentaho Report Designer 5 and Pentaho BA Server 5 were not available. If the stable versions are still not available, when you have this book, you can download TRUNK versions from the following links:

- Pentaho Report Designer TRUNK (`http://ci.pentaho.org/view/Reporting/job/git-report-designer/`)
- Pentaho BA Server TRUNK (`http://ci.pentaho.com/view/Platform/job/BISERVER-CE/`)

Who this book is for

This book is ideal for a wide variety of profiles, irrespective of whether you have recently taken your first steps or are experienced in the world of Business Intelligence; whether you need to make professional reports in your organization or business or you are a developer and want to improve reporting in your applications. This book assumes that you understand the basic notions of databases and the SQL language, and that you have a computer with a Windows or Linux operating system and have Internet access.

Conventions

In this book, you will find several headings appearing frequently.

To give clear instructions of how to complete a procedure or task, we use:

Time for action – heading

1. Action 1
2. Action 2
3. Action 3

Instructions often need some extra explanation so that they make sense, so they are followed with:

What just happened?

This heading explains the working of tasks or instructions that you have just completed.

You will also find some other learning aids in the book, including:

Pop quiz – heading

These are short multiple-choice questions intended to help you test your own understanding.

Have a go hero – heading

These practical challenges give you ideas for experimenting with what you have learned.

You will also find a number of styles of text that distinguish between different kinds of information. Here are some examples of these styles, and an explanation of their meaning.

Code words in text are shown as follows: "We made a copy of the report `05_Adding_Groups.prpt` and saved it with the name `15_Adding_Hyperlinks_Sparklines.prpt`."

A block of code is set as follows:

```
SELECT country.country_id, country.country, customer.first_name,
customer.last_name, SUM(payment.amount) sum_amount,
payment.customer_id
FROM payment
INNER JOIN customer ON customer.customer_id=payment.customer_id
INNER JOIN address ON address.address_id=customer.address_id
INNER JOIN city ON city.city_id=address.city_id
INNER JOIN country ON country.country_id=city.country_id
WHERE country.country_id IN (20,24,29,34,48,67,74)
GROUP BY payment.customer_id
ORDER BY country.country, customer.first_name
```

When we wish to draw your attention to a particular part of a code block, the relevant lines or items are set in bold:

```
SELECT country.country_id, country.country, customer.first_name,
customer.last_name, SUM(payment.amount) sum_amount,
payment.customer_id
FROM payment
INNER JOIN customer ON customer.customer_id=payment.customer_id
INNER JOIN address ON address.address_id=customer.address_id
INNER JOIN city ON city.city_id=address.city_id
INNER JOIN country ON country.country_id=city.country_id
WHERE country.country_id IN (20,24,29,34,48,67,74)
GROUP BY payment.customer_id
ORDER BY country.country, customer.first_name
```

New terms and **important words** are shown in bold. Words that you see on the screen, in menus or dialog boxes for example, appear in the text like this: "On the **Select Destination Location** screen, click on **Next** to accept the default destination.".

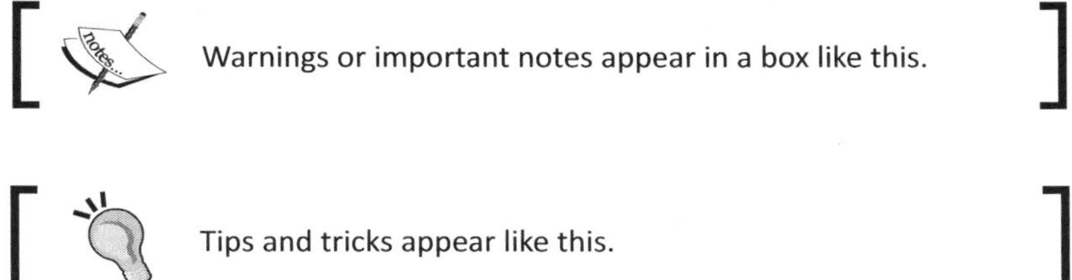

Warnings or important notes appear in a box like this.

Tips and tricks appear like this.

Reader feedback

Feedback from our readers is always welcome. Let us know what you think about this book—what you liked or may have disliked. Reader feedback is important for us to develop titles that you really get the most out of.

To send us general feedback, simply send an e-mail to `feedback@packtpub.com`, and mention the book title through the subject of your message.

If there is a topic that you have expertise in and you are interested in either writing or contributing to a book, see our author guide on `www.packtpub.com/authors`.

Customer support

Now that you are the proud owner of a Packt book, we have a number of things to help you to get the most from your purchase.

Errata

Although we have taken every care to ensure the accuracy of our content, mistakes do happen. If you find a mistake in one of our books—maybe a mistake in the text or the code—we would be grateful if you would report this to us. By doing so, you can save other readers from frustration and help us improve subsequent versions of this book. If you find any errata, please report them by visiting `http://www.packtpub.com/submit-errata`, selecting your book, clicking on the **errata submission form** link, and entering the details of your errata. Once your errata are verified, your submission will be accepted and the errata will be uploaded to our website, or added to any list of existing errata, under the Errata section of that title.

Piracy

Piracy of copyright material on the Internet is an ongoing problem across all media. At Packt, we take the protection of our copyright and licenses very seriously. If you come across any illegal copies of our works, in any form, on the Internet, please provide us with the location address or website name immediately so that we can pursue a remedy.

Please contact us at `copyright@packtpub.com` with a link to the suspected pirated material.

We appreciate your help in protecting our authors, and our ability to bring you valuable content.

Questions

You can contact us at `questions@packtpub.com` if you are having a problem with any aspect of the book, and we will do our best to address it.

1
What is Pentaho Report Designer?

In this chapter, we will explain what Pentaho Report Designer (PRD) is, and we will discuss its engine and its Graphical User Interface (GUI). We will also discuss the advantages that its open source license entails.

We will describe the two most common uses of PRD, which are embedding in Java projects and publishing to the Pentaho BA Server.

We will present the principal types of reports: Transactional Reporting, Tactical Reporting, Strategic Reporting, and Helper Reporting. As we will see throughout this book, PRD supports all of these types of reports.

Later, we will list the main features of PRD; this includes inserting charts (sparklines and JFreeCharts), a variety of export formats, parameterization, style expressions, crosstab reports, interactive reports, Java API, integration with the Pentaho suite, and abstraction layers.

We will make a brief review of the landmarks in the evolution of PRD and its different versions.

At the end of the chapter, we will display a series of PRD reports in order to show the scope of the potential capacities that PRD possesses.

Pentaho Reporting is a technology that allows you to design and build reports for the Pentaho BA platform and other application servers. **Pentaho Report Designer** (**PRD**) is a graphics tool that implements the report-editing function. The project from which PRD originated was originally called JFreeReport.

PRD is an open source tool licensed under the **GNU Lesser General Public License** (**GNU LGPL**). This license provides the four basic freedoms of free software and the GNU GPL. And the *L* (Lesser) in LGPL indicates that this software can be used as part of or in combination with proprietary software, which provides greater flexibility for different licenses and software to coexist.

> For more information about free software and the GNU project, visit `http://www.gnu.org/`.
>
> To read more about the GNU GPL and GNU LGPL licenses, visit `http://www.gnu.org/licenses/licenses.en.html`.

PRD contains a Java-based report engine that provides scalability, portability, and integration. Additionally, the editor's UI is implemented with Swing widgets, which give it a friendly, multiplatform look and feel. This UI is very intuitive, and it allows you to become familiar with the tools quickly.

PRD lets you create simple reports, wizard-based reports, advanced reports, reports with charts, subreports, parameterized reports, and others. Once a report has been created, PRD lets you export it in a variety of formats, such as PDF, Excel, HTML, and CSV, or preview it using Swing.

Since the beginning, PRD has benefitted from multiple contributions from the community, and currently the community supporting this project is growing and becoming more stable and contributing regularly in the form of code, wikis, documentation, forums, bug reports, tutorials, and so on.

> Here are some interesting links about PRD:
>
> 
>
> - **Official blog**: `http://www.on-reporting.com`
>
> 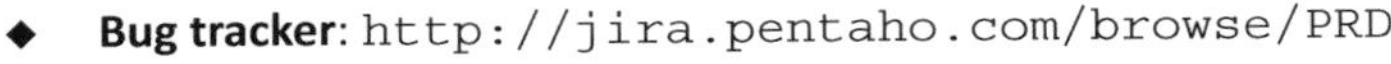
>
> - **Bug tracker**: `http://jira.pentaho.com/browse/PRD`
>
> 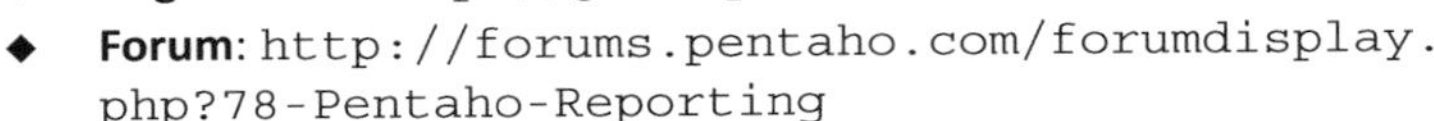
>
> - **Forum**: `http://forums.pentaho.com/forumdisplay.php?78-Pentaho-Reporting`
> - **Wiki**: `http://wiki.pentaho.com/display/Reporting/Report+Designer`

PRD has two typical uses as follows:

- It can be embedded in Java projects in desktop and web applications. In this book, we will develop a good example of how to embed PRD reports in web applications.
- It can, in a few steps, publish reports to the Pentaho BA Server to be used from there. It can, furthermore, be embedded in other application servers. These points will also be addressed in this book.

Types of reports

There are various categories that reports can be grouped into. From our perspective, the following categories are the most important:

- **Transactional reports**: Data for these reports comes from transactions and their objective is to present data at a very detailed and granular level. This type of report is usually used in an organization's day-to-day business. Examples of this kind of report are sales receipts, purchase orders, and so on.
- **Tactical reports**: Data for these reports comes from summaries of transactional data. The level of summary is low, usually not more than daily or weekly. This type of report contains information to support short-term decision making. For example, a stock inventory allows us to place orders to replace merchandise.
- **Strategic reports**: These reports commonly used data sources clean, reliable and stable, for example of a data warehouse, and their goal is to create business information. This kind of report supports medium and long-term decision making and is usually highly summarized; it allows for parameterization and includes charts and subreports. For example, a seasonal analysis of sales lets us determine what marketing campaigns should be carried out at given periods of time.
- **Helper reports**: Data for these reports comes from diverse origins and contains information that may not be normalized, including photos, images, and bar codes. This kind of report is not aimed at supporting decision making but serves a variety of interests. Examples of this kind of report are technical product descriptions, letterheads, ID cards, and so on.

Defining data

Data is an expression that describes some characteristic of an entity. For example, in saying that a box is black, we are specifying data (black) regarding a characteristic (color) of an entity (box).

Defining information

Information is obtained through data processing. Data can be processed through summary, classification, grouping, and ordering.

Main features of Pentaho Report Designer

The following are some of PRD's principal characteristics:

- **Reporting algorithm**: PRD avoids compiling reports, a method that other reporting tools use, and combining the report layout with data as it is acquired. Initially, the algorithm calculates and determines how to separate the data into groups, subgroups, and so on, and calculates the height, width, position, and style of the elements (text, images, and so on); later, the data is placed where it belongs in order to obtain the desired output.
- **Diverse data sources**: This includes JDBC (this allows access to most databases), Pentaho Metadata, Pentaho Data Integration, OLAP, XML, in-line table, Sequence Generator, Query Scripting, Java Method Invocation, Hibernate, Open ERP, CDA, and so on.
- **Diverse output formats**: These are PDF, Excel, Excel 2007, HTML, RTF, CSV, XML, and Text. PRD renders reports with high image quality.
- **Insertable objects**: PRD lets you add text fields, labels, images, charts, subreports, shapes, lines, sparklines, hyperlinks, bar codes, and other objects to your reports. Objects are inserted in the UI by simply dragging and dropping.
- **Charts**: There are two categories of charts that can be added to reports in PRD; they are as follows:
  - **Sparklines**: These are inline charts. PRD supports bar, line, and pie sparklines.
  - **JFreeChart charts**: These are traditional charts. PRD supports bar, line, area, pie, multipie, barline, ring, bubble, scatter-plot, XY-bar, XY-line, XY-area, extended XY-line, waterfall, radar, and XY-area-line charts.
- **Parameterization**: PRD allows you to define parameters that can be used in different parts of the report; for example, as a filter for a SQL query, as the text of a label, as part of a formula, and as a style attribute, among others. Regarding the type of presentation, PRD provides the following widgets to supply parameter values: drop-down menus, simple-value lists, multivalue lists, radio buttons, checkboxes, single selection buttons, multiselection buttons, textboxes, text areas, and date pickers.
- **Formulas and style expressions**: PRD allows you to assign a style property according to the value of a formula, expression, or fixed value. For example, if the value of the field "quantity" is greater than 50, you can make the background color of a given shape green. You can also use formulas to create new fields and calculate their values.

- **Crosstab report**: PRD lets you create powerful reports based on cross tabs using a simple wizard.
- **Interactive reports**: PRD lets you add interactivity to your reports, making it possible to expand/collapse groups, add hyperlinks to other reports, and so on.
- **Wizard**: PRD includes a wizard that lets you create a report through simple and intuitive steps.
- **Publication**: From the PRD UI, you can publish directly to the Pentaho BA Server.
- **Java API**: PRD includes a very extensive API that lets you execute, create, and modify reports without using the UI.
- **Extendibility**: PRD lets you add new functionality through the incorporation of plugins.
- **Stylesheet support**: PRD supports internal storage or external access to CSS3 stylesheets.
- **Integration with the Pentaho suite**: PRD is easily integrated with the other tools in the Pentaho suite, including **Pentaho Data Integration** (**PDI**) and C-Tools (CDF and CDA).
- **Pentaho Data Integration**: PDI implements a transformation step that lets you execute and parameterize PRD reports; this allows you to implement mailing and report bursting, among many other possibilities.
- **Community Dashboard Framework** (**CDF**): This implements a component for working with PRD reports. **Community Data Access** (**CDA**) can be added as a plugin PRD, with the goal that our reports can get their data from a CDA connection.
- **Abstraction layers**: When an end user creates a report, they usually see the process as a whole. The process of creating a report in PRD can be separated into three parts: the selection of data source to use, the design/layout of the report, and the final presentation format. PRD defines two layers of abstraction between these three parties, allowing each party to become independent of the other and the report to be adapted to different contexts and needs. For example, if a report is created based on a data source developed in MySQL and is later published to a Pentaho BA Server connected to a PostgreSQL production database, the report will be adapted to this context and will be able to be executed without change.

The following illustration demonstrates before to publish in Pentaho BA Server using MySQL and a presentation in PDF:

The following diagram illustrates after to publish in Pentaho BA Server using PostgreSQL and a presentation in HTML:

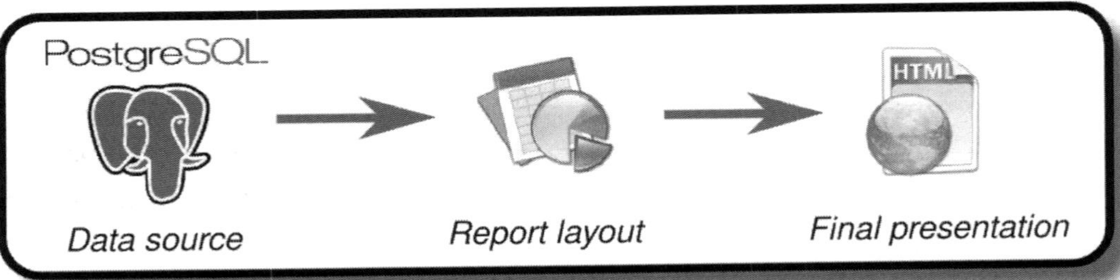

History

Landmarks in the evolution of PRD are as follows:

- **2002**: *David Gilbert* (author of JFreeChart) implements the first version of JFreeReport. Soon after, *Thomas Morgner* becomes the lead developer. The JFreeReport project is very successful and many people begin to contribute to it.
- **2006**: *Thomas* joins Pentaho, changing the name to Pentaho Reporting. Thomas becomes a developer for the **Pentaho Reporting Engine** and other suite tools.
- **January 2006**: Pentaho announces that Pentaho Report Designer (PRD) Wizard is available for creating reports. *Mike D'Amour* becomes the initial author of this wizard.

- **June 2006**: *Martin Schmid* contributes the first version of PRD to the community. From this point forward, the designer is developed in parallel with the engine.
- **November 2006**: (BA Server, Version 1.6) Pentaho Reporting is integrated with the Pentaho Metadata Engine to create ad hoc reports.
- **April 2007**: The Pentaho team joins OpenOffice.org to distribute a reports solution for the OOo database tool. This project is led by *Thomas Morgner* and comes to be known as the **Pentaho Reporting Flow Engine**.
- **December 2007**: The development of version 1.0 of the PRD Classic Engine begins.
- **March 2008**: A native data source is added for Pentaho Data Integration.
- **June 2008**: The Olap4j data source is added; it provides connectivity to Mondrian and other OLAP sources and the possibility of executing MDX queries. Implementing cross tabs is discussed.
- **June 2009**: PRD supports **Rich Text Format** (**RTF**) and script-based data sources are added (Scriptable Datasource).
- **June 2010**: The Table of Contents component is added.
- **October 2010**: The Drill Linking characteristic is added.
- **November 2010**: Execution environment information is available via ENV Fields.
- **December 2010**: The development of the Community Data Access (CDA) data source begins.
- **January 2011**: PRD cache development begins.
- **July 2011**: Sparklines are added.
- **November 2011**: Version Checker is added.
- **April 2011**: 10 years since the creation of JFreeReports.

The evolution of different versions of PRD can be seen in SourceForge via the link `http://sourceforge.net/projects/pentaho/files/Report%20Designer/` as follows:

- 2007 – November: Version 1.6
- 2008 – June: Version 1.7
- 2009 – January: Version 2.0
- 2009 – August: Version 3.0
- 2009 – November: Version 3.5
- 2010 – March: Version 3.6

- 2010 – December: Version 3.7
- 2011 – March: Version 3.8
- 2012 – May: Version 3.9
- 2013 – Version 5.0

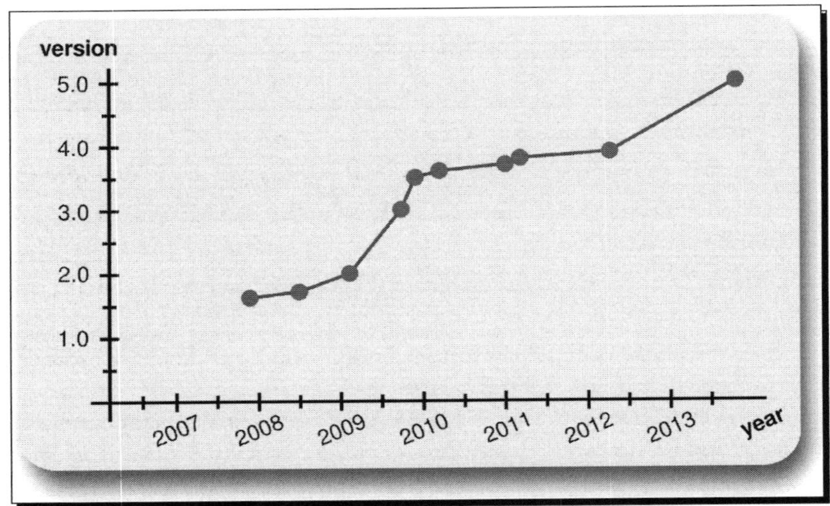

Examples of typical reports

In the following sections, we present a series of PRD reports typically included as examples of Pentaho solutions and in the sample reports of PRD.

The buyer report

The buyer report is found at the following location in the top menu:

Help | Sample Reports | Operational Reports | Buyer Report

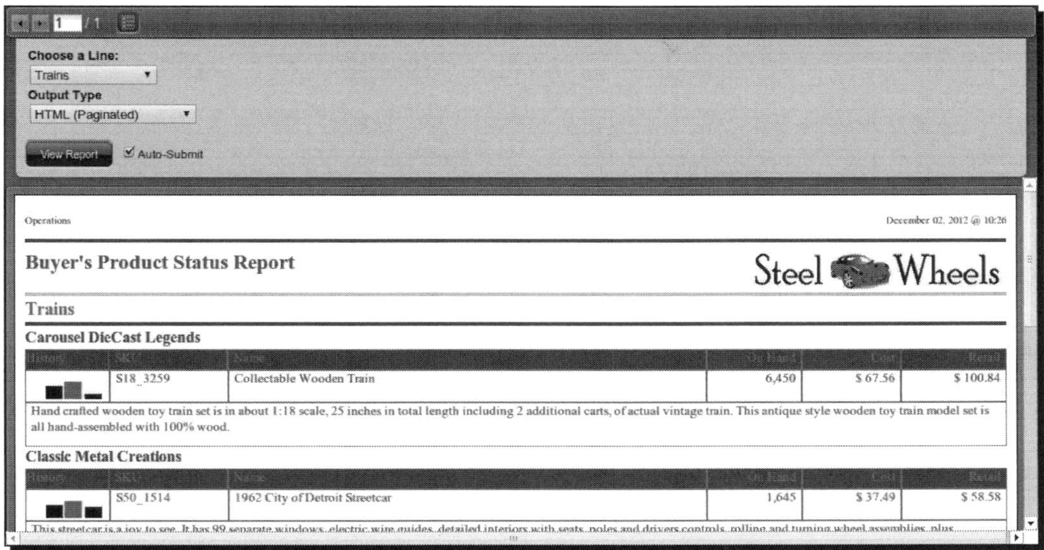

This report presents an analysis of the products belonging to each product line grouped by the vendor. For each product, it shows a sparkline with information about the sales of this product in the last three years. This report allows the end user to select the product line to be displayed.

As can be seen in the top part of the report, there are two selectors for passing parameters to the report:

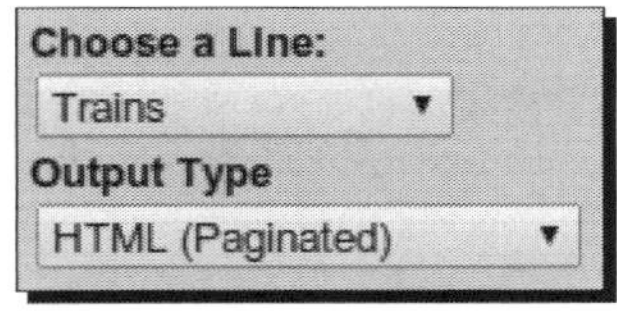

The selectors will then show a report of the product line (**Choose a Line:**) indicated in the parameter, in this case **Trains**, and its visualization format will be the one chosen in **Output Type**, in this case **HTML (Paginated)**.

To show information about each product, this report uses sparklines, text, numbers, and monetary values (in dollars):

History	SKU	Name	On Hand	Cost	Retail
	S18_3259	Collectable Wooden Train	6,450	$ 67.56	$ 100.84

Also, an image has been placed in the report title (see the first screenshot of this section).

The income statement

The income statement report is found at the following location in the top menu:

Help | Sample Reports | Financial Reports | Income Statement

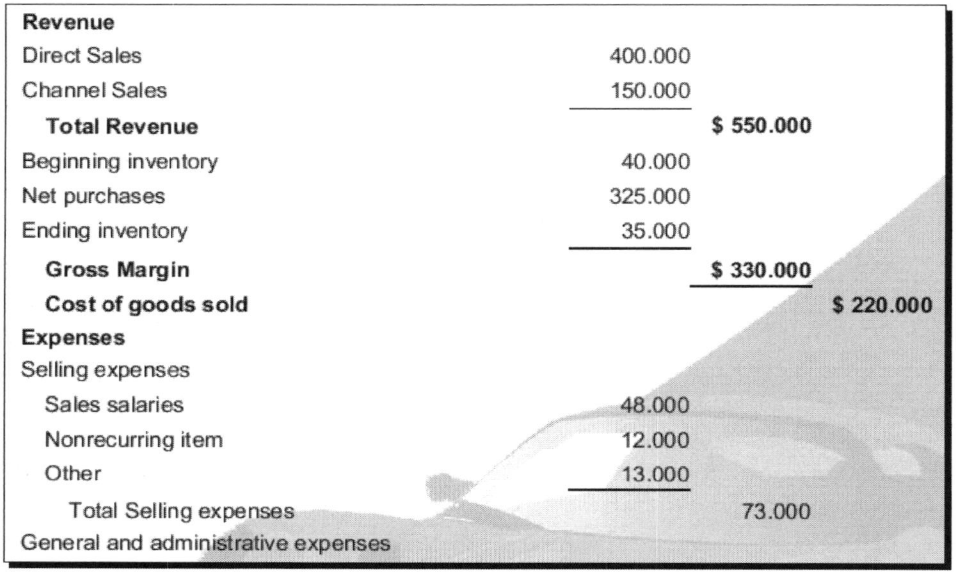

Revenue			
Direct Sales	400.000		
Channel Sales	150.000		
Total Revenue		**$ 550.000**	
Beginning inventory	40.000		
Net purchases	325.000		
Ending inventory	35.000		
Gross Margin		**$ 330.000**	
Cost of goods sold			**$ 220.000**
Expenses			
Selling expenses			
Sales salaries	48.000		
Nonrecurring item	12.000		
Other	13.000		
Total Selling expenses		73.000	
General and administrative expenses			

This report shows the current income statement of the company and shows calculations of totals and subtotals, grouping each item in its respective category (Revenue, Cost of Goods, and so on).The default for the **Output Type** parameter value has been set to PDF, so when it is executed, it will download the file `Income Statement.pdf`. If you prefer to view the report in another format, you only have to change the value of the **Output Type** parameter.

This report has an image as a background.

The inventory list

The inventory list report is found at the following location in the top menu:

Help | Sample Reports | Operational Reports | Inventory List

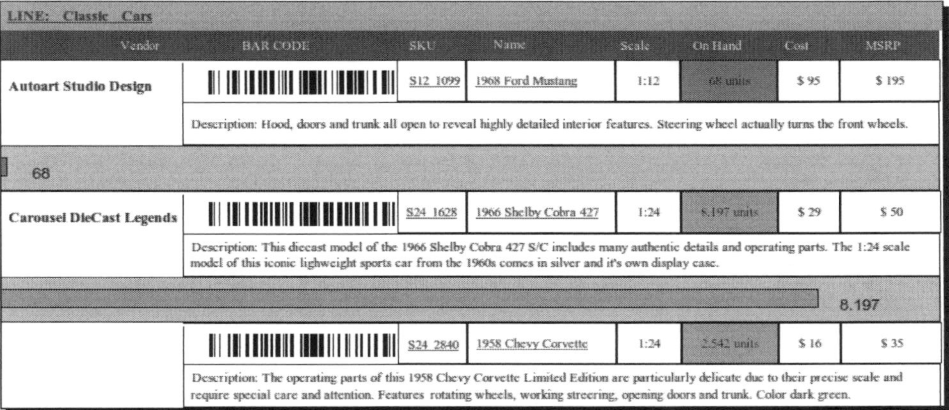

LINE: Classic Cars

Vendor	BAR CODE	SKU	Name	Scale	On Hand	Cost	MSRP
Autoart Studio Design		S12 1099	1968 Ford Mustang	1:12	68 units	$ 95	$ 195
	Description: Hood, doors and trunk all open to reveal highly detailed interior features. Steering wheel actually turns the front wheels.						
68							
Carousel DieCast Legends		S24 1628	1966 Shelby Cobra 427	1:24	8.197 units	$ 29	$ 50
	Description: This diecast model of the 1966 Shelby Cobra 427 S/C includes many authentic details and operating parts. The 1:24 scale model of this iconic lighweight sports car from the 1960s comes in silver and it's own display case.						
8.197							
		S24 2840	1958 Chevy Corvette	1:24	2.542 units	$ 16	$ 35
	Description: The operating parts of this 1958 Chevy Corvette Limited Edition are particularly delicate due to their precise scale and require special care and attention. Features rotating wheels, working streering, opening doors and trunk. Color dark green.						

This report shows information about the stock of products and allows the end user to select one or more product lines that need to be shown.

This report uses bar codes:

It uses hyperlinks (drill through) to other reports:

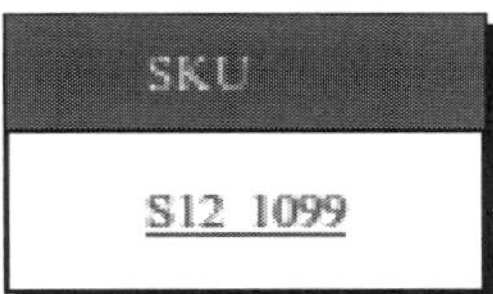

If you click on the values in the field **SKU**, a new tab will open displaying a report with additional information about this SKU. In this case, if we click on **S12_1099**, a report shown in the following screenshot will appear:

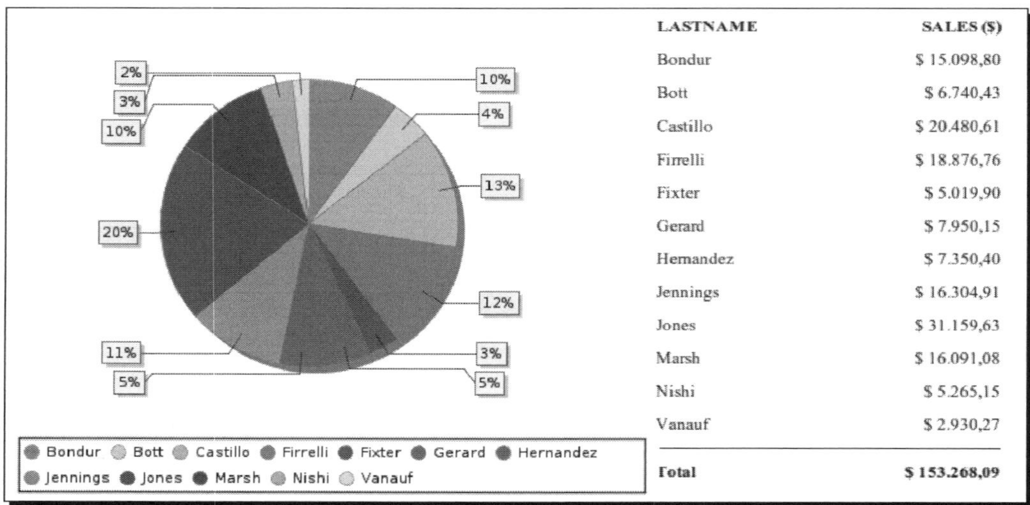

LASTNAME	SALES ($)
Bondur	$ 15.098,80
Bott	$ 6.740,43
Castillo	$ 20.480,61
Firrelli	$ 18.876,76
Fixter	$ 5.019,90
Gerard	$ 7.950,15
Hernandez	$ 7.350,40
Jennings	$ 16.304,91
Jones	$ 31.159,63
Marsh	$ 16.091,08
Nishi	$ 5.265,15
Vanauf	$ 2.930,27
Total	**$ 153.268,09**

It also uses links of web pages:

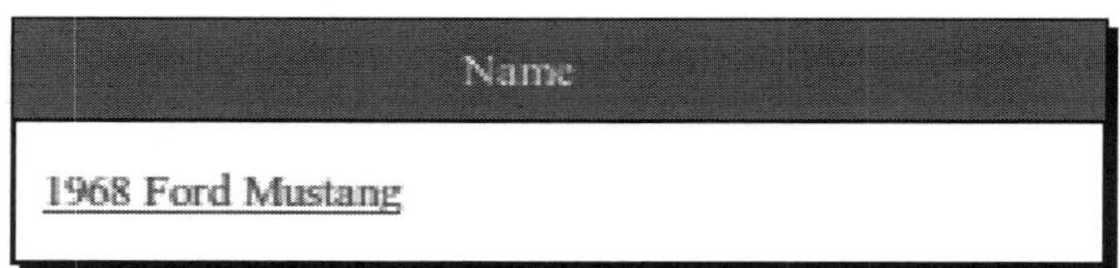

Name
1968 Ford Mustang

If you click on the values in the field **Name**, a new web browser tab opens with a web page that searches for Google Images.

This report uses conditional formatting, that is, the background color of the field **On Hand** is determined according to certain values and conditions. This allows for the viewing of the statuses of the reports through indicators in a very simple way, that is, the indicator is green when the values are good, yellow when they are acceptable, and red when they are bad.

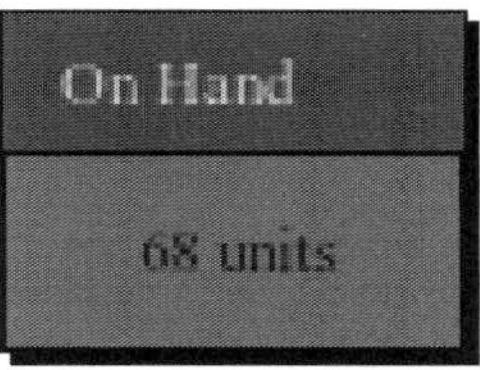

Invoice

The invoice report is found at the following location in the top menu:

Help | Sample Reports | Production Reports | Invoice

TO: Australian Gift Network, Co
31 Duncan St. West End,
South Brisbane, Queensland 4101 Australia

INVOICE

Attn: Tony Calaghan
Sales Rep: 1611
Terms: Net 30 days

Invoice #: 10152
Account Number: 333
Date: septiembre 25, 2003

SKU	Product Description	Price/Unit	Qty..	Total Price
S18_4027	1970 Triumph Spitfire	$4.524,10	35	$4.524,10
S32_3207	1950's Chicago Surface Lines Streetcar	$1.681,35	33	$1.681,35
S24_4048	1992 Porsche Cayenne Turbo Silver	$2.802,09	23	$2.802,09
S24_1444	1970 Dodge Coronet	$1.632,75	25	$1.632,75
				$10.640,29

Payment History

Date	Check#	Amount
11-15-03	HL209210	$ 27.098,80
10-17-03	JK479662	$ 10.640,29
03-01-05	NF959653	$ 21.730,03

Send Payment and Remittance Slip to:
Steel Wheels
500 International Speedway
Daytona Beach FL 32114

Thank you for your business!

This report shows all the invoices that have been issued to customers. Each invoice is presented on a separate page, and the end user has the ability to select the client they want to analyze.

This report, showing **Payment History**, uses sub-reports.

Product Sales

The product sales report is found at the following location in the top menu:

Help | Sample Reports | Operational Reports | Product Sales

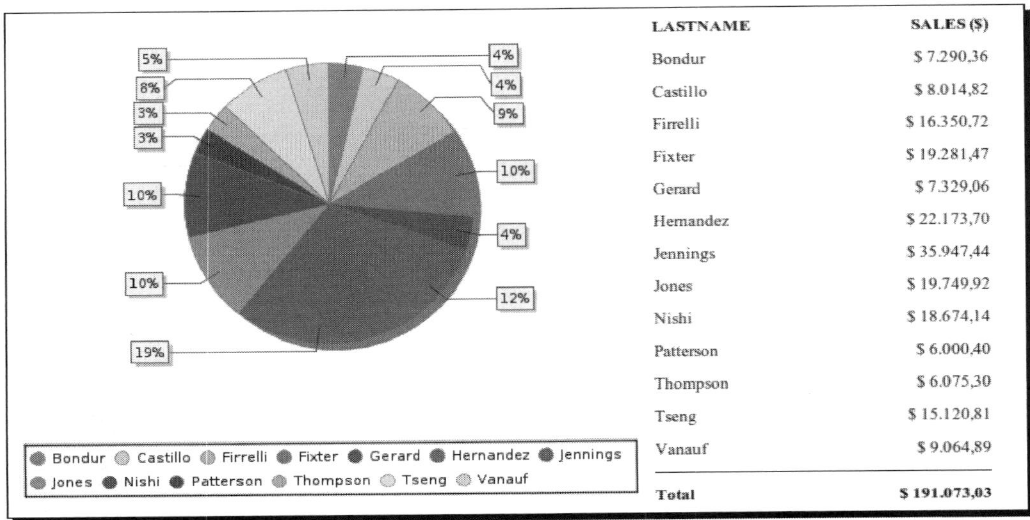

5%
8%
3%
3%
10%
10%
19%
4%
4%
9%
10%
4%
12%
Bondur Castillo Firrelli Fixter Gerard Hernandez Jennings
Jones Nishi Patterson Thompson Tseng Vanauf
LASTNAME SALES ($)
Bondur $ 7.290,36
Castillo $ 8.014,82
Firrelli $ 16.350,72
Fixter $ 19.281,47
Gerard $ 7.329,06
Hernandez $ 22.173,70
Jennings $ 35.947,44
Jones $ 19.749,92
Nishi $ 18.674,14
Patterson $ 6.000,40
Thompson $ 6.075,30
Tseng $ 15.120,81
Vanauf $ 9.064,89
Total $ 191.073,03

This report shows information about sales made to the customers. On the left-hand side, a pie chart shows the percentage of sales made to each customer and on the right-hand side, a sub-report shows a list of the amount of sales in detail.

It is important to point out that the parameter selectors are related, that is, once a value is chosen for **Line**, only products belonging to that line will be shown in the options of the selector **Product**:

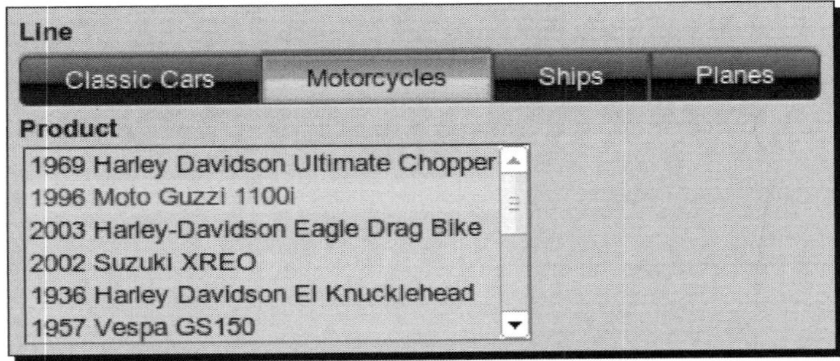

Top N Customers

This report is found at the following location in the top menu:

Help | Sample Reports | Operational Reports | Top N Customers

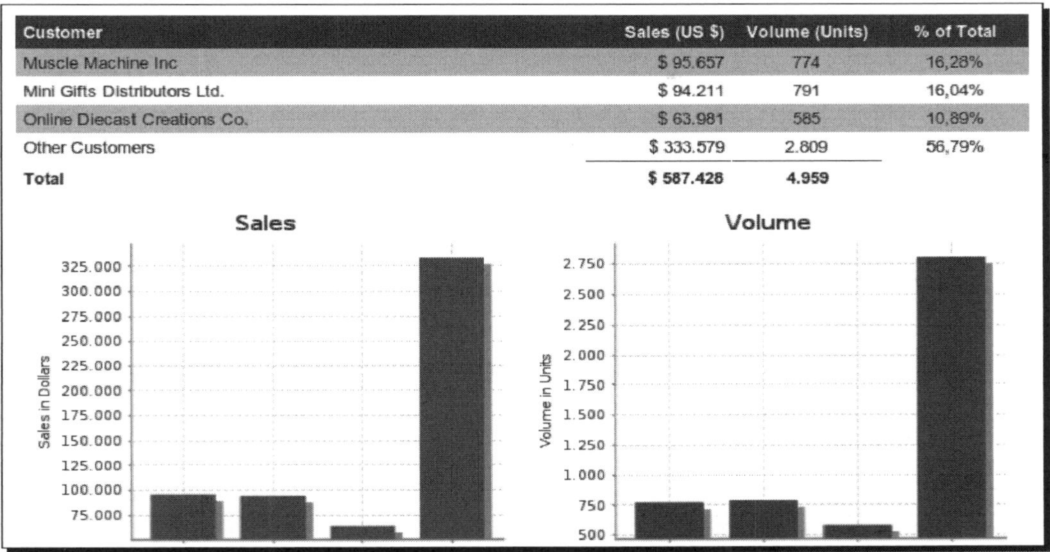

Customer	Sales (US $)	Volume (Units)	% of Total
Muscle Machine Inc	$ 95.657	774	16,28%
Mini Gifts Distributors Ltd.	$ 94.211	791	16,04%
Online Diecast Creations Co.	$ 63.981	585	10,89%
Other Customers	$ 333.579	2.809	56,79%
Total	**$ 587.428**	**4.959**	

This report shows an analysis of the top *N* customers; here *N* can be defined via a parameter. It also displays information amount and percentage of the total sales, and uses a table and two bar charts.

HTML actions

This report is found at the following location in the top menu:

Help | Sample Reports | Advanced | HTML Actions

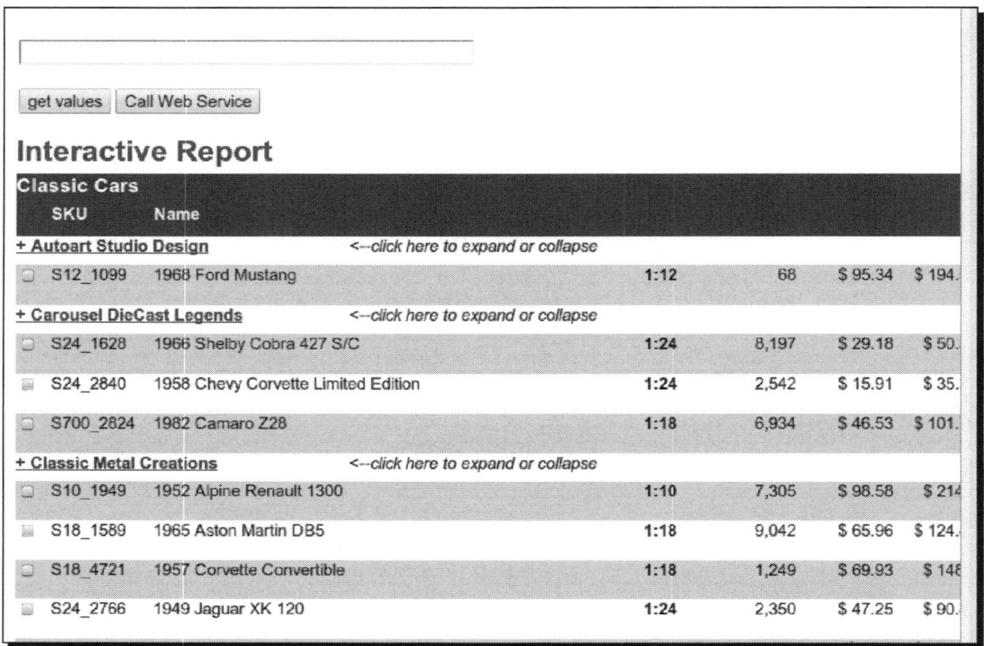

This report shows a list of products grouped by the vendor and provides information about their code, name, purchase price, and so on. Furthermore, it lets us expand or collapse the different groups. That is, if you click on **+ Autoart Studio Design**, all the child nodes collapse.

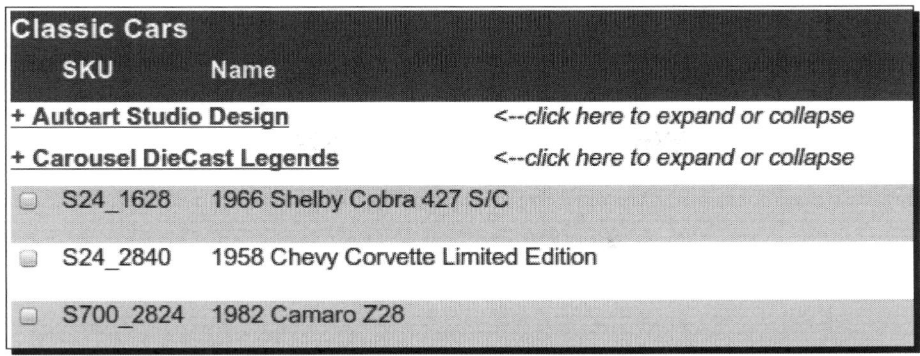

This report lets us search for the models of the cars we choose in Google Images. For example, choose **1966 Shelby Cobra 427 S/C** as shown in the following screenshot:

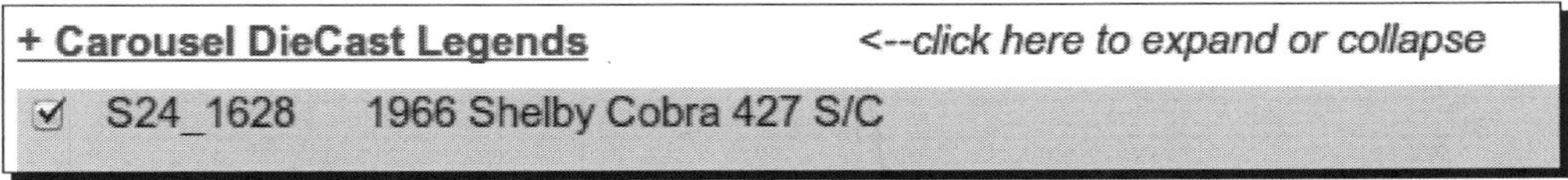

Click on the **get values** button. You will see that all the auto models will be shown in the following screenshot:

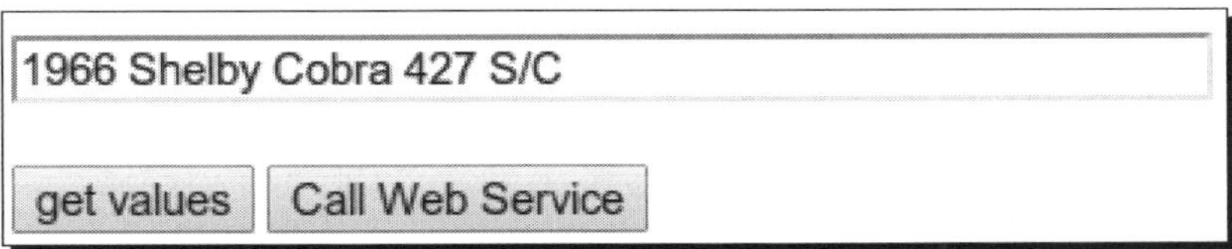

Click on the **Call Web Service** button; a new web browser window will open with a web page that searches for Google Web.

Summary

In this chapter, we saw that Pentaho Report Designer (PRD) is a very powerful tool for report editing and that it is licensed under the GNU LGPL. We also saw that it has a Java-based report engine and that the editor's UI is implemented with Swing widgets.

We saw that it can be embedded in Java projects in desktop and web applications, and that it can publish reports to the Pentaho BA Server.

We discussed the different types of reports, such as Transactional Reports and Tactical Reports, and their principal characteristics. We also discussed that what makes each of these reports different from others is their data source, their granularity, and their final goal.

We detailed the principal characteristics of PRD through which we were able to show its robustness, flexibility, and interactivity.

We listed each landmark in the development of PRD, following its evolution with each new contribution and functionality. We also showed in a small graph how PRD versions advanced over time.

By the end of this chapter, we are able to appreciate the quantity and variety of reports that PRD lets us create.

In the next chapter we will look at the system requirements to be able to execute PRD. We will download, install, and configure PRD 5.0. Furthermore, we will download and install a database sample.

2
Installation and Configuration

In this chapter we will look at the system requirements to be able to correctly execute the Pentaho Report Designer (PRD), and we will explain how to meet these requirements step-by-step.

We will download PRD 5.0 from `SourceForge.net` *and explain how different versions of PRD are organized on the download site.*

Once we have downloaded PRD, we will install it in our operating system. We will also explain how to configure the drivers that will be used and how to assign more RAM to the PRD execution environment.

Throughout this book we use the MySQL example database Sakila DB for creating different reports. We will explain what Sakila DB is and how to download and install it using the MySQL command-line processor (CLP).

We will show the tables of Sakila DB and their relations using entity relationship diagrams (ERD).

In this chapter we will learn how to:

- Install the JDK
- Set the `JAVA_HOME` and `PATH` variables
- Download and install Pentaho Report Designer 5.0
- Configure the memory for PRD
- Configure JDBC drivers to be used in PRD
- Download and install the sample database, Sakila DB

Configuring the environment

The system requirements needed to run PRD are installing JDK and configuring the environment variables.

System requirements

To correctly execute PRD, the following are necessary:

- The **Java Runtime Environment** (**JRE**) 1.7 or higher installed
- The `JAVA_HOME` variable configured
- The `PATH` variable entry configured, pointing to `[JAVA_HOME]/bin`

While only JRE is necessary to execute PRD and the other applications that we will discuss in this book, we will also need the Java Development Kit (JDK) to develop one of the applications in the last chapters. For this reason, we will install JDK 1.7.

JDK also includes the **Java Virtual Machine** (**JVM**), a series of tools that lets us develop Java applications, including a compiler, a debugger, the API source code, the JRE, and so on.

Time for action – installing JDK and configuring the environment variables

To configure the `JAVA_HOME` and `PATH` variables, follow these steps:

Installing on a LINUX environment:

1. Install JDK 1.7. You can go to the official Java website (`www.java.com`), download the installer file and then execute it in your operating system. Or you can execute the following commands in a terminal:

   ```
   shell> sudo add-apt-repository ppa:webupd8team/java
   shell> sudo apt-get update
   shell> sudo apt-get install oracle-java7-installer
   ```

2. Write the following command in the terminal:

   ```
   shell> sudo gedit /etc/environment
   ```

3. Add a line in this file that contains the following (or similar, depending on each environment):

   ```
   JAVA_HOME="/usr/lib/jvm/java-7-oracle"
   ```

4. To the beginning of the value of the `PATH` variable, add the `/usr/lib/jvm/java-7-oracle/bin:` string.

The separator for the `PATH` entries in Linux environments is ":".

5. The `/etc/environment` file should look like this:

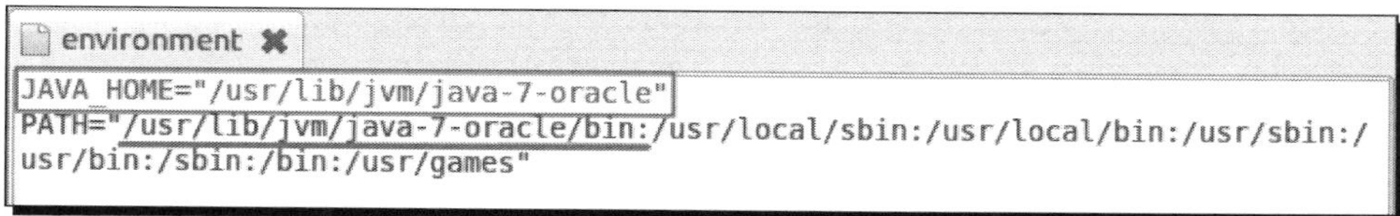

6. Restart the session.

In Windows environments:

1. Install JDK 1.7. Go to the official Java website (`www.java.com`), download the installer file, and then execute it in your operating system.
2. Click on the **Environment Variables...** option:

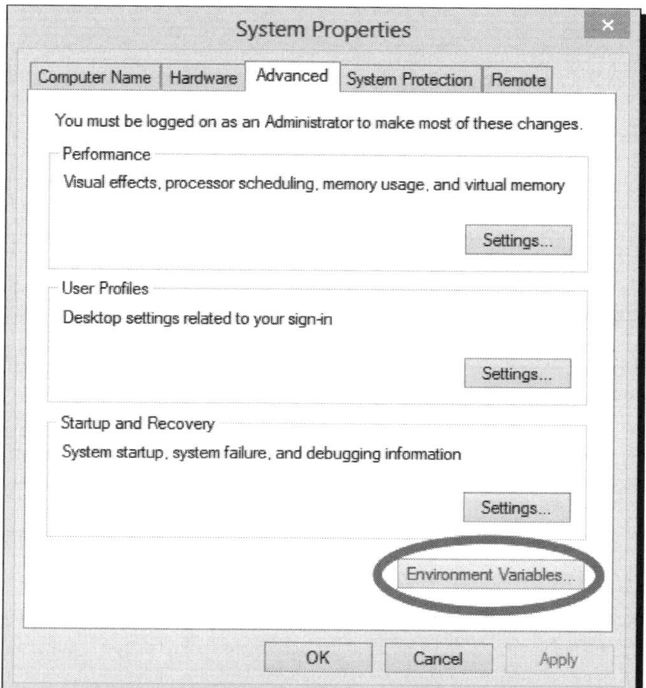

3. To add the `JAVA_HOME` system variable, click on the **New...** button that is found in the **System variables** section:

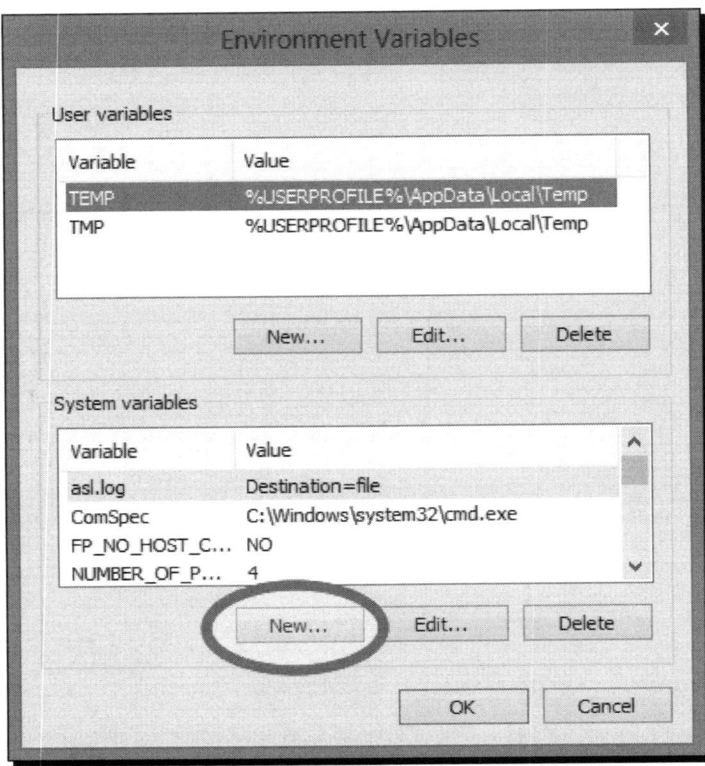

4. This action will open a new window, where we must fill in the following values:

- In **Variable name:**, type `JAVA_HOME`.
- In **Variable value:**, type the path that corresponds to the JDK installation. For example, add a system variable with the name `JAVA_HOME` and complete its value with the corresponding path, say, **C:\Program Files\Java\jdk1.7.0_04**, as shown in the following screenshot:

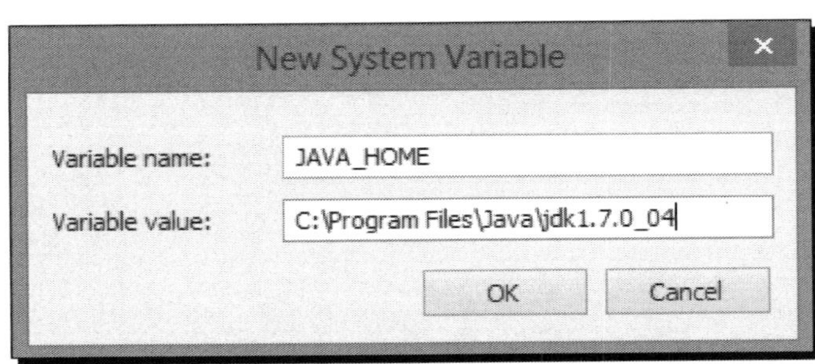

5. Click on **OK** to save the changes and exit.
6. In the **System variables** section, select the `PATH` variable and click on the **Edit...** button.
7. At the beginning of the value of the `PATH` variable, add the `%JAVA_HOME%\bin;` string.
8. The separator for `PATH` entries in the Windows environment is **;** as shown in the following screenshot:

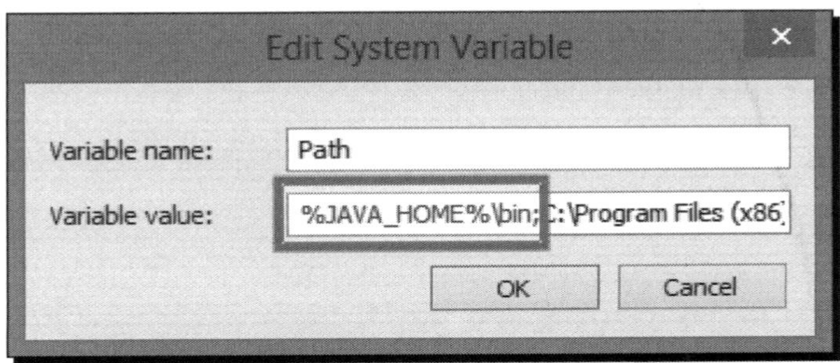

9. Press **OK** to save changes and exit.
10. Restart your computer.

To confirm the correct installation in Linux as well as in Windows, we can execute the following command in a terminal:

```
shell> java -version
```

We should obtain a result similar to the following:

```
java version "1.7.0_04"
Java(TM) SE Runtime Environment (build 1.7.0_04-b20)
Java HotSpot(TM) Server VM (build 23.0-b21, mixed mode)
```

In 2009, Oracle acquired Sun Microsystems, which gave Oracle Java technology the MySQL RDBMS and the Solaris operating system. This is why in Linux environments, the package corresponding to Java Version 1.6 is called `sun-java6-jdk`, and in Version 1.7, it's called `oracle-java7-installer`.

What just happened?

We installed JDK and configured the `JAVA_HOME` and `PATH` environment variables. Configuration was performed for both the Linux and Windows operating systems. We defined the `JAVA_HOME` environment variable that points to a local Java installation. We also added the Java `bin` directory to the `PATH` variable so that we can call Java from anywhere.

Time for action – downloading, installing, and configuring PRD

We will download PRD from the `SourceForge.net` repositories, install PRD, and set your RAM:

1. To download PRD, paste `http://sourceforge.net/projects/pentaho/files/Report%20Designer/` in your web browser.

   Different versions of PRD are stored here, each version in its own folder.

   In the latest versions, we can recognize the type of content of the packages according to the following pattern:

   - `prd-source-[version].zip`: This contains the PRD source code
   - `prd-ce-[version].zip`: This contains the Windows distribution
   - `prd-ce-mac-[version].tar.gz`: This contains the Mac distribution
   - `prd-ce-[version].tar.gz`: This contains the Linux distribution

   In our case, we download Version 5.0.0; therefore, in Linux environments, we should download the following file:

   - `prd-ce-5.0.0.stable.tar.gz`

   And in Windows environments, we should download the following file:

   - `prd-ce-5.0.0.stable.zip`

2. Now we will install PRD.

   We choose a folder and unzip the file according to our operating system. As a result, we obtain a folder with the `report-designer` name. From here on, we will call the complete path to this folder `[PRD_HOME]`.

> As such, the location of the JDBC drivers is `[PRD_HOME]/lib/jdbc`. This is where we should copy the drivers for the JDBC data sources we want to connect to. Some drivers are included by default, for example, the `HSQLDB` driver. A JDBC driver is a software component that allows a Java application to connect and interact with a database. A different implementation is required for each database to which we connect.

3. Next we will configure PRD.

   We can assign more RAM to the PRD execution environment in the following way:

   In Linux environments:

   1. Open a terminal and edit the `report-designer.sh` file:

      ```
      shell> gedit [PRD_HOME]/report-designer.sh
      ```

   2. Place the desired value in the following line:

      ```
      "$_PENTAHO_JAVA" -XX:MaxPermSize=512m -jar "$DIR/
      launcher.jar" $@
      ```

      For example:

      ```
      "$_PENTAHO_JAVA" -XX:MaxPermSize=512m -Xmx768M -jar "$DIR/
      launcher.jar" $@
      ```

   In Windows environments:

   1. Go to the `[PRD_HOME]` folder and edit the `report-designer.bat` file.
   2. Place the desired value in the following line:

      ```
      start "Pentaho Report Designer" "%_PENTAHO_JAVA%"
      -XX:MaxPermSize=256m -Xmx512M -jar "%~dp0launcher.jar" %*
      ```

      For example:

      ```
      start "Pentaho Report Designer" "%_PENTAHO_JAVA%"
      -XX:MaxPermSize=256m -Xmx768M -jar "%~dp0launcher.jar" %*
      ```

What just happened?

We downloaded PRD 5.0 from `SourceForge.net`, in accordance with our operating system, and we have learned about the pattern of names for various packages.
We installed PRD, unzipping the respective package, and explained that the path where we should place the JDBC drives is `[PRD_HOME]/lib/jdbc`. We also edited the `PRD_HOME]/report-designer.[sh|bat]` file in order to explain how to assign more RAM to the PRD execution environment.

Learning the Sakila database

Sakila DB is an example database developed by *Mike Hillyer*, who is a member of the MySQL AB documentation team. The goal of Sakila DB is to be the example database used in books, articles, tutorials, examples, and so on. Sakila's development dates back to 2005. Since then, it has grown and become stronger through various community contributions.

Sakila DB is designed to store information for a video rental store: actors, movies, clients, rentals, payments, and so on.

Sakila is the name of the dolphin used in the official MySQL logo:

About MySQL in this book

In this book, we assume that the reader has MySQL Server 5 or later installed. The installation and configuration of MySQL Server is beyond the scope of this book. There are many good tutorials on how to install MySQL in different operating systems, for example, `http://dev.mysql.com/doc/workbench/en/wb-starting.html`.

Time for action – downloading and installing Sakila DB

Sakila DB can be downloaded from `http://dev.mysql.com/doc/index-other.html`.

After browsing to that URL, follow these steps to download and install Sakila:

1. In the **Example Databases** section, you will find the links to download Sakila DB, as shown in the following screenshot.
    - In Linux environments, choose the TGZ option: `http://downloads.mysql.com/docs/sakila-db.tar.gz`.
    - In Windows environments, choose the Zip option: `http://downloads.mysql.com/docs/sakila-db.zip`.

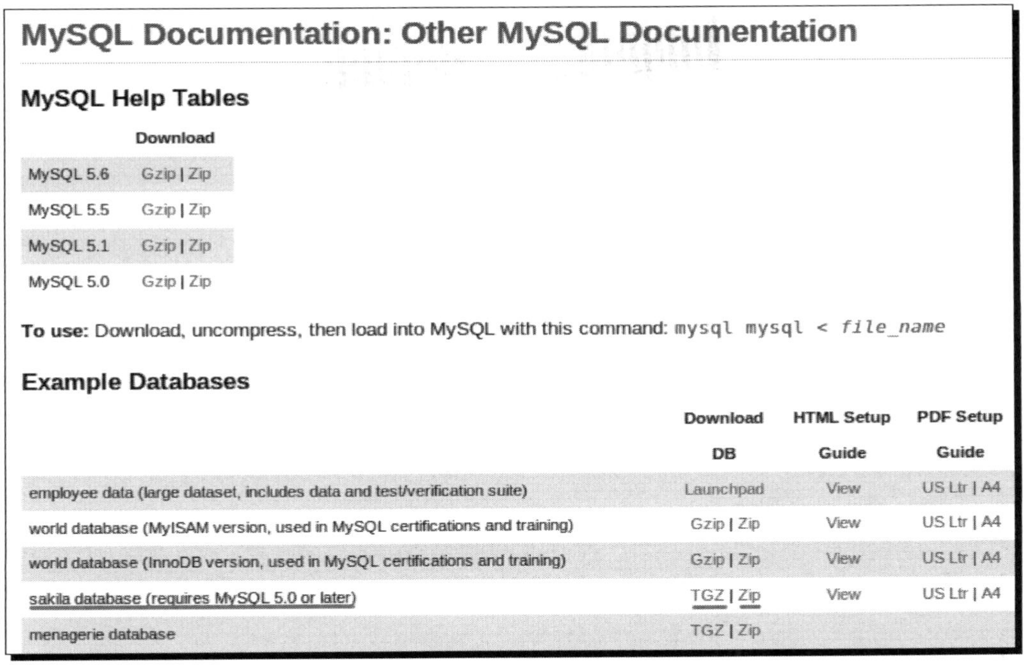

MySQL Documentation: Other MySQL Documentation

MySQL Help Tables

	Download
MySQL 5.6	Gzip | Zip
MySQL 5.5	Gzip | Zip
MySQL 5.1	Gzip | Zip
MySQL 5.0	Gzip | Zip

To use: Download, uncompress, then load into MySQL with this command: `mysql mysql < file_name`

Example Databases

	Download DB	HTML Setup Guide	PDF Setup Guide
employee data (large dataset, includes data and test/verification suite)	Launchpad	View	US Ltr | A4
world database (MyISAM version, used in MySQL certifications and training)	Gzip | Zip	View	US Ltr | A4
world database (InnoDB version, used in MySQL certifications and training)	Gzip | Zip	View	US Ltr | A4
sakila database (requires MySQL 5.0 or later)	TGZ | Zip	View	US Ltr | A4
menagerie database	TGZ | Zip		

2. Once the correct file has been downloaded, we will unzip it in a temporary folder that we will call `[SAKILA_TMP]`.
3. Then, we will execute two commands in a terminal to create the database and populate it with data.
4. First, we will execute the `sakila-schema.sql` script to create the general schema of the Sakila database, that is, the tables, views, and so on. After executing the following command, we will be asked for the root user password. This is determined by the following command:

```
p.shell> mysql -u root -p <[SAKILA_TMP]/sakila-schema.sql
```

5. Next, we will execute the `sakila-data.sql` script to insert the example data in Sakila DB. Here too, we must enter the root user password: `shell> mysql -u root -p <[SAKILA_TMP]/sakila-data.sql`. Next, we will perform a small test to verify that everything is okay. First, we log in to MySQL through the following command (remember to enter the root user password):

   ```
   shell> mysql -u root -p
   ```

6. We then connect to the Sakila database:

   ```
   mysql> use sakila;
   ```

7. Now, we will display a list of all the tables in the Sakila database:

   ```
   mysql> show tables;
   ```

8. Type the `exit` command to quit MySQL CLP.

What just happened?

We have downloaded the `sakila-db` package and executed scripts to create the database and populate it with data using the MySQL command-line processor (CLP).

The Sakila database schema

With the script files that contain the physical schema and the data, the package we downloaded contains a third file called `sakila.mwb`. This file contains a diagram of the database to be used with MySQL Schema Workbench. In the following sections, we show the database model, and we divide it into the following three subdiagrams for easy understanding:

- Customer Data
- Inventory
- Business

The information about Sakila DB in this chapter is based on the official documentation, which can be found at `http://dev.mysql.com/doc/sakila/en/index.html`.

In the *Appendix*, *Sakila DB Data Dictionary*, we have a detailed data dictionary (DD) complete with a sample of data from each table in the Sakila DB.

Customer Data

Client information is stored in four tables, three of which contain information about the addresses that will be used for other entities, such as `staff` and `store`.

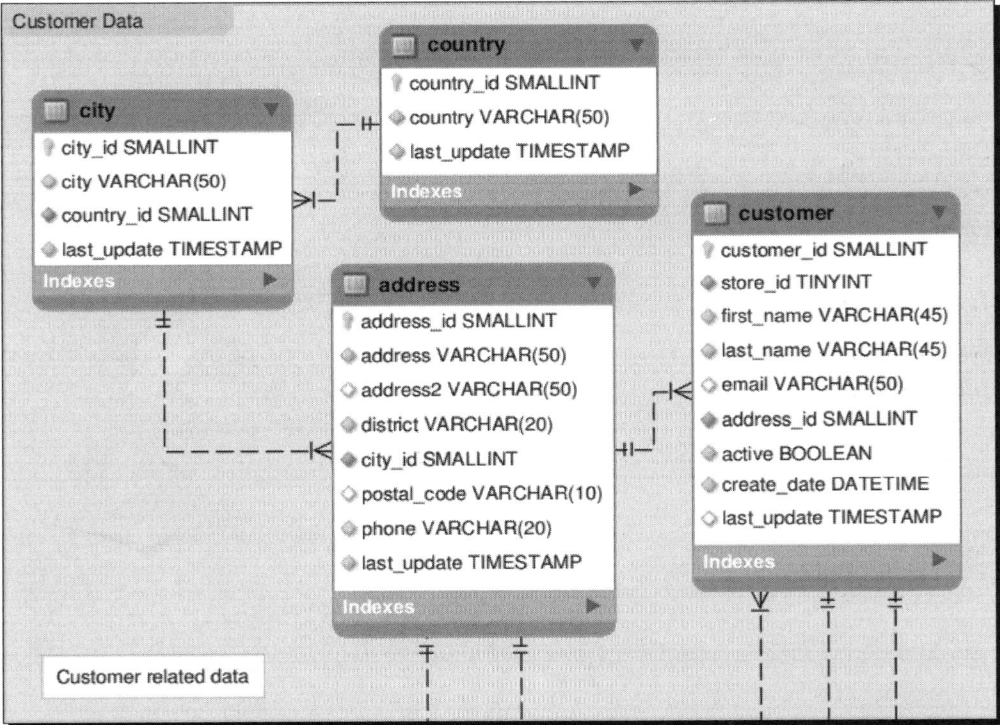

Inventory

Information about movies is stored in eight tables. We can distinguish between the logical definition of a movie and its physical copies that are stored in the `inventory` table.

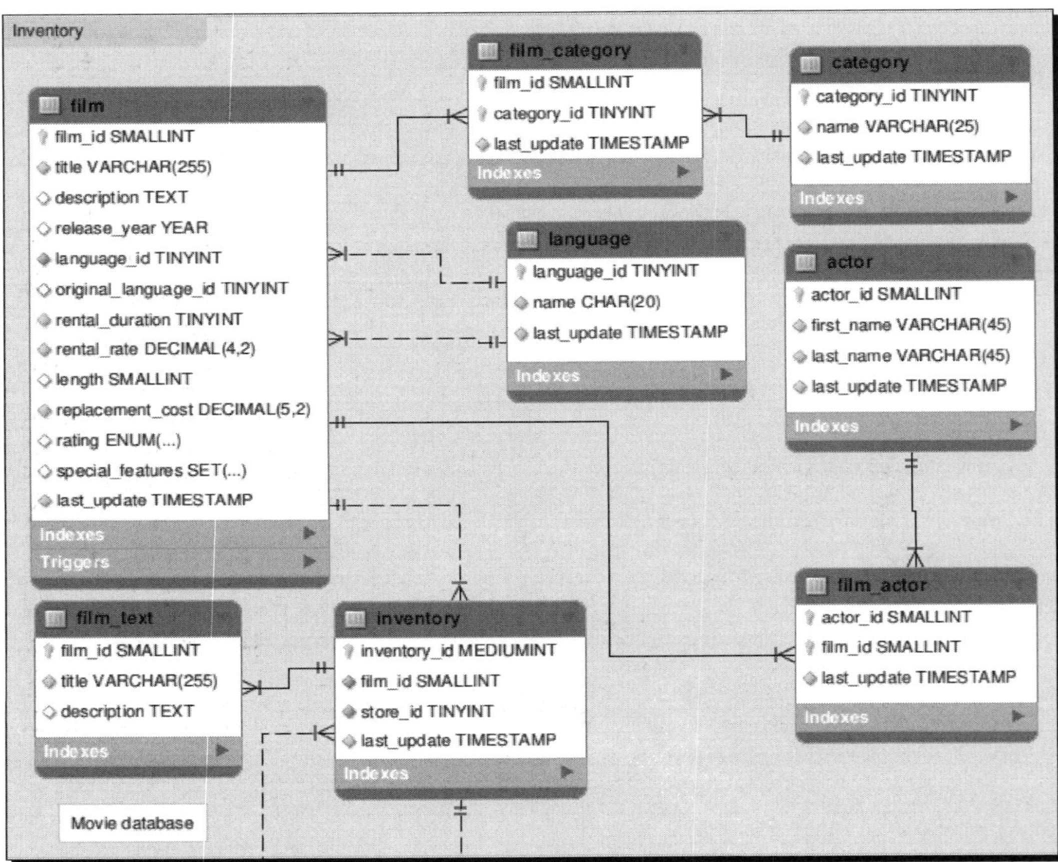

Business

Information about business is stored in four tables. The structure allows us to store information about the employees of each store and information about rentals and payments.

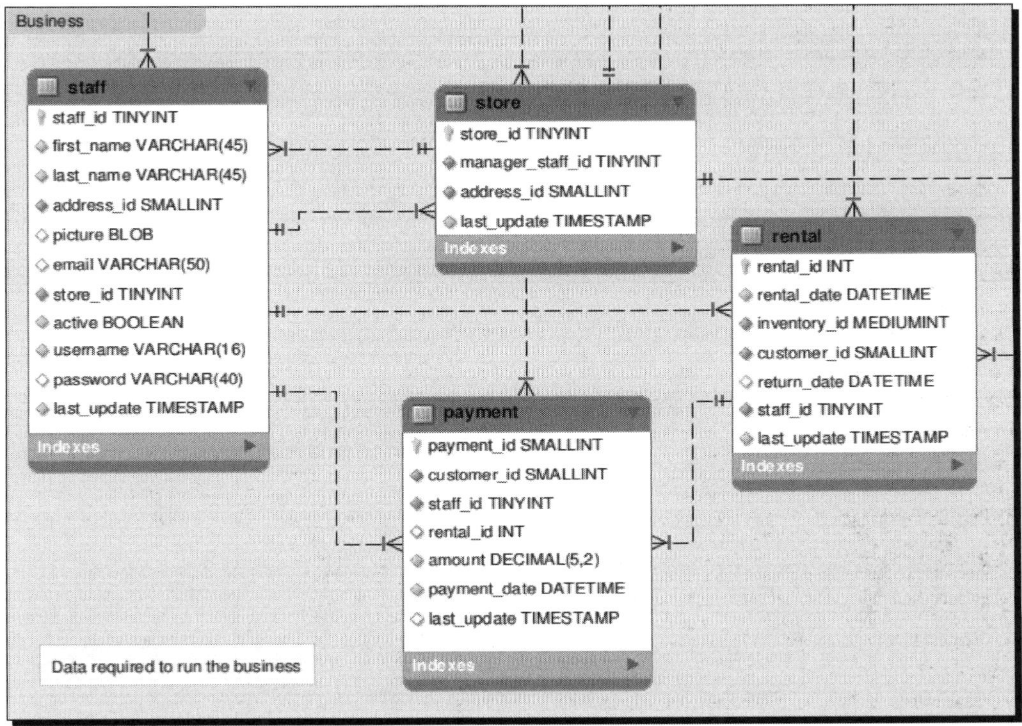

Have a go hero

We propose that you investigate the folder structure of Pentaho Report Designer and their respective content.

To do this, you must go to the PRD installation path, that is, `[PRD_HOME]` and seek answers to the following questions:

- Which files are in the root?
- What's in the `lib` folder?
- What's in the `plugins` folder?
- What's in the `samples` folder?
- What's in the `templates` folder?

Pop quiz – system requirements, JDBC driver, Sakila DB, and RAM

Q1. Which of the following affirmations are true?

1. In order to run Pentaho Report Designer, JDK must be installed first.
2. A JDBC driver is an implementation of a relational database.
3. To include a JDBC driver in PRD, you must copy it in the `[PRD_HOME]/lib/jdbc` path.
4. The database we use to practice this book is called Sakila, and it stores information about sales and purchases.
5. To add more RAM to PRD, it's necessary to edit the `report-designer.sh` file or `report-designer.bat` file, as appropriate.

Summary

After finishing this chapter, we should be able to correctly configure the PRD work environment. We have installed JDK and configured the `JAVA_HOME` and `PATH` environment variables.

We have downloaded PRD 5.0 from `SourceForge.net` in accordance with our operating system, and learned about the pattern of names for various packages. For example, the `prd-ce-[version].tar.gz` package corresponds to the Linux-type operating systems and the `prd-ce-[version].zip` package corresponds to Windows operating systems.

Next, we installed PRD, unzipping the respective package, and explained that the path where we should place the JDBC drives is `[PRD_HOME]/lib/jdbc`. We also edited the `[PRD_HOME]/report-designer.[sh|bat]` file in order to explain how to assign RAM to the PRD execution environment.

We explained that the reports in this book are based on the example database, Sakila DB. This database stores information about a video rental store: movies, rentals, payments, and so on.

We also explained how to download the Sakila DB package and how to execute its scripts to create the database and populate it with data using the MySQL command-line processor (CLP).

Finally, we divided the Sakila DB example database in three sub diagrams: Customer Data, Inventory, and Business based on these entity relation diagrams.

In the next chapter, we will take a closer look at PRD. After starting with PRD, we will detail each part of our UI layout and analyze each option.

3
Start PRD and the User Interface (UI) Layout

In the last chapter, we installed and configured **Pentaho Report Designer** *(***PRD***). Now it's time to execute PRD and begin to familiarize ourselves with the* **user interface** *(***UI***).*

In this chapter we will see:

- How to start PRD in different operating systems
- An explanation of the layout of the PRD UI
- The use and the goal of each area within the UI of PRD, for example, the Work area, the Insertable objects, the Report tree structure, Style and Attributes, the Data panel, the Menu bar, and so on

We will present each part of the PRD layout through screenshots and provide details about the most important buttons and options. We hope that by the end of the chapter, you will have a fairly clear idea of the structure of the PRD UI and its different functions so that in the following chapter, when we make our first report, it will not be difficult to follow the steps described.

Starting PRD

We will start PRD and create a new report, and finally we will explain each of the areas of the PRD UI layout.

Time for action – starting PRD and creating a new report

In the following steps, we will start PRD and create a new report:

1. For starting PRD, we will follow the instructions according to our operating system:
   - **In Linux environments**: Open a terminal and type the following commands:

```
shell> cd [PRD_HOME]
shell> sh report-designer.sh
```

Remember that where it says `[PRD_HOME]`, you should type the complete path to the `PRD` folder.

   - **In Windows environments**: Go to the folder `[PRD_HOME]` and execute (press *Enter* or double-click on) the file `reportdesigner.bat`

   After doing this, as PRD loads its configuration and starts up, it will show us the following screenshot:

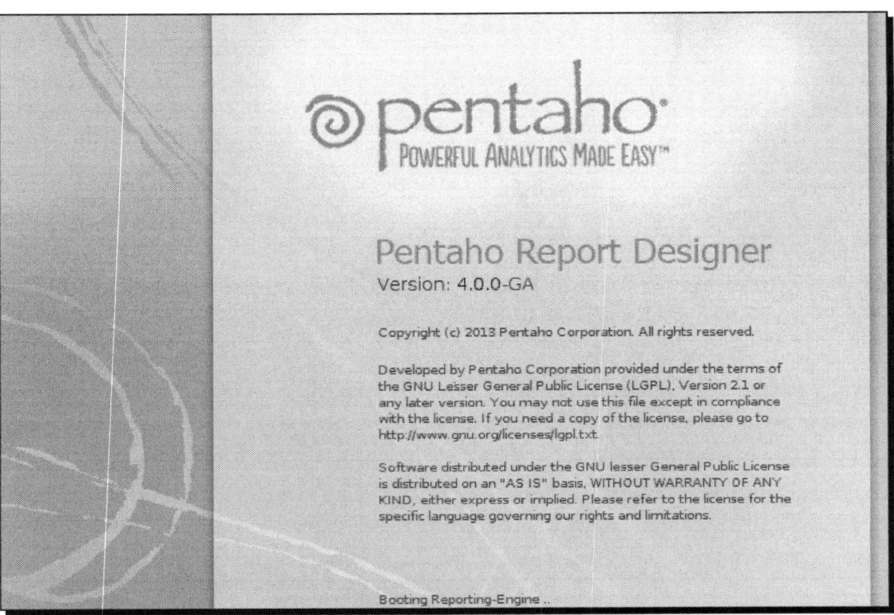

   Once PRD has been executed, we will see the following:

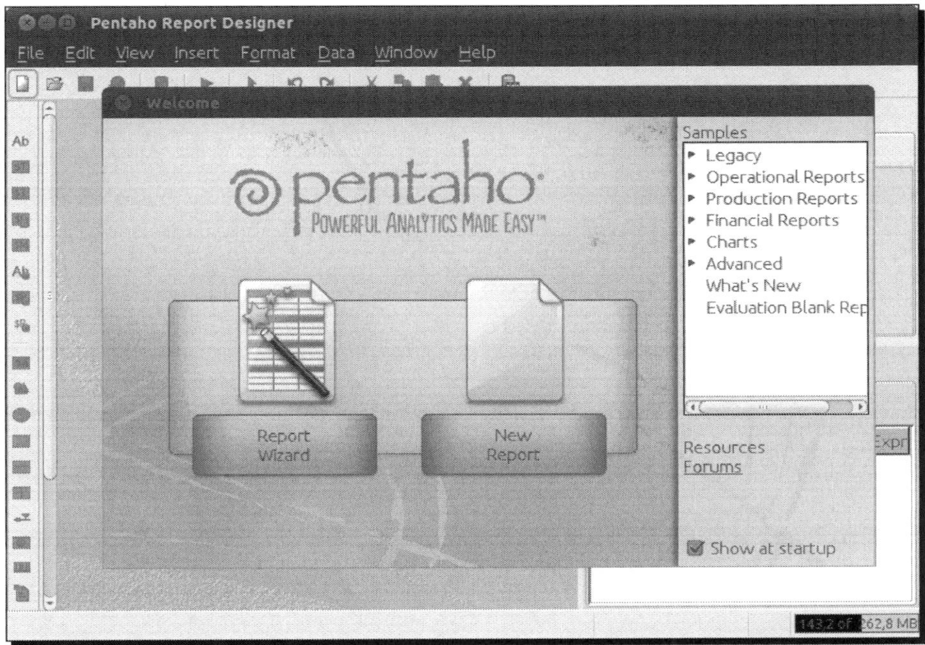

[Before continuing, we should make clear that PRD version 4 is still in development as this book is being written. The reader may find some minimal differences in the UI.]

2. Now we will create a new report. This can be done in several ways:

    1. Choose the option **New Report** in the **Welcome** window.
    2. Click on the following icon in the **Shortcuts** bar.
    3. Click on **File** | **New**.
    4. Press *Ctrl* + *N*.

Based on the following screenshot, we will explain each area of the layout of PRD:

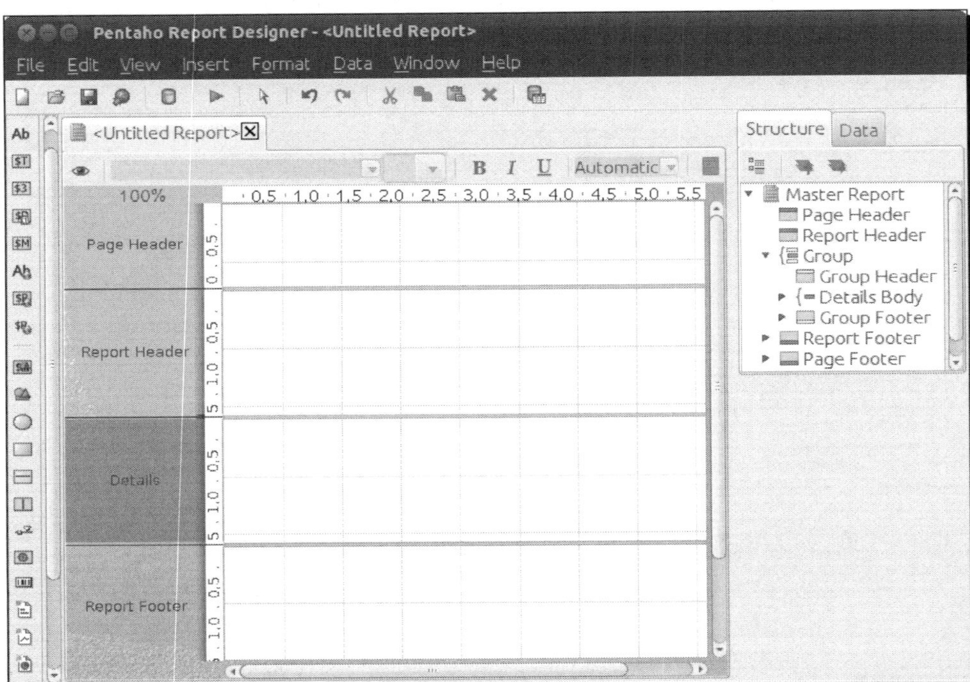

What just happened?

We started PRD according to our operating system, and we saw the window that PRD shows us when it loads its configuration and the UI's general window. If PRD does not start, check the system requirements.

We created a new report, and we saw the different ways to do it. Furthermore, we presented the screenshot that we will consider in explaining the layout of PRD.

PRD layout

Now we will analyze the PRD layout bit by bit.

We can identify the following sections in the layout:

1. Work area
2. Insertable objects
3. Report tree structure
4. Style and Attributes
5. Data panel
6. Menu bar
7. Shortcuts
8. Tab section
9. Format tools
10. Message section and memory indicator

We will see the most important options in each section, and we will specify the area of the PRD layout where each of these sections are located.

The Work area

This is found at the center of the screen. This area is more commonly called Canvas, and this is where we will place the fields, charts, lines, and so on that we want to see in the report.

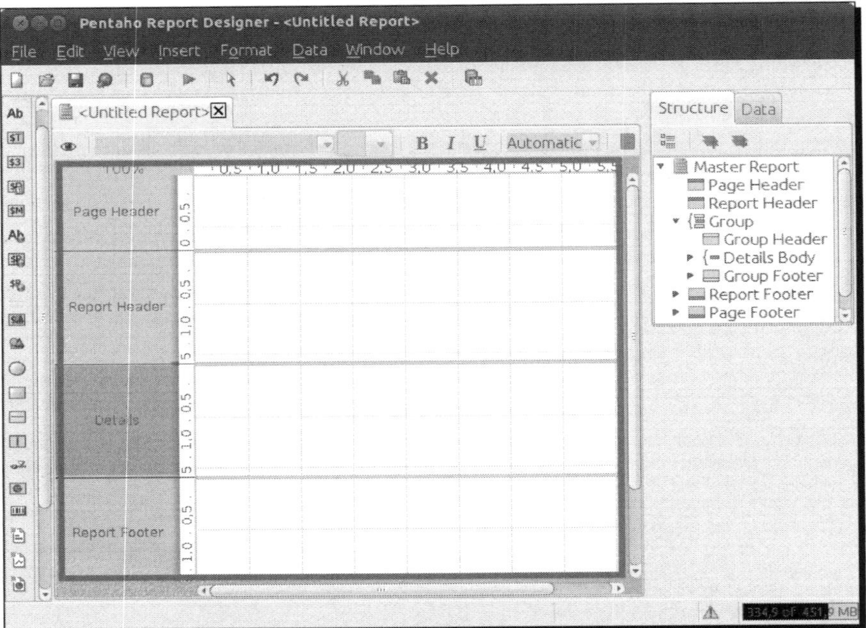

To the left of the Work area, we will find the following sections:

- **Page Header**
- **Report Header**
- **Details**
- **Report Footer**
- **Page Footer**

By default, only these sections are visible in the Work area of the new reports. There are other predetermined sections that are initially invisible, such as **Group Footer** and **Group Header**. New sections can also be added as subgroups.

Insertable objects

These are found on the left-hand side of the screen. Here we will find all of the elements that we can add to our reports. Among these elements are fields, graphics, text, lines, subreports, sparklines, and so on.

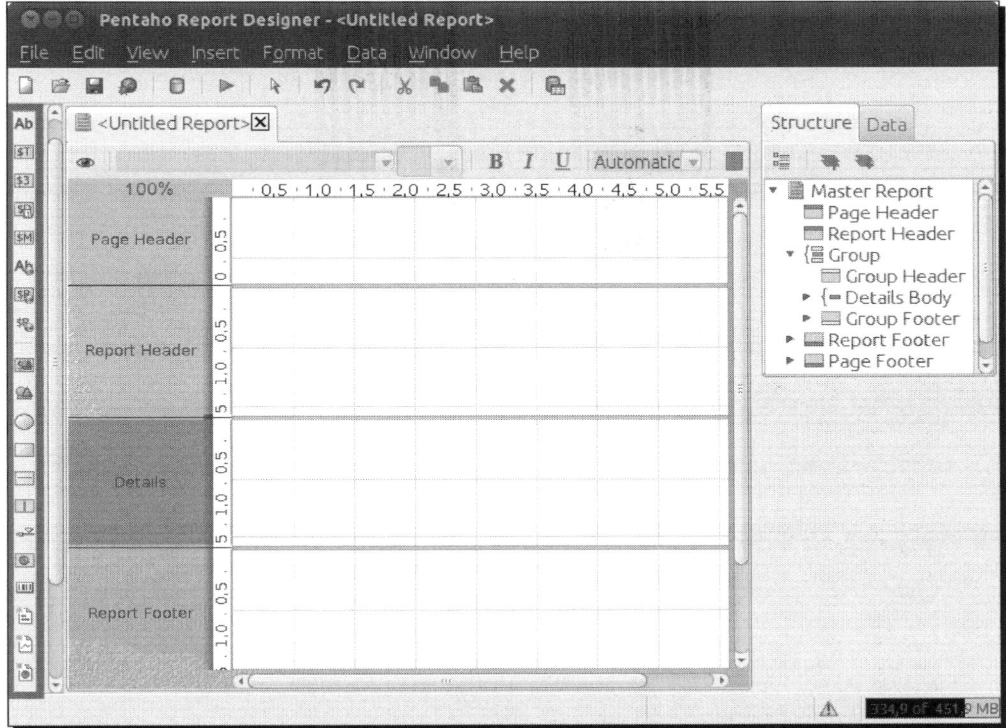

Now we will describe each of the insertable objects' labels:

- **Label**: This lets us insert a static text. This is often used for titles, subtitles, legends, labels, headers, and so on. This field appears as an icon on the left-hand side pane as follows:

- **Text field**: This field appears as an icon on the left-hand side pane as follows:

  This lets us insert text fields from our data source in the report and represent values of type text. When we insert a text field in the report, we are using a Text field component.

- **Number field**: This field appears as an icon on the left-hand side pane as follows:

  This lets us insert number fields from our data source in the report and represent values of type number. When we insert a number field in the report, we are using a Number field.

- **Date field**: This field appears as an icon on the left-hand side pane as follows:

  This lets us insert date/time fields from our data source in the report and represent values of type date/time. When we insert a date/time field in the report, we are using a Date field.

- **Message**: This field appears as an icon on the left-hand side pane as follows:

  This lets us insert fields with large texts and lets us combine various fields and texts in expressions. They are used, for example, to create strings such as "Today is the $(day) of $(month), $(year)". To obtain the same result, we would have to use multiple instances of the following objects: Label, Text field, Number field, and Date field.

- **Resource label**: This field appears as an icon on the left-hand side pane as follows:

  This object behaves similarly to Label (Ab) with the difference that Resource label takes its value from an internationalized file. These are used when text in the report has to change based on the user's location.

- **Resource field**: This field appears as an icon on the left-hand side pane as follows:

  This is similar to the Resource label (Ab). The only difference is how the key for obtaining the resource is established. In this case, the value is not constant but is obtained from the data source.

- **Resource message**: This field appears as an icon on the left-hand side pane as follows:

  This is similar to Message () in its possibilities but in this case, the expression can be obtained from a resource file and, as such, internationalized.

- **Image field**: This field appears as an icon on the left-hand side pane as follows:

  This lets us insert images obtained from our data source. When we insert an image field in the report, we are using an Image field. They are used to display product images, photos of people, logos, and so on.

- **Image**: This field appears as an icon on the left-hand side pane as follows:

  This lets us insert images obtained from a physical location. The images can be linked or embedded in the report. This is mainly used for images that are placed at the head or foot of the report, for example, the logo that represents the organization or a report's background image.

- **Ellipse**: This field appears as an icon on the left-hand side pane as follows:

  This lets us insert an ellipse in our report.

- **Rectangle**: This field appears as an icon on the left-hand side pane as follows:

  This lets us insert a rectangle in our report.

- **Horizontal line**: This field appears as an icon on the left-hand side pane as follows:

  This lets us insert a horizontal line in our report.

- **Vertical line**: This field appears as an icon on the left-hand side pane as follows:

  This lets us insert a vertical line in our report.

- **Survey scale**: This field appears as an icon on the left-hand side pane as follows:

  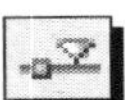

  This lets us insert a widget that displays quantitative values graphically. The possible values are defined as a continuous line, the displayed value as a point on this line, and the limits of different ranges as figures. They are used to graphically and simply display the values of surveys, evaluations, indicators, and so on.

- **Chart**: This field appears as an icon on the left-hand side pane as follows:

  This lets us insert charts in our reports. There is a great variety of charts that we can use. Charts are commonly used to represent information in a simplified manner.

- **Simple bar codes**: This field appears as an icon on the left-hand side pane as follows:

  This lets us insert bar codes in our reports. Bar codes are commonly used in order to be read and decoded by a specialized machine later. Bar codes are habitually used in billing, library management, inventory control, movement control, shipping control, receipts, documents, and so on.

- **Bar sparkline**: This field appears as an icon on the left-hand side pane as follows:

  This lets us insert bar sparklines. They are generally used to graph comparative information in detail.

- **Line sparkline**: This field appears as an icon on the left-hand side pane as follows:

  This lets us insert line sparklines. They are generally used to graph information on tendencies or evolution in time in detail.

- **Pie sparkline**: This field appears as an icon on the left-hand side pane as follows:

  This lets us insert pie sparklines. They are generally used to graph comparative percent information in detail.

- **Band**: This field appears as an icon on the left-hand side pane as follows:

  This lets us insert a band in our report. This band lets us group other Insertable objects and treat them as a whole. This facilitates managing and editing complex reports.

- **Subreport**: This field appears as an icon on the left-hand side pane as follows:

  This lets us insert a subreport in our report. These are usually used when we need to show different levels of granularity or information that comes from diverse queries in the same report.

- **Table of content**: This field appears as an icon on the left-hand side pane as follows:

  This lets us insert a table of contents based on report data. These are used when there is a large quantity of data in the report, and we want to exactly know on which page each group begins.

- **Index**: This field appears as an icon on the left-hand side pane as follows:

  This lets us insert an index based on report data. These are commonly used when we want to know on which page of the report the data from a particular column is found.

Report tree structure

This is found in the upper-right area and the **Structure** tab should be chosen. This is where the report layout is displayed. This facilitates navigating in the report and editing its components.

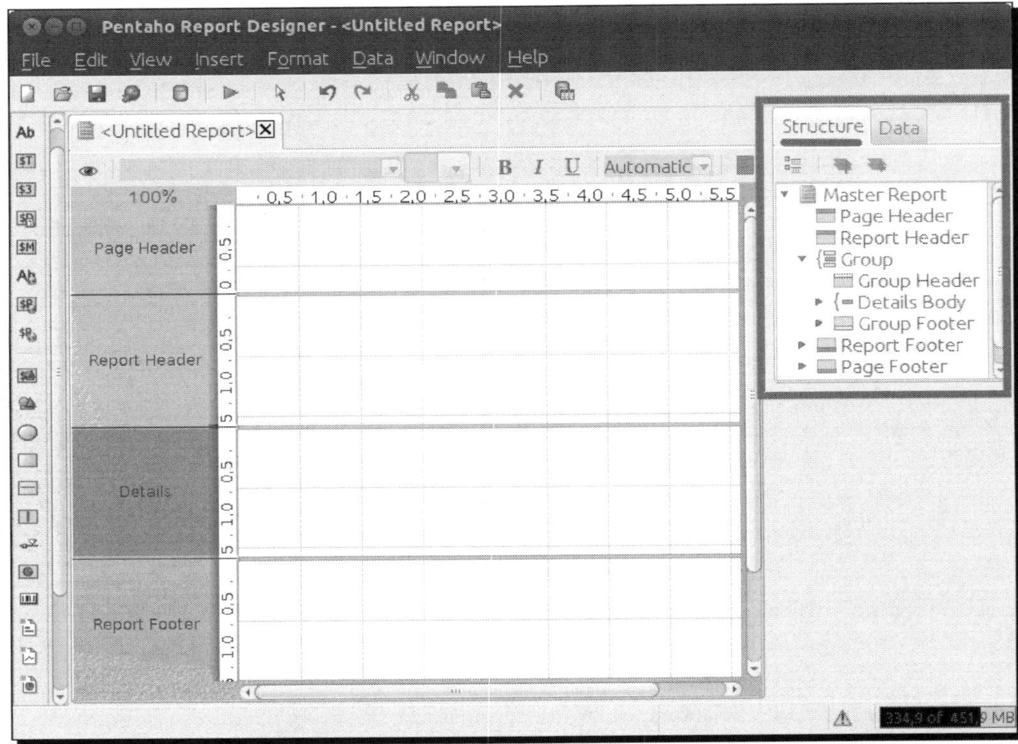

As you can see, the organization of the report's sections is presented in a tree hierarchy. For example, the sections **Group Header**, **Details Body**, and **Group Footer** are child nodes of **Group**. Similarly, the Insertable objects added to each of the sections will be their child nodes.

The Insertable object Band () creates a new level in the hierarchy.

Style and Attributes

This is found in the lower-right area and is activated by selecting a branch in the tree structure or an Insertable object. This panel lets us configure all of the details of the selected object.

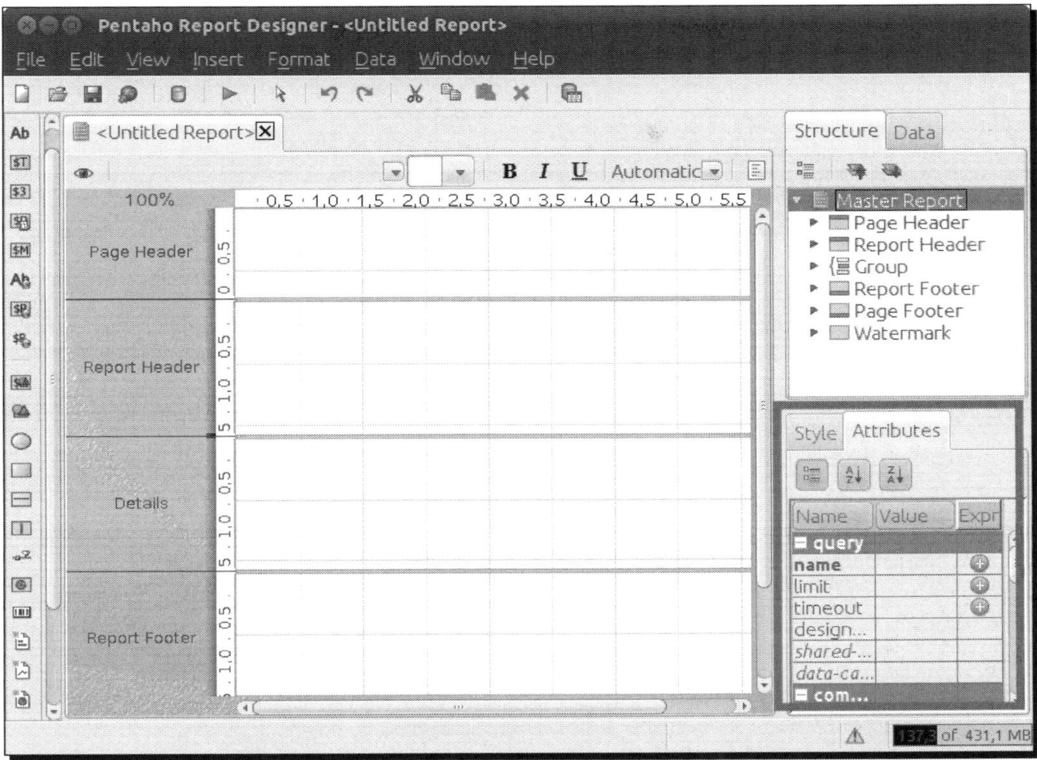

Once an object is selected, this panel lets us configure its characteristics. To facilitate editing, the characteristics are grouped in two tabs as follows:

- **Style**: These let us configure how the object is rendered
- **Attributes**: These determine the object's behavior and interaction with the report

Additionally, the characteristics in each of these tabs are grouped according to their function. For example, when adding `Label` in the **Style** tab, in the **size & position** group, we can see the attributes **x**, **y**, **width**, **height**, and **visible**.

All of the characteristics should have a value. If a value is not specified, a default value will be used. In many cases, the default value is null; moreover, the configuration of sections will be inherited by the Insertable objects that are placed on it. If we want to specify a value, we can do it in the **Value** column or use the graphic expression editor (⊕). This is a very important characteristic that PRD offers, as once a value is established, a constant value can be specified or a value can be generated using a complex expression.

Another important point is that in the **Style** tab, when a characteristic's default value is modified, the box **Inh** is unchecked (☐). This lets us quickly determine which characteristics have been modified. In the **Attributes** tab, something similar happens when the ⊞ option is used but in this case, the icon is replaced by ✎.

The Data panel

This is found in the upper-right area and the **Data** tab should be chosen.

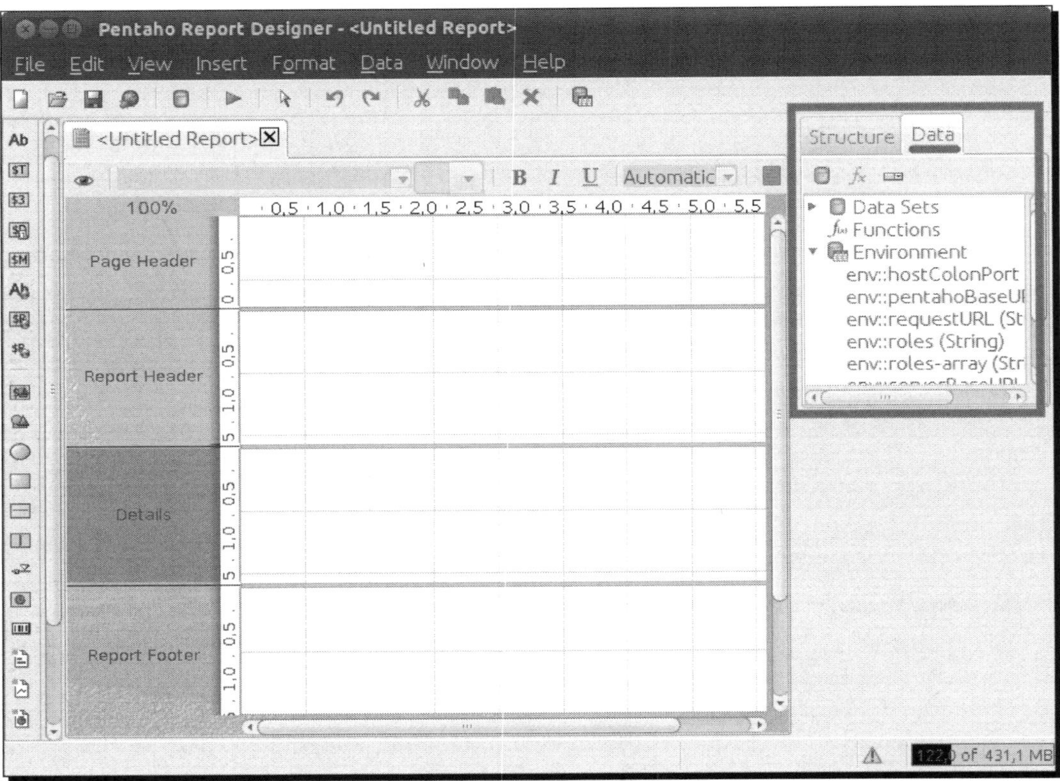

This is where the following fields are configured:

- **Data sets**: These are data sources that will be used in the report. We can define one or more data sets in our report but only one will be the Main. Using Data Sets Main, we will be able to drag-and-drop your fields in the Work area. Other Data Sets can be used for other purposes, for example, to fill selectors (lists, combos, checks, and so on).

- **Functions**: Functions that are once defined can be inserted in the report or used as variables. Using functions, we can create totals and subtotals, calculate the maximum, minimum, and average, create mobile calculations, and so on.
- **Environment**: These are environment variables whose values can be used to design our report. For example, we can make a graph visible or invisible according to the value of the variable, `userName`.
- **Parameters**: These are input parameters and filters. For example, we can use parameters for the user to select a year so that the report displays information related to this year.

The menu bar

The Menu bar lets us access PRD's functions in the traditional form, which is context free. In other words, all of the available options are found in the same menu and grouped into submenus.

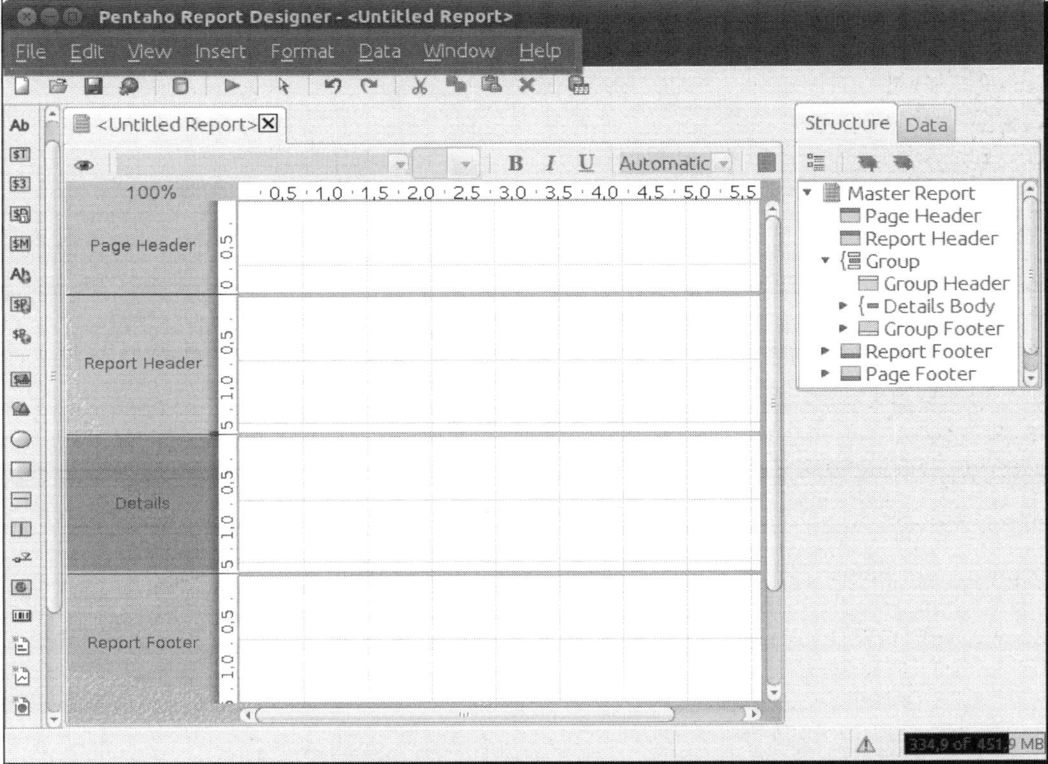

Shortcuts

PRD displays the most used functions in the shortcut bar.

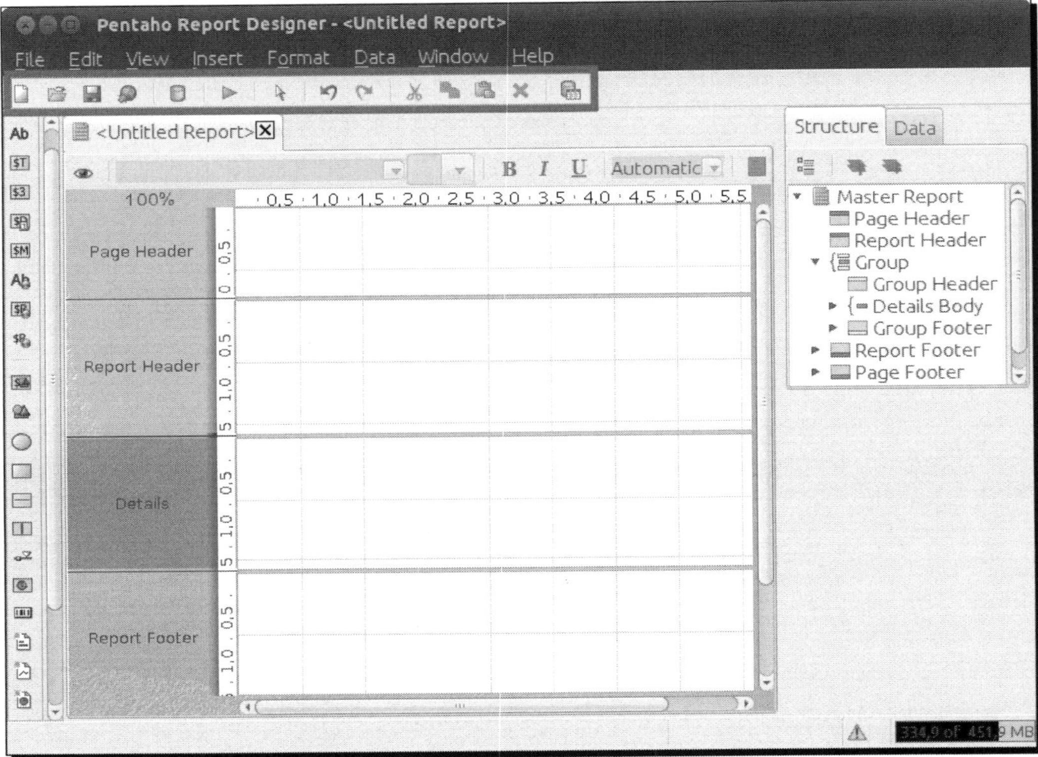

Now we will introduce each of the options and their respective functions:

- To create a new report, click on the following icon:

- To open an existing report, click on the following icon:

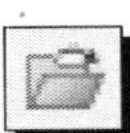

- To save changes made to the report, click on the following icon:

- To publish the report to the Pentaho BI Server, click on the following icon:

- To add a new data source, click on the following icon:

- To visualize the report in different formats, click on the following icon:

- To activate the option that lets us select various objects added to the report, click on the following icon:

- To undo the changes, click on the following icon:

- To redo the changes, click on the following icon:

- To cut objects from the report and place them on the clipboard, click on the following icon:

- To copy objects in the report and add them to the clipboard, click on the following icon:

- To paste objects from the clipboard into the report, click on the following icon:

- To delete objects from the report, click on the following icon:

- To open a window with a list of all the report's available fields, click on the following icon:

The tab section

PRD organizes open reports and subreports in tabs allowing us to alternate among the different reports in the main window. The title of each report is used as the title of each tab; if the report is untitled, the name of the file is used.

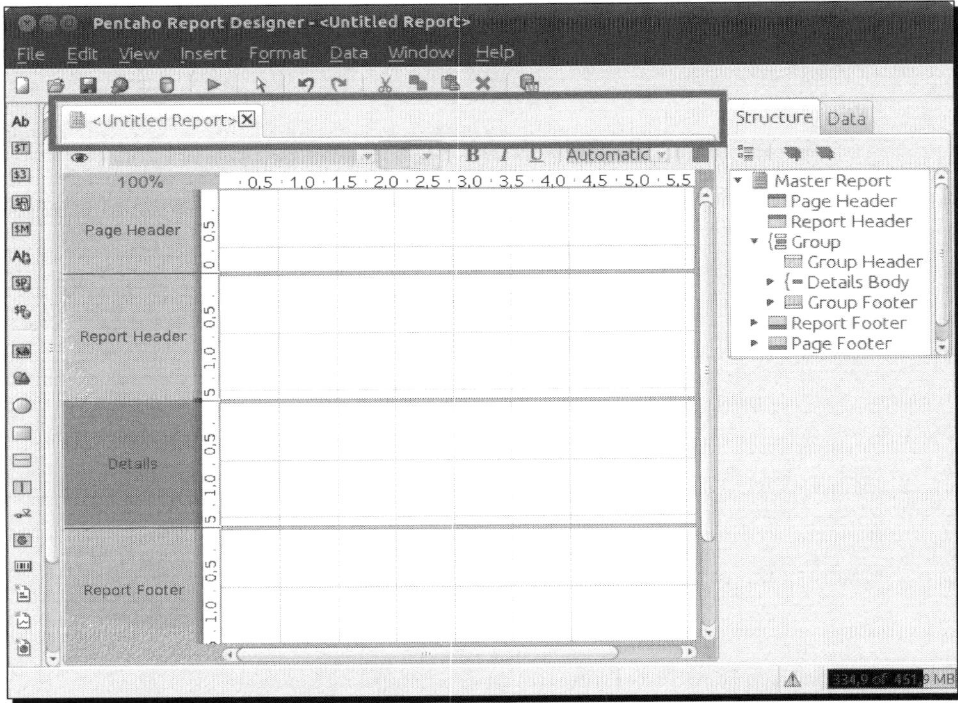

> The title of a report is a part of the report's descriptive metainformation. To access this information, we should choose the option **File | Report Properties...** from the Menu bar. Also, if we select the node **Master Report** in the tab **Structure**, we can modify/see the report title in **Attributes.name** (the **common** category).

Format tools

It is located above the Work area.

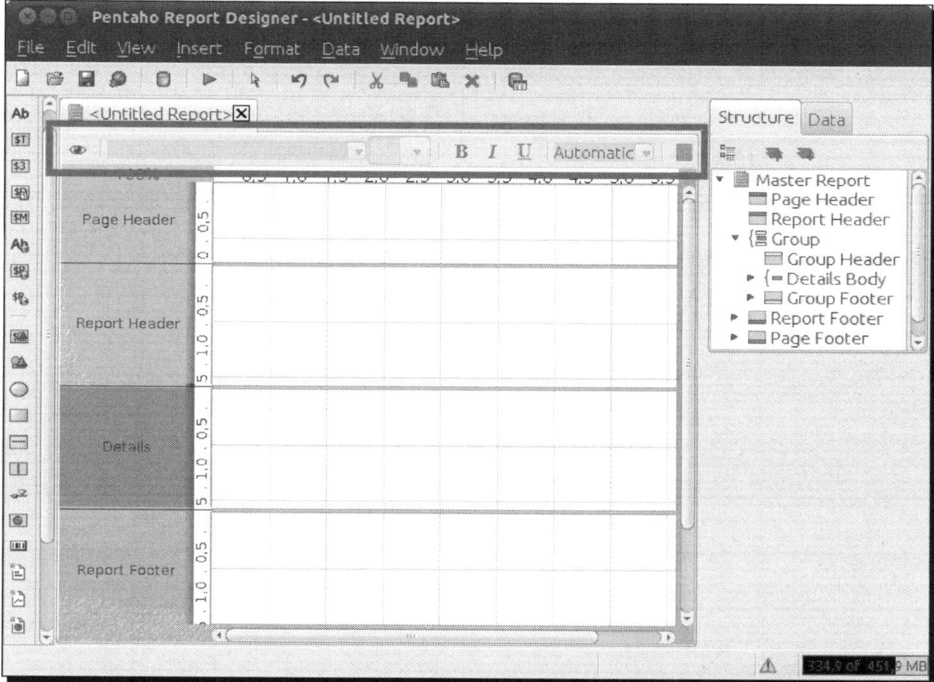

Here we find the following options:

- The following icon displays the report in preview mode:

  To return to the editing mode, click on the icon again.

- The following icon lets us change the font type and size:

- The following icon lets us make the font bold, italic, and underlined and change the font's color:

- The following icon lets us change the justification of texts:

- The following icon lets us create hyperlinks:

Message section and memory indicator

This is the section that PRD uses to communicate to us if an exception occurs or there is a warning.

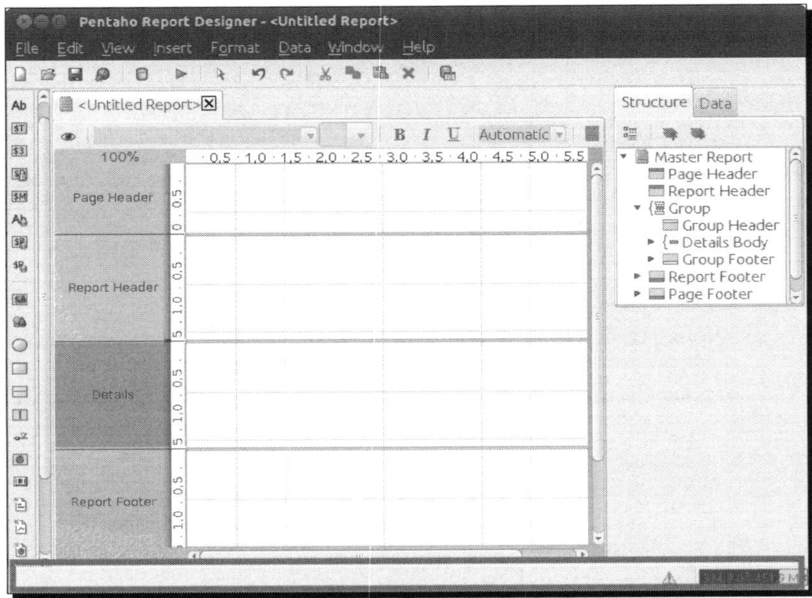

A widget is also constantly displayed with information about the RAM used and the assigned limit as follows:

The RAM information widget can warn us if we need to assign more RAM to PRD. *Chapter 2, Installation and Configuration*, explains how to configure this.

The icon indicates warnings.

If we click on this icon, a panel will be opened at the bottom of the screen as follows:

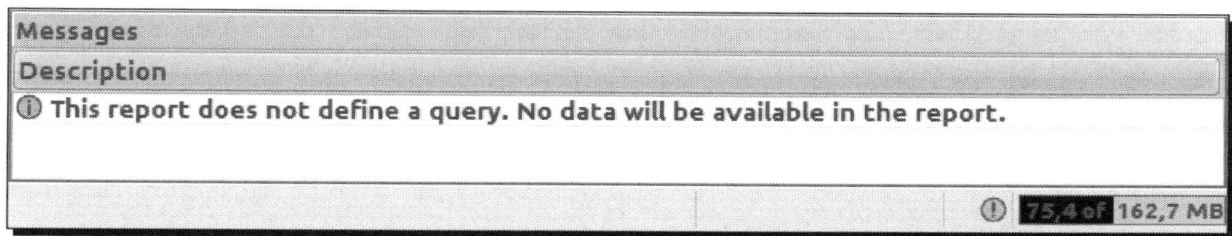

The icon indicates exceptions. If we click on this icon, a new window will be opened as follows:

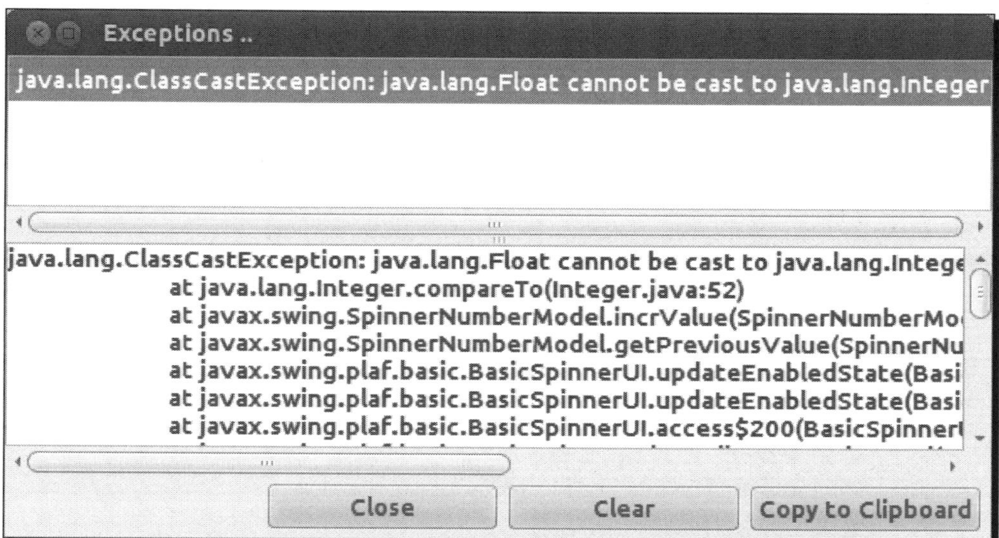

Have a go hero

We propose you to open a sample report (**Buyer Report**) and analyze their design through the layout areas.

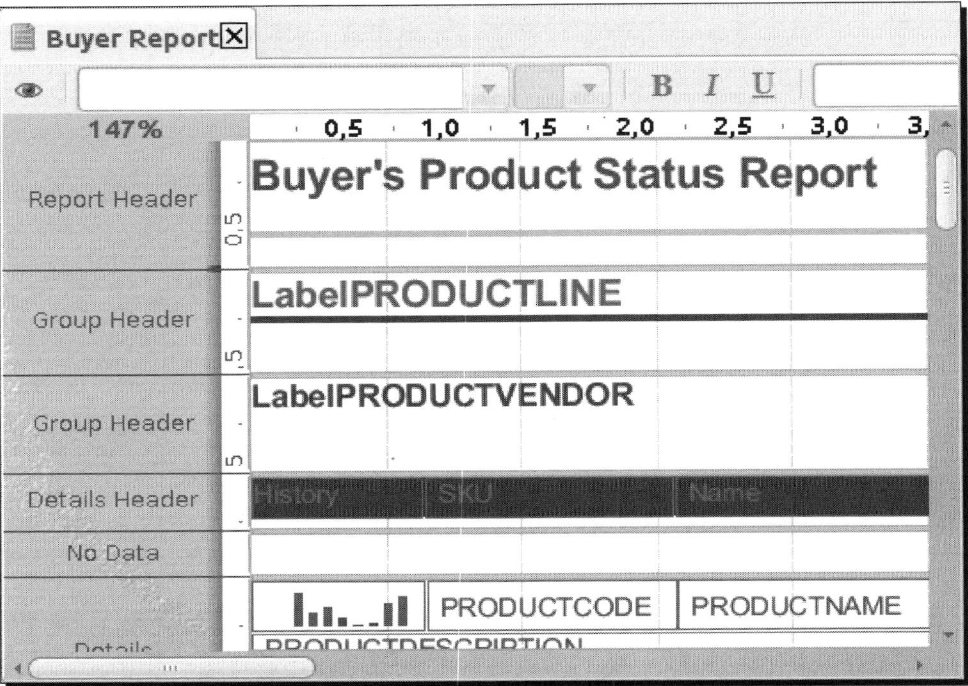

The steps you should be following are roughly the following:

1. To open this report, you must navigate to **Help** | **Sample Reports** | **Operational Reports** | **Buyer Report** in the top menu.
2. Select the objects in the Work area and see what are the kind of objects (**Attributes.type**).
3. See how the inserted objects are organized in the hierarchical tree.
4. See the data sets used and their respective fields.
5. See how the functions are configured.
6. See the parameter line and view its settings.

Pop Quiz – layout of PRD

Q1. Which of the following affirmations are true?

1. Work area is the place where we will design our reports.
2. The object number field is similar to the object label, with the particularity that the number field allows us to assign a numerical value.
3. The difference between image and image field is that image field can get the image of our data source.
4. We can add objects to our reports only from the Insertable objects area.
5. We can configure all the details of our objects on Style and Attributes.
6. Every time we open a new report, it is shown in a new window.
7. The **Structure** tab shows all sections and objects of our report organized in the hierarchical tree.
8. From the Data panel area, you can only manage data sets, functions, and parameters.

Summary

After finishing this chapter, we have the foundation needed to continue with the exercises in the following chapters. We have covered the following topics:

- We have started PRD in different operating systems, and we have differentiated among a series of sections in the PRD UI. This division in sections correspond to the physical location of each part but principally to the function that each performs in the UI.
- We defined the Work area as the place where we add fields, graphics, and so on that we want to include in the report.
- We described the function of each object that we can add to our reports, which are found in Insertable objects.
- In the Report tree structure, we saw how the objects in our report are structured.
- We explained in Style and Attributes that we can configure the details of each object selected.
- We also explained that in the Data panel we can create and edit data sets, functions, environments, and parameters.

These are the most important sections in the PRD layout, as they are the sections that let us create our reports; however, we also defined the *Menu bar*, *Shortcuts*, *Tab section*, *Format tools*, and *Messages and memory indicator* sections.

In the next chapter, we will create our first report. We will define the data sets based on a table, add some Insertable objects, create several functions, and export the report in different formats.

4

Instant Gratification – Creating Your First Report with PRD

In this chapter, we will create our first report with PRD. As we perform each step in the creation of this report, we will see the PRD UI's functions in action. It is important to understand the concepts presented in the previous chapters in order to be able to put them in practice without difficulty.

In this chapter, we will cover the following:

- We will see how to configure the report's sections: **Page Header**, **Report Header**, **Details Header**, **Details**, and **Details Footer**
- We will add different insertable objects to our report, such as labels, horizontal lines, vertical lines, text fields, number fields, and images
- We will create the following functions and explain how they are used: `RowBanding`, `Count (Running)`, and `Sum (Running)`
- We will see how to preview our report and the different formats that PRD lets us export to, such as PDF, HTML, and Excel/Excel 2007

Each step will be explained in detail and screenshots will be included where necessary. Once the report is finished, we suggest that you modify it and add some extra functions.

Creating your first report with PRD

In this chapter, we will create a report that, at first glance, appears simple. In fact, it is simple. However, by the end of the chapter, we will have carried out the principal steps that are normally followed in creating reports.

Initially, it can be very difficult to adapt to working with a tool as complex as PRD. This is why we will explain its principal functions and characteristics gradually as we develop our examples. Understanding these things allows us to work with PRD and learn to use it at the same time. Our methodology will be to present a concept and put it in practice.

The report that we will now create is shown in the following screenshot:

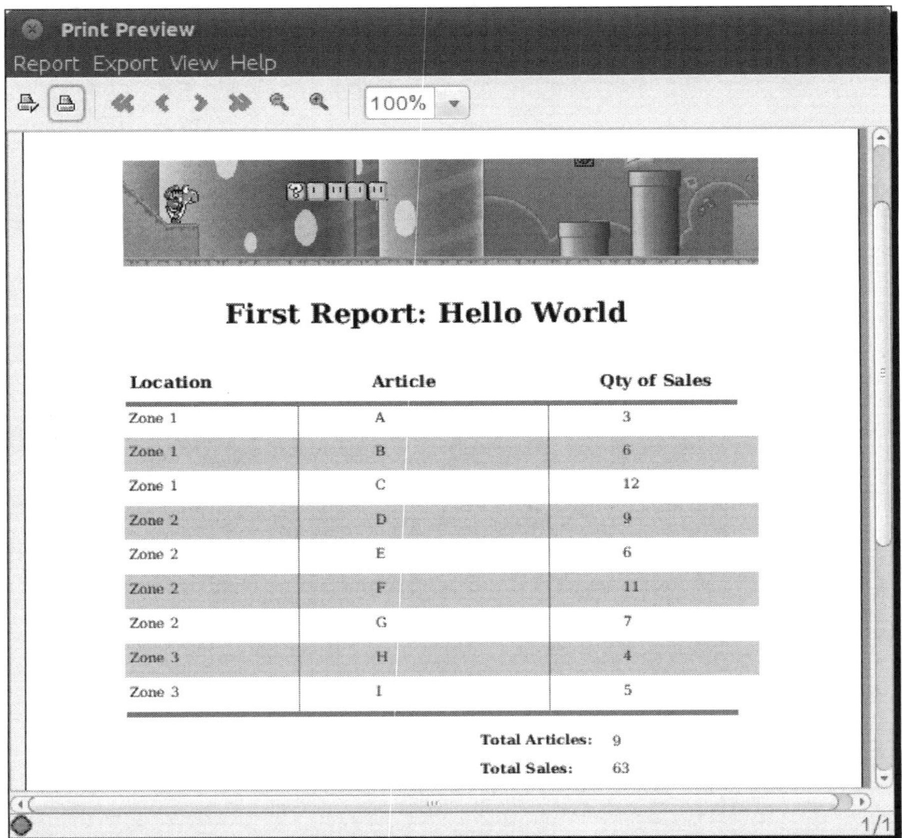

Time for action – creating a new report and creating a table based on data sets

We will create a new report, and later we will create a `Table` type data source and configure its columns and data types. Finally, we will populate the table with the example data.

1. Start PRD if it is not yet running.
2. Create a new report. Remember that there are different ways to create a new report as follows:
   - Choose the **New Report** option in the **Welcome** window
   - Click on the following icon in the shortcuts bar:

   - Navigate to **File** | **New**
   - Press *Ctrl* + *N*
3. Save the report as `01_Hello_World.prpt` using the following icon:

4. We will define `Table` as a data source. The `Table` is a static data source; it is stored with the report's metadata and remains constant. This type of data source is often used for demonstrations, examples, testing, prototyping, and so on.

5. In the **Data** tab, right-click on **Data Sets** and choose **Table**.

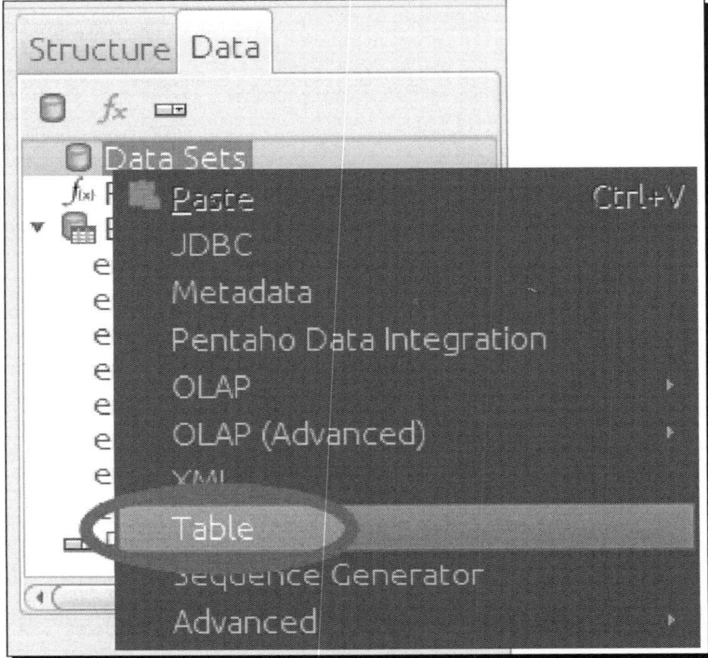

6. We define three columns in our data sets: `Zones`, `Products`, and `Quantity`.

7. To create the table, click on the icon. By default, this will create a query with the name set as **Query 1** and with two columns **ID** and **Value**. We will do the following:

    1. We will change the query's name to `ZoneProductQty`.
    2. We click on the heading of the **ID** column and press on the button to eliminate it.
    3. We repeat this process now for the heading of the **Value** column.
    4. We press on the button to add a new column. Next, we double-click on the heading of this column to modify it. We give it the name `Zones` and then click on the button and choose **class.java.lang.String** as `Zones` will have a `String` type data.
    5. We follow the same steps to create another column with the name `Products` using the `String` data type (`class.java.lang.String`).
    6. We follow the same steps to create another column with the name `Quantity` using the `Integer` data type (`class.java.lang.Integer`).

7. After following these steps, we will obtain a result like this:

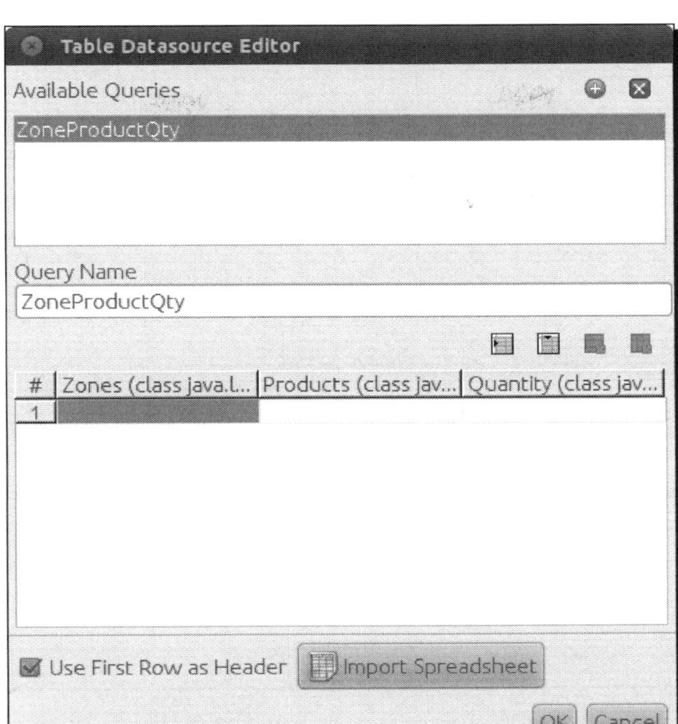

8. Next, we will populate the table with data.

9. To do so, we press on the button and fill in the values that correspond to each column. Each time we have to create a new row, we press on the button. We need to populate the table with the data that is shown in the following screenshot:

#	Zones (class java.l...	Products (class jav...	Quantity (class jav...
1	Zone 1	A	3
2	Zone 1	B	6
3	Zone 1	C	12
4	Zone 2	D	9
5	Zone 2	E	6
6	Zone 2	F	11
7	Zone 2	G	7
8	Zone 3	H	4
9	Zone 3	I	5

> Another way of populating the table with data is by pressing the **Import Spreadsheet** button. With this option, we can extract data from a spreadsheet.

10. Press **OK** to save the changes and return to the previous screen. Now we can see how our new data source turned out in the following screenshot:

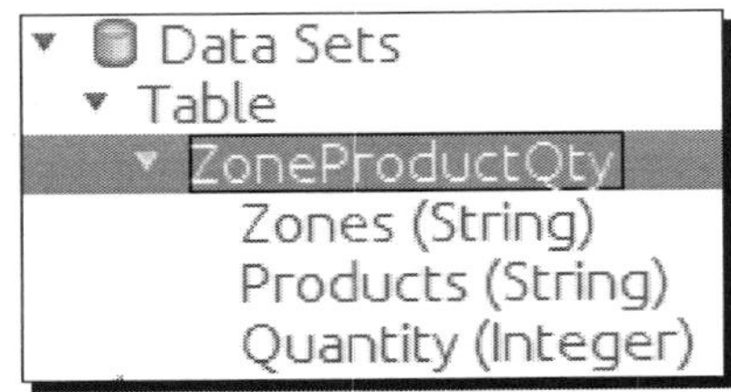

What just happened?

Initially we created a new report, and then we created a data set of the type `Table`. We added three columns (`Zones`, `Products`, and `Quantity`) to the table and defined its data types. Finally, we populated the table with some example data.

Time for action – configuring the Report Header and Details Header sections

In the ensuing steps, we will configure the **Report Header** and **Details Header** sections so that it looks as follows:

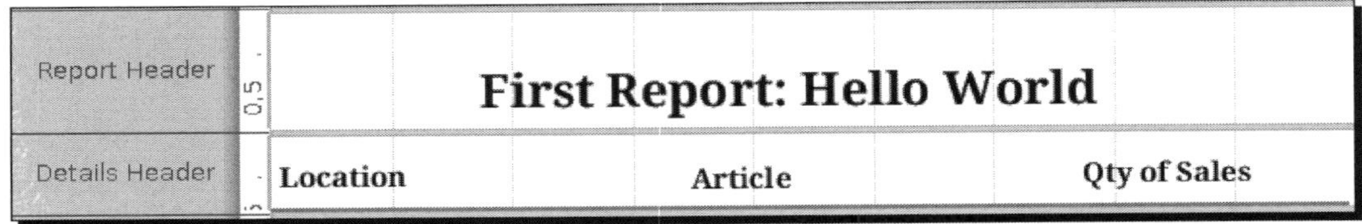

1. In the **Report Header** section, we will add a label with the header text.
2. To do this, we must drag-and-drop the insertable object `Label` (Ab); this means that we need to drag it and release it in the work area that belongs to the **Report Header** section. Next, we will configure this label so it includes the text **First Report: Hello World** in bold face, centered, and large font size.
3. To do so, we will select the label we just added in the work area and configure its **Attributes** and **Style** properties.

4. In the **Attributes** tab, as the value of the characteristic value, we enter `First Report: Hello World`.
5. In the **Style** tab, as the value of the **bold** characteristic, we enter `true`.
6. In the **Style** tab, as the value of the **font-size** characteristic, we enter `20`.
7. In the **Style** tab, as the value of the **h-align** characteristic, we enter `CENTER`.

From now on, to indicate that a certain value should be entered in a certain characteristic of **Attributes** or **Style**, we will use the following notations:

Attributes.value = `First Report: Hello World`

Style.bold = `true`

Style.font-size = `20`

Style.h-align = `CENTER`

8. We will make the **Details Header** section visible in our report. The **Details Header** section is commonly used to place information of what you will see in **Details**.
9. Go to the tab structure, and in the hierarchical tree, navigate to **Master Report** | **Group:** | **Details Body** | **Details Header**. Then set **Attributes.hide-on-canvas** to **false** as shown in the following screenshot:

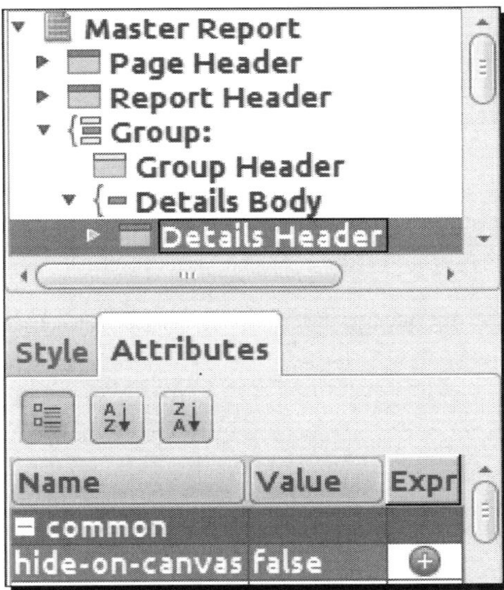

10. Place three labels in the work area of this section (by dragging-and-dropping) with the following text:
    - `Location`
    - `Article`
    - `Qty of Sales`
11. Finally, configure the following characteristics:
    - **Style.font-size** = 12
    - **Style.bold** = `true4.`

    We insert a horizontal line ( ) under the preceding labels and configure it in the following way:
    - **Style.stroke** = `solid, 4.0`
    - **Style.text-color** = `#009933`

What just happened?

We customized the report's **Report Header** and added and configured a title. Also, in the **Details Header** section we added and configured three column headings and a horizontal line.

Time for action – configuring details

Next, we will configure **Details** to get the following result:

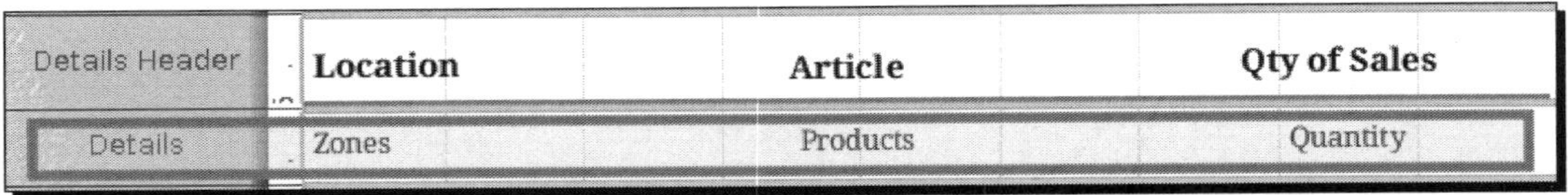

1. We select the **Data** tab and drag-and-drop **Zones**, **Products**, and **Quantity**, placing each under the corresponding label.

> As we saw before, these objects that we just added to the report are actually the text field ($T) and number field ($3). This is because PRD makes mapping the data type dragged to the work area with the required insertable object.

2. Now we will execute the report to see the results it is giving us.

   We press the icon found in the shortcut bar. This will give us different format options to output the report.

   In this case, we choose **Print Preview** as follows:

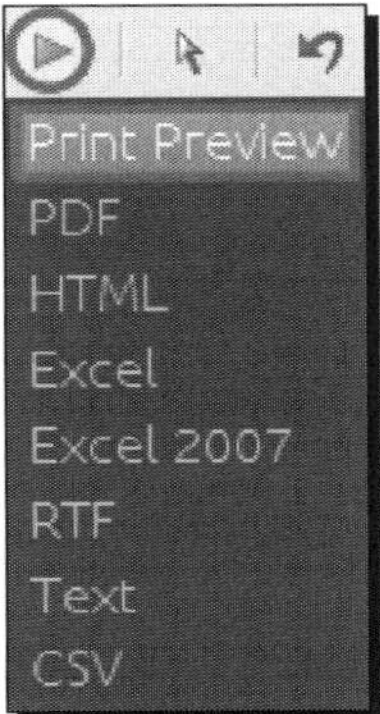

3. This will give us the following preview:

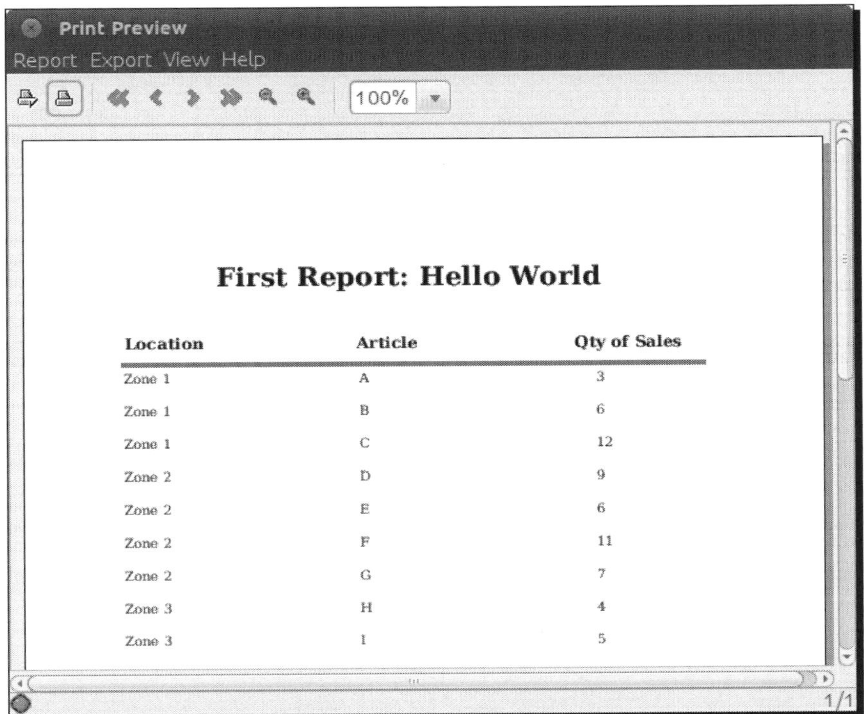

What just happened?

We added the fields **Zones**, **Products**, and **Quantity** to the **Details** section of our report. Then we executed our report in preview mode.

The second half of the report

So far we have completed the first part of the guide, more precisely the creation of our first report. We have created a data set type **Table** and configured the **Report Header**, **Details Header**, and **Details** sections.

Now, we will move on to the second part of the report. We will add functions, configure the **Details Footer** section, and give final touches to the design.

Time for action – adding functions

We will add a function to color the rows in an alternating manner, differentiating between the even and odd rows, just as they appear in the finished report.

1. In the **Data** tab, we right-click on **Functions**, and in the drop-down menu, we select the **Add Functions...** option.

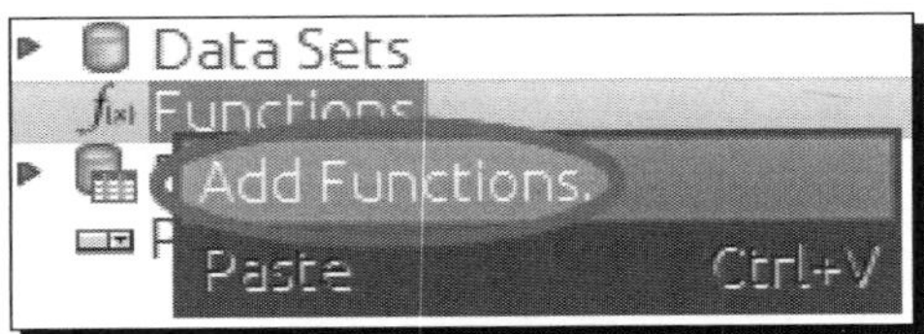

2. Now we will see the following window:

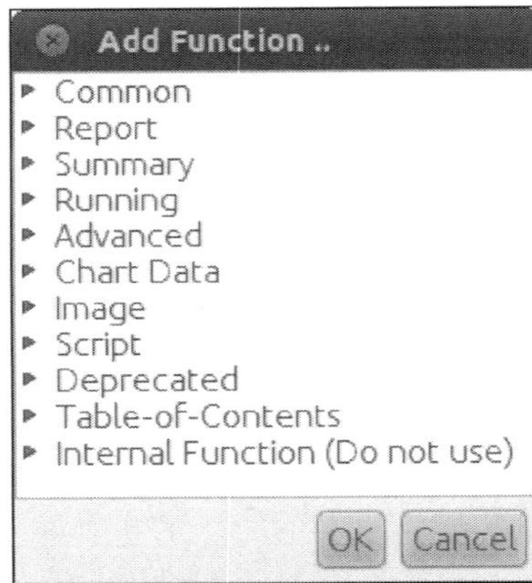

3. This window contains all of the functions that we can create in PRD grouped into categories. In this case, we choose the **Row Banding** function in the **Report** category and click on **OK** to create it:

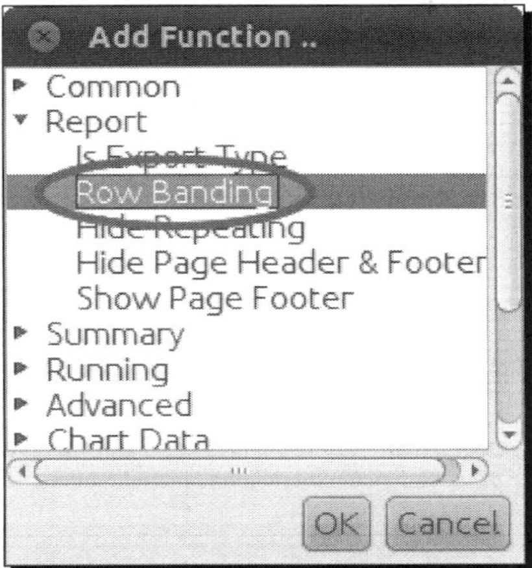

4. Next, we configure its name, background color, and the name of the element/object that the function will be applied to:
   - **Function Name** = `RowBanding`
   - **Active Banding Color** = `#ccff66`
   - **Apply Element(s) Named** = `oddEvenRowBanding`
   - Now that the function has been defined, we can apply it

5. In the **Structure** tab, navigate to **Master Report** | **Group** | **Details Body** | **Details**:

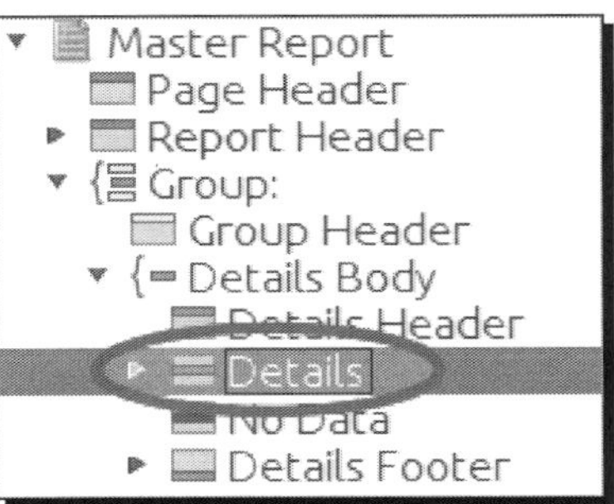

6. In this tab, we configure the following:
   - **Attributes.name** = `oddEvenRowBanding`

   This will apply the `oddEvenRowBanding` function to this object.

7. We see what the report looks like at this point. Press the preview button. We should obtain the following result:

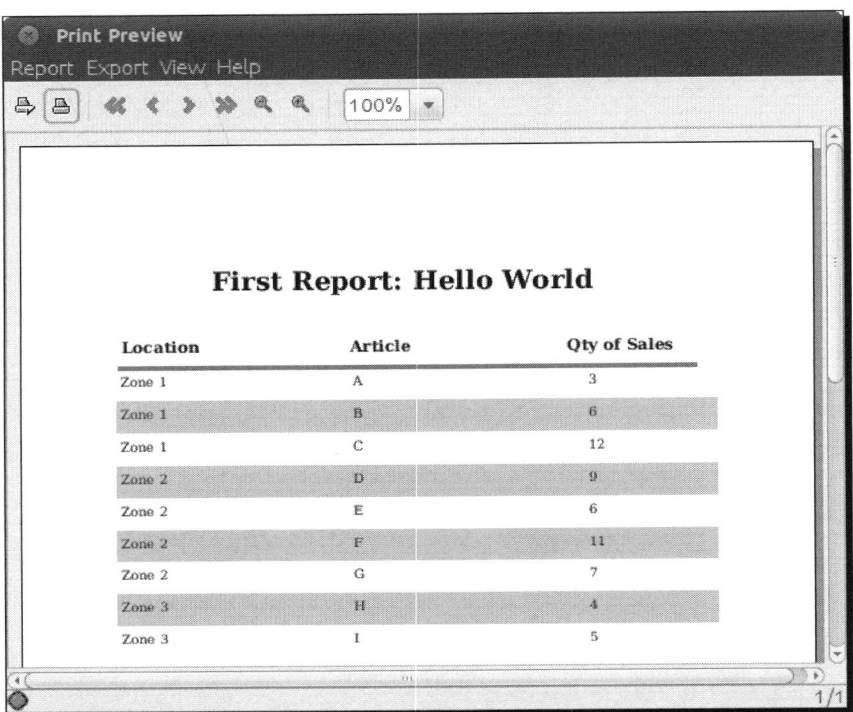

What just happened?

We added a function to alternately color the rows of our report. We configured this function according to our needs and we applied it to our report.

Time for action – configuring the Details Footer section

Next, we will configure the **Details Footer** section as seen here:

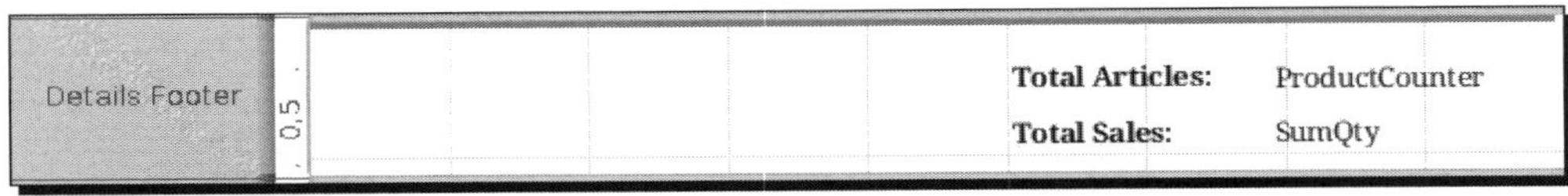

1. We will make the **Details Footer** section visible in our report. The **Details Footer** section is commonly used to place a summary of what was seen in **Details**.

2. Go to the **Structure** tab, and in the hierarchical tree, navigate to **Master Report | Group: | Details Body | Details Footer**. Then configure **Attributes.hide-on-canvas** with the value **false**:

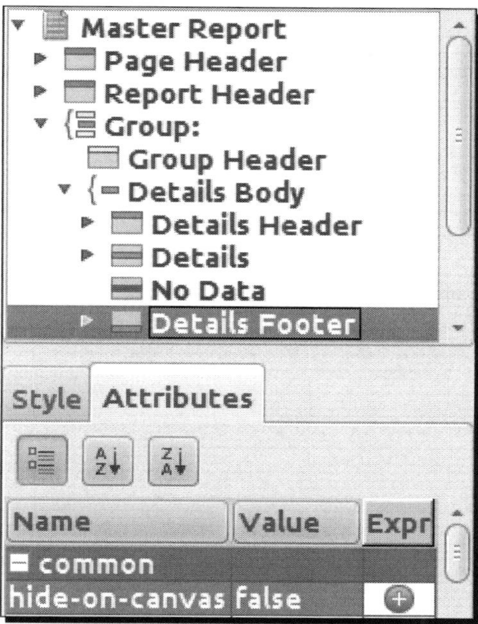

3. We will add the following two labels in the work area of this section:
   - `Total Articles:`
   - `Total Sales:`
4. And we will set the following value for both of them:
   - **Style.bold** = `true`
5. Next, we will create a function to count the rows, in this case, of the products sold.

   We create the `Count (Running)` function, found in the **Running** category, and configure it with the following characteristic:
   - Function name = `ProductCounter`

The functions that include the word `Running` as part of their name tell us that they are executed as the data is processed, that is, on the fly. In this case, `Count (Running)` will count the report's rows as they are presented in the **Details** section of each page.

6. Similarly to the previous step, we create a function that will take a sum of the sales made.

   We create the `Sum (Running)` function, found in the **Running** category, and configure it with the following characteristics:

   - Function name = `SumQty`
   - Field name = `Quantity`

> In this case, `Sum (Running)` will take a sum of the `Quantity` field as the data is presented in the **Details** section of each page.

7. Now we place the two recently created functions to the right of the label that corresponds to each, that is, we will place `ProductCounter` to the right of the first label and `SumQty` to the right of the second label.

   Let's consider, when we are laying out the report, that an object we have inserted becomes red; refer to the following example:

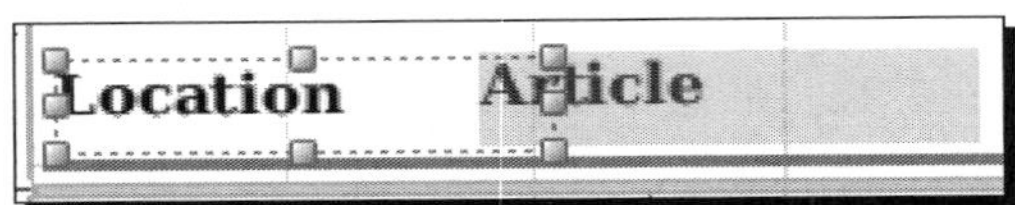

   This indicates that this object is superimposed on another object and that it is possible that when the report is executed, this object will not be viewable normally. In these cases, we should arrange and resize the objects so that none are superimposed.

8. We copy the horizontal line ( ) created earlier by pressing the icon. We select the **Details Footer** section and paste the horizontal line by pressing the icon. Then we position it in the upper part of this section.

9. We see what the report looks like at this point. Press the preview button. We should obtain the following result:

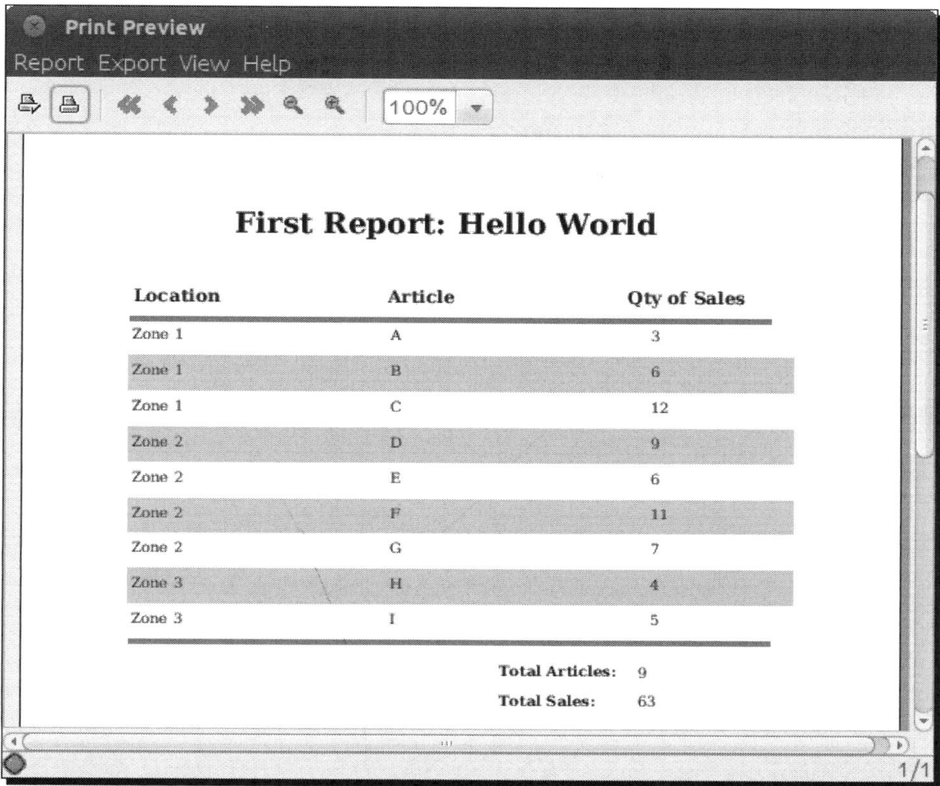

What just happened?

We customized our report's **Details Footer** section. We created and added two functions, one to calculate the quantity of articles sold and another to calculate the sum of the sales.

Time for action – adding more details

Next, we will add two vertical lines in the **Details** section and add an image in the **Page Header** section:

1. We add another detail in the **Details** section.

   We add two vertical lines ( ) to separate our report's columns. It should look as follows:

Details Header	Location	Article	Qty of Sales
Details	Zones	Products	Quantity

2. Establish the following characteristics for both lines:
   - **Style.stroke** = `solid, 1.0`
   - **Style.text-color** = `#0099333`; to finish this example, we add an image in the **Page Header** section

3. In the **Page Header** section, place the **Image** object ( ). Right-click on this object, and in the drop-down menu, choose the **Edit Content...** option.

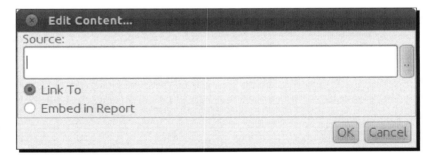

4. We need to indicate our image's path and choose how we want the image connected to our report:
   - **Link To**: This option only stores the image's path. The image is obtained when the report is executed.
   - **Embed In Report**: This option stores the image as a resource with the report's metadata.

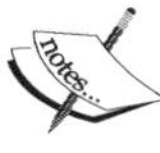

> The advantage of **Link To** is that the size of the report is smaller. Also, the image can be changed, maintaining the same name, and the report will continue using it. The disadvantage is that it depends on the image's location. The advantage of **Embed in Report** is that it does not depend on the image's location. The disadvantage is that the image will always be the same and the report will be larger in size.

In this case, we choose Embed In Report, press the ... button, and search for an image to be put in our report. Next, we press on the OK button to save our changes.

5. Let's see what our first report looks like. Press the preview button. We should obtain the following result:

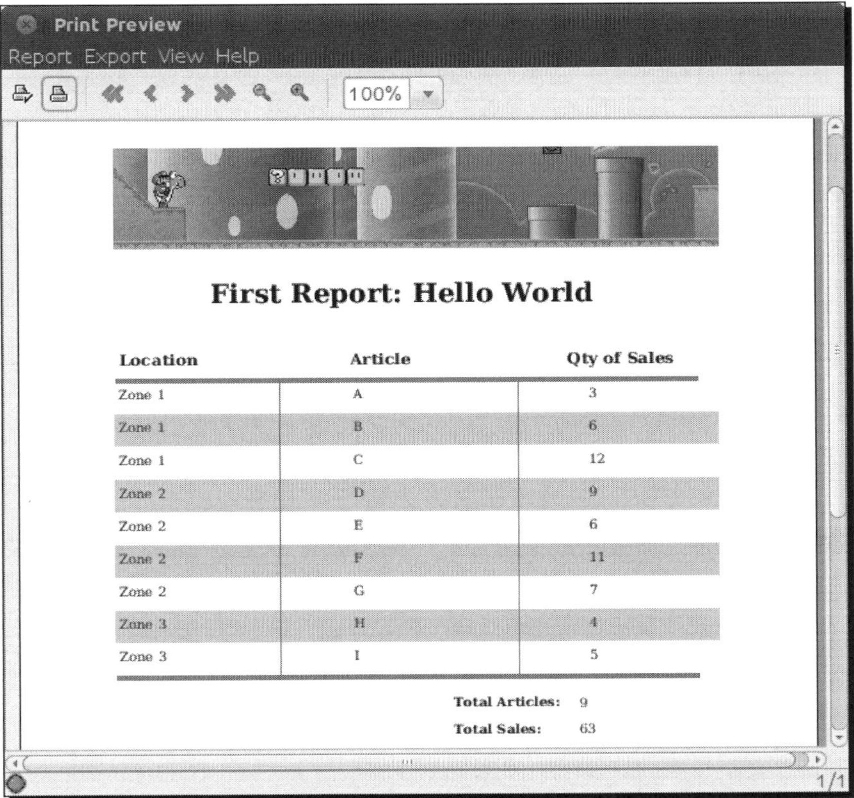

What just happened?

We added a vertical line in the **Details** section to separate the fields it contains. We added an image in the **Page Header** section. Finally, we executed the report in the preview mode.

Output types

We will now see some examples of the main output types of PRD.

Time for action – exporting in different formats

Next, we will see how to present the report we just created by exporting it to different formats:

1. Press on the icon found in the shortcut bar. In this case, we choose **PDF**:

2. Now press on the icon and choose **HTML**:

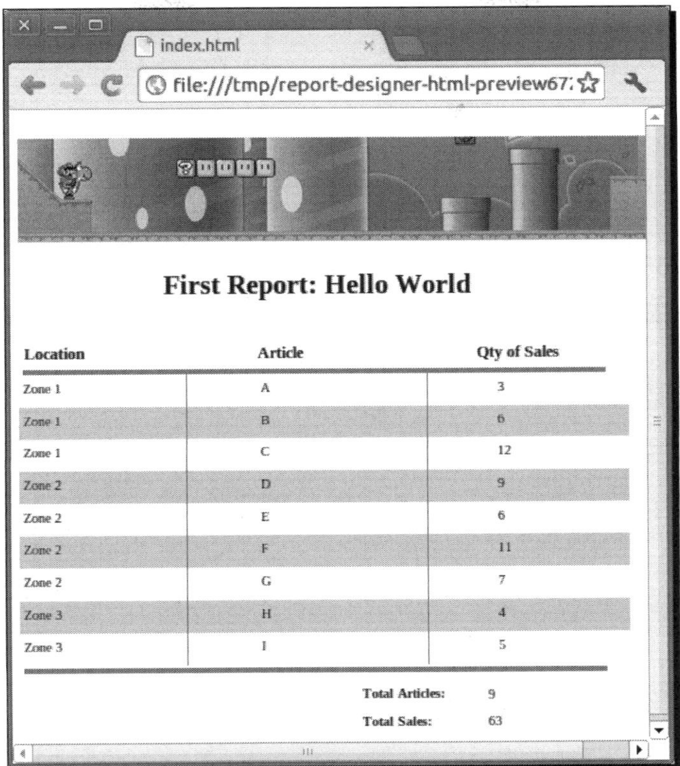

First Report: Hello World

Location	Article	Qty of Sales
Zone 1	A	3
Zone 1	B	6
Zone 1	C	12
Zone 2	D	9
Zone 2	E	6
Zone 2	F	11
Zone 2	G	7
Zone 3	H	4
Zone 3	I	5

Total Articles: 9

Total Sales: 63

3. Press on the icon and choose **Excel** (or **Excel 2007**).

What just happened?

We exported our report to different formats, that is, to PDF, HTML, and Excel/Excel 2007.

Have a go hero

Now that we have made our first report, it is time for you to put into practice what we have been learning. We propose that you make some small modifications to the `01_Hello_World.prpt` report so that it looks as follows:

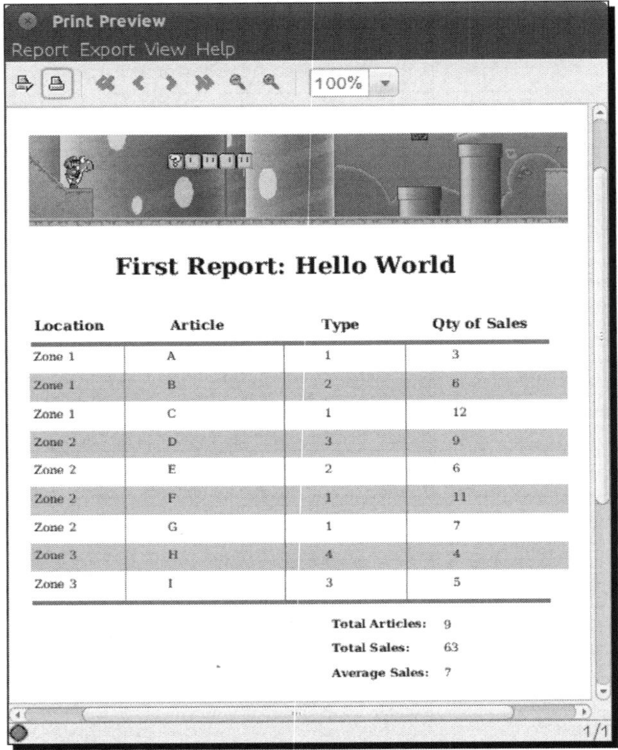

The steps you should perform, broadly speaking, are as follows:

1. Save the report with the name `01_Hello_World_Plus.prpt`.
2. Edit the `ZoneProductQty` data set, adding the **Type** column with its corresponding values.
3. Create a function that returns the average of the quantities sold, that is, that calculates it based on the `Quantity` field.

Pop Quiz – data sets, functions, and objects

Q1. Which of the following affirmations is true?

1. The **Table** data set uses a table of our database.
2. We can create a data set by extracting data from a spreadsheet.
3. To assign a value to a label to display it, we have to configure **Style.value**.
4. The `RowBanding` function can give background colors to the rows in the **Details** section, but always alternately coloring the rows.
5. The **Image** object allows either embedding an image in the report or taking it from a path.
6. The **Print Preview** option shows the report in the HTML format by default.

Summary

In this chapter, we created our first report by following a series of steps that we listed and explained in detail.

We created a **Table** type data set and configured its data manually. We defined three columns: **Zones**, **Products**, and **Quantity**. We specified the type of data that each would contain (`String`, `Integer`, and so on). Then we populated the table with the example data.

We configured the **Report Header** and **Details Header** report sections, adding labels and a horizontal line. Also, we configured the characteristics of these insertable objects.

In the **Details** section, we added the fields from the table we created initially.

We created and added various functions to the report. We created and added `RowBanding` to alternately color the data in the **Details** section, and in the **Details Footer** section, we added `Count (Running)` and `Sum (Running)` to count and sum up respectively.

To add a personal touch, in the **Page Header** section we added an image of our liking.

We saw how useful the preview option is to see what the report we are designing looks like.

We also saw how PRD exports the report in diverse formats: PDF, HTML, and Excel/Excel 2007. We also showed screenshots of these different formats. Finally in the *Time for action* sections, we proposed that you make some modifications to the recently created report. Among them, we added a new column to our data sets and created a function of the type `Average (Running)`. In the next chapter, we will explain how to create/edit JDBC-type data sets and how to create a JDBC connection to our Sakila database with its corresponding SQL query.

5

Adding a Relational Data Source

In this chapter, we will create a copy of the report created in the previous chapter and modify it so that it takes its data from a relational source. We will explain what JDBC is, what a JDBC driver is, and how it is used.

The topics we will be covering in the chapter include the following:

- Downloading the JDBC driver for MySQL and copying it inside Pentaho Report Designer (PRD)
- Using the UI to create/edit JDBC-type data sets and creating a JDBC connection to our sakila database, with its corresponding SQL query
- Modifying the following sections: **Report Header**, **Group Header**, **Details Header**, and **Details Footer**; we will configure the last two to be repeated on each page
- Deleting certain objects from the report, adding some new ones, and modifying others so that they all correspond to our new data source
- Aggregation functions, explaining the most used ones; we will add a new function into our report and use its output in order to modify the style of a message
- Understanding and modifying the charset of our report

As an extra, we will invite you to create your own report from the ground up, as well as give you a few tips to assist you in its creation.

Learning about JDBC driver

Java Database Connectivity (**JDBC**) is an **Application Programming Interface** (**API**), which defines how a client should access and interact with a database from Java. Each provider (IBM, Oracle, Sun, Microsoft, and others) implements the mechanism (the "How To") for its own product, allowing the client not to be bothered with the details of each implementation and worrying only about its interface. In Java slang, this is known merely as a controller or JDBC driver.

A JDBC driver, generally speaking, consists of one or various files with a `.jar` extension, which must be copied on a certain path (Java `CLASSPATH`, that is) so that applications can make use of it instead.

In order for a JDBC driver to be used, Java programs require the following information:

- **URL**: This is a string that specifies, among other things, the protocol, location of the server, port, and name of the database.
- **Driver**: This is the name of the class that implements the `java.sql.Driver` interface.
- **User**: This is the user with the necessary privileges on the database engine (this parameter might be optional depending on the case).
- **Password**: This is the password corresponding to the user (this parameter might also be optional).

In some cases, the inclusion of the user and password is supported within the URL, so we only need to define the **URL** and **Driver** parameters.

The syntax to indicate the URL and driver class name should always be present in the implementation documentation of each provider.

For example, in the case of MySQL, the information regarding the implementation can be found in the following web page:

`http://dev.mysql.com/downloads/connector/j/5.1.html`

The implementation details are as follows:

- **Driver**: `com.mysql.jdbc.Driver`
- **URL**: `jdbc:mysql://localhost:3306/MyDataBase`
- **Protocol**: `jdbc:mysql`
- **Name server**: `localhost (local address)`
- **Port**: `3306 (default port)`
- **Database**: `MyDataBase`

Time for action – configuring drivers

At this time, we will download the JDBC driver from the official MySQL assets and then copy it into the Pentaho Report Designer.

In order to download the MySQL JDBC driver we will open the following web page: `http://dev.mysql.com/downloads/connector/j/5.1.html`.

1. Move downwards in the page and find the tab named **Generally Available (GA) Releases**. We will choose the right file, depending on our operative system, from the following choices:
   - **mysql-connector-java-x.x.xx.tar.gz**
   - **mysql-connector-java.x.x.xx.zip**
2. Click on the **Download** button and follow the steps to perform the download.

   In order for PRD to be able to make use of the recently downloaded JDBC driver, we need to copy it to a certain path.
3. Open the compressed file we just downloaded and browse its contents until we locate the JDBC driver: `mysql-connector-java-x.x.xx-bin.jar`.
4. Copy this `.jar` to `[PRD_HOME]/lib/jdbc`.
5. For the PRD to load the JDBC driver we just added, we need to restart the PRD.

What just happened?

We just downloaded the MySQL JDBC driver and copied it into the PRD library folders and later restarted PRD.

Creating a new data set

In this section, we will see how to create a new data set.

Time for action – creating a new data set

Now we will open the previously created report and save it with a different name. This copy shall serve as the base report, which we will use throughout this chapter. Later we will create a new data set of JDBC type.

1. Open the `01_Hello_World.prpt` report from the PRD UI. To do so, click on the icon from the **Shortcuts** menu, and search for the report `01_Hello_World.prpt`; select it, and click on the **OK** button.

2. Now navigate to **File** | **Save As...** and save the current report with the following name: `03_Adding_Relational_DS.prpt`.
3. We will now create a new data set of JDBC type. In order to do so, go to the **Data Panel** (inside the **Panel** tab), right-click on **Data Sets** and select the **JDBC** option.
4. We will be presented with a new window on the left side of which we will be able to observe the connections that have already been defined by the current user:

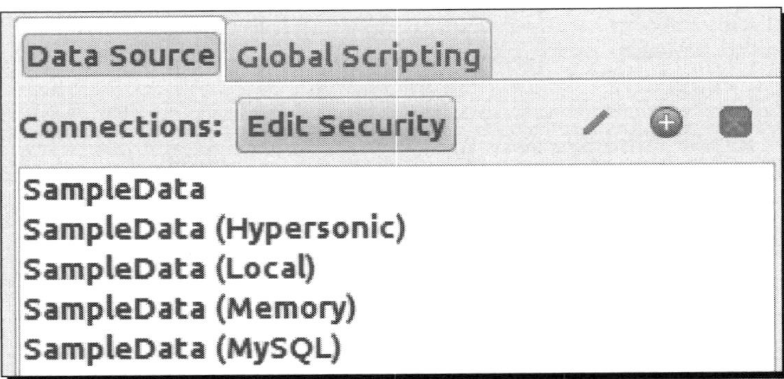

> By default, PRD brings a series of example data sets. To see these connections in detail, we can go to the following folders:
>
> - **On a Linux system**: `/home/userName/.pentaho/report-designer/user/org/pentaho/reporting/ui/datasources/jdbc/Settings`
> - **On a Windows system**: `C:\Documents and Settings\userName\.pentaho\report-designer\user\org\pentaho\reporting\ui\datasources\jdbcSettings`

5. Now we will create a new connection to our `sakila` database. To do so we will select the option and complete the newly opened form with the following data:
   - **Connection Name**: `sakila db`
   - **Connection Type**: `MySQL`
   - **Access**: `Native (JDBC)`
   - **Host Name**: `localhost`
   - **Database Name**: `sakila`
   - **Port Number**: `3306`
   - **User Name**: `root`
   - **Password**: `root`

This **Connection Configuration** window is used by every tool in the Pentaho Suite.

6. Once the form is completed, click on the **Test** button to verify that the data we entered is correct, and then click on **OK** to continue.

7. At this stage, we will create a new query and in order to do so click on the icon found on the **Available Queries** section. We should now select the new query and modify the **Query Name** section to have the value `CountryCustomerAmount`. Finally, in the **Query** section, we will copy the following query:

```
SELECT country.country, customer.first_name, customer.last_name,
SUM(payment.amount) sum_amount
FROM payment
INNER JOIN customer ON customer.customer_id=payment.customer_id
INNER JOIN address ON address.address_id=customer.address_id
INNER JOIN city ON city.city_id=address.city_id
INNER JOIN country ON country.country_id=city.country_id
GROUP BY payment.customer_id
ORDER BY country.country
LIMIT 0,30
```

8. To verify that we have performed every step correctly, click on the **Preview** button to obtain a quick view of the relevant data.

Preview

country	first_name	last_name	sum_amount
Afghanistan	VERA	MCCOY	67.82
Algeria	JUDY	GRAY	96.75
Algeria	MARIO	CHEATHAM	112.72
Algeria	JUNE	CARROLL	173.63
American Samoa	ANTHONY	SCHWAB	71.80
Angola	MARTIN	BALES	103.73
Angola	CLAUDE	HERZOG	111.75
Anguilla	BOBBY	BOUDREAU	106.65
Argentina	JASON	MORRISSEY	128.72
Argentina	LYDIA	BURKE	82.76
Argentina	DARRYL	ASHCRAFT	76.77
Argentina	JORDAN	ARCHULETA	132.70
Argentina	WILLIE	HOWELL	101.74
Argentina	PERRY	SWAFFORD	117.76
Argentina	MICHEAL	FORMAN	102.74
Argentina	WILLIE	MARKHAM	101.75
Argentina	LEONARD	SCHOFIELD	109.68
Argentina	FLORENCE	WOODS	126.70

Close

In the **Query** section, we can find the button. It brings up a quite useful visual editor, which can assist us in the creation of queries. With this editor you can drag-and-drop tables to use, check the fields that will be included, and so on. It is ideal for users who have no knowledge of SQL.

9. Finally, click on **OK**.

   PRD supports simultaneous data sets on the same report, but only one of them can be selected to be used in the report. At this point, we have two data sets available in our report, but **ZoneProductQty** is selected.

10. Right-click on our newly created **CountryCustomerAmount** data set and select the **Select Query** option.

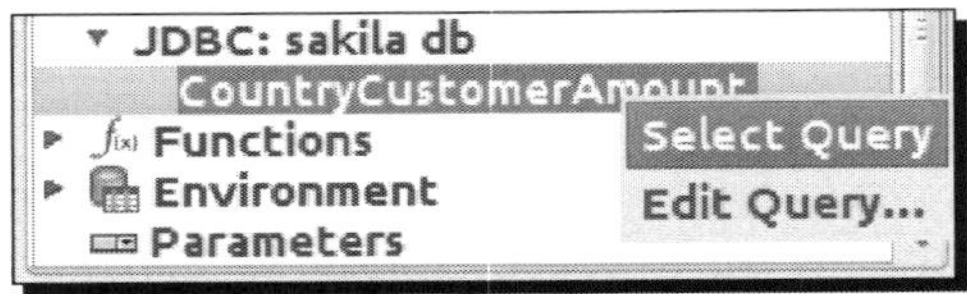

11. Now select the parent node of our old data set, that is, **Table**, and then click on the option (available on the **Shortcuts** menu).

What just happened?

We just opened the previously created `01_Hello_World.prpt` report and saved it with a different name: `03_Adding_Relational_DS.prpt`. We created a JDBC-type data set and defined the connection to our `sakila` database. Then we created a new query and performed a preview on the data. We also discarded the old data set and selected the new one.

Time for action – modifying the header and detail

Next, we will modify our report's layout. We will delete the old objects from the **Report Header** section and the **Details Header** section, hide the **Page Header** section and enable the **Group Header** section of our report. Then, we will add three new labels (**Country**, **Customer**, and **Amount**) and modify the data to be shown on the **Details** section. Also, we will configure the behavior of **Details Header**.

1. We should now delete every **label** (Ab) as well as the **horizontal-line** () from the **Report Header** section and the **Details Header** section.
2. Then we will go to **Report tree structure** (**Structure tab**) and search the tree for the following node: **Master Report** | **Group** | **Group Header**. We will select this node and modify **Attributes.hide-on-canvas** to `false`.

This modification will enable the visualization of the **Group Header** in the Work Area.

3. Then we will go to Report tree structure (**Structure tab**) and search the tree for the following node: **Master Report** | **Group** | **Details Body** | **Details Header**. We will select this node and modify its behavior:

   - **Style.repeat-header**: `true`

   This modification will make this section present on every page.

> In all sections of our report we can configure its behavior (**Style**, **category page-behavior**). For example, **Style.pagebreak-before** and **Style.pagebreak-after** are used to add a page break before or after the section is presented in the report.

4. Now we will delete the **image** ( ) from the **Page Header** section.
5. Go to Report tree structure (**Structure tab**) and search the tree for the following node: **Master Report** | **Page Header**. Select this node and perform the following change:

   - **Attributes.hide-on-canvas**: `true`

   This modification will hide the **Page Header** section from the UI.

6. We will now add a new label in the **Details Header** section, and configure the following values:

   - **Attributes.value**: `Adding Relational Data Source`
   - **Style.font-size**: `18`
   - **Style.bold**: `true`

7. We will now add three labels to the **Details Header** section and modify their text so that they look like the ones shown in the following screenshot:

Details Header	**Country**	**Customer**	**Amount**

To modify the text of the labels we should change the value present in **Attributes.value** for every label. We will also style these labels a little bit by changing the following fields:

   - **Style.font-size**: `12`
   - **Style.bold**: `true`

PRD allows for multiple objects to be selected simultaneously and then change their **Attributes** and **Styles** in a single action.

To select multiple objects at the same time we can use the option available on the Shortcuts menu of the UI.

Now, we need to draw a line beneath the three labels so that it looks like this:

Details Header | **Country** | **Customer** | **Amount**

But this time we will not add a horizontal-line object. What we will do is set the bottom border of the **Details Header** section. We will go to Report tree structure (**Structure** tab), select the node **Master Report** | **Group** | **Details Body** | **Details Header** and set the following:

- **Style.bottom-style**: `solid`
- **Style.bottom-size:** `4.0`
- **Style.bottom-color**: `#009933`

8. Now delete the **text-field** ( ) and **number-field** ( ) objects available on the **Details** section and add to this very section a **text-field** object, as well as a **Message** ( ) and a **number-field**:

9. On the **Message** and **number-field** objects, we will configure the **Style.h-align** to have a value `CENTER`, so that the text on them is horizontally centered on display. Now, we will modify the values of these three objects so that they show the data from our **CountryCustomerAmount** data set.

   - In the first object (**text-field**) we will modify **Attributes.field** and select the value `country`.
   - In the second object (**Message**) we will modify **Attributes.value** with the following: `$(first_name), $(last_name)`.
   - In the third object (**number-field**) we will modify **Attributes.field** and select the value `sum_amount`.

The **Details** section of our report should look like the following:

Details	country	$(first_name), $(last_name)	sum_amount

To visualize what our reports are looking like we can use the **Preview** option.

What just happened?

We deleted the labels and horizontal-line, which were present on the **Report Header** and **Details Header** sections of our report. We hid the **Page Header** section, and then enabled the **Group Header** section. We configured the **Details Header** section to be repeated on every page. We also added and styled three new labels to the mentioned section: **Country**, **Customer**, and **Amount**. We then deleted the old objects present in the **Details** section and added three new objects: **text-field**, **Message**, and **number-field**. Finally, we modified these objects to contain information coming from our **CountryCustomerAmount** data set.

Time for action – modifying the report's footer

We will configure the **Details Footer** section for it to be repeated on every page of our report. We will configure the top border of the **Details Footer** section. We will modify the name of the labels on the **Details Footer** section to match the ones in our data set. Finally, we will modify the **SumQty** function to perform a sum on the `sum_amount` field.

1. We will go to Report tree structure (**Structure** tab) and search the tree for the node by navigating to: **Master Report** | **Group** | **Details Footer**. We will select this node and modify it in the following way:

   - **Style.repeat-header**: `true`

   This modification will make this section present on every page.

2. We will delete **horizontal-line** from the **Details Footer** section.
3. We will go to Report tree structure (**Structure** tab), navigate to **Master Report** | **Group** | **Details Body** | **Details Footer**, and set the following:

   - **Style.top-style**: `solid`
   - **Style.top-size**: `4.0`
   - **Style.top-color** : `#009933`

4. At this point, we will modify the text belonging to the two labels of the **Details Footer** section. On the upper label, we will place the text **Total Customers**, on the lower one we will put **Total Amount**:

5. We will now modify the **SumQty** function so that it performs a sum on the `sum_amount` field. We will access the Data Panel (**Panel tab**), inside **Functions** we will select **SumQty** and change the following:

    - **Field Name**: `sum_amount`

We should modify the **Function Name** of this function, as well as the **Product Counter** one, but these modifications will not be done now so that we do not introduce too many extra steps. Feel free to perform these changes in your report.

To see what our report looks like so far we can use the **Preview** option.

What just happened?

We configured the **Details Footer** section to be repeated on every page. Also, in this section, we delete the horizontal-line and we set its border top. We configured two labels and the function so that they match our current data set.

Aggregation functions

So far, we have introduced two functions into our report:

- `ProductCounter`: This performs a cumulative count on the rows in the **Details** section. This function belongs to the **Running** category.
- `SumQty`: This performs a cumulative count on the **sum_amount** fields of the rows present in the **Details** section. This function also belongs to the **Running** category.

Every function in the **Running** category performs calculations, sum, counts, and so on in a cumulative fashion, that is, they take into consideration the values obtained on previous pages. For example, the **Count** function appearing on the first page performs a count of the rows of the said page, from the second page on it will add the current page count to the total count of the previous one. In the same way, the functions **Maximum** and **Minimum**, when applied to the first page only take into consideration the minimum and maximum values, respectively, as shown on the first page. In the following pages, they will only update these values if a bigger or lesser value is to be found on the current page, otherwise they will remain the same.

In the **Summary** category, we will find functions that perform calculations on a per page or total basis. In this category, the **Count** function will count the total number of rows present in our whole report. Something similar applies to the **Maximum** and **Minimum** functions, the maximum and minimum values are calculated only once, taking into consideration every row in our report. The functions **Count** for **Page** and **Sum** for **Page** perform these calculations for every page, that is, the first one counts the row present in every page, and the second one performs a sum of the values present in every page.

Inside the **Common** category, we will find functions used to manage the pages of our report: **Page**, **Total Page Count**, and **Page** of **Pages**. Within this category, we will also find **Open Formula**, which allows the introduction of more complex calculations and provides a very powerful and useful Formula Editor. This editor is the same one we see when we click on the ⊕ button on the **Attributes** and/or **Style** options of an object.

Later we will talk in detail about Open Formula.

Another function that is very commonly used is **Row Banding** under the **Report** category, which is the one we have used on our reports to color the rows in an interleaved fashion. If we take the time to explore the rest of the categories and functions, we will find a great amount of them, each one with a specific mission.

Time for action – using functions to configure styles

We will now create a function to obtain the maximum value for **sum_amount** present in our report. We will then use the said value to obtain its corresponding customer and apply a bold style onto it.

1. In the **Summary** category, we will create a new function **Maximum** and configure the following:
   - **Function Name** = `MaxSumAmount`
   - **Field Name** = `sum_amount`

2. Now we will select the **Message** object we placed in the **Details** section of our report and configure the following:
   - **Style.bold**: `=IF([sum_amount]=[MaxSumAmount];"true";"false")`

   This formula will analyze row by row if the current value of **sum_amount** equals **MaxSumAmount** (the maximum value for **sum_amount**). If such a condition is `true`, the name of the customer shall be put in bold, if it is `false`, it will retain the current style.

In later chapters, we will discuss greater detail the definition of formulas.

3. If we now perform a preview on our report, we will be able to see how the style for the customer with the greatest amount has been changed:

Adding Relational Data Source

Country	Customer	Amount
Afghanistan	VERA, MCCOY	67,82
Algeria	JUNE, CARROLL	173,63
Algeria	JUDY, GRAY	96,75
Algeria	MARIO, CHEATHAM	112,72

What just happened?

We created a function **Maximum** of the type **Summary** so that it obtains the greatest value for **sum_amount**. We selected the message object, which contains the description of the current customer, and configured its style to be **Style.bold** when the current customer is the one who possesses the maximum amount value.

Encoding charset

The encoding charset is a method that allows the conversion of a character in a natural language into a symbol of a different representation system as a number in an electronic system. The conversion is performed after applying a series of codification rules. This concept is very important since its application allows us to show symbols belonging to different languages into our reports.

To modify the encoding charset of our report, we must go to Report tree structure (the **Structure** tab), search the tree for the **Master Report** node, select it, and put into **Style.encoding** the charset we wish to use, for example:

- **Style.encoding** = `LATIN1`

> If you are having encoding problems and the report is correctly configured, check that Java and data base are correctly configured.

Have a go hero

In this section, we will invite you to create your own report from the ground up, and to employ in this endeavor the knowledge you have acquired up to this point. The report we are inviting you to create should look like the following:

Group Header	**Adding Relational Data Source Plus**	
Details Header	**Country**	**Amount**
Details	country	sum_amount
Details Footer	**Count Country:**	RunningCount
	Total Country:	SummaryCount
Page Footer	PageOfPages	

Pop quiz – JDBC, Functions, and Encoding Charset

Q1. Which of the following affirmations are true?

1. JDBC is a driver to connect to databases.
2. MySQL's JDBC driver is included by default in the whole Pentaho suite.
3. When a new connection is created on PRD, it is available to every user in the system.
4. The **Count** functions of the **Running** and **Summary** categories perform the same calculations, the difference lies in which section of the report they are placed.
5. PRD's feature to enable the modification of the encoding charset of our reports makes it possible to show symbols from different languages in the said reports.

Summary

In this chapter, we created a copy of the previously created report and modified it to use a relational source to obtain its data. We then learned about JDBC and JDBC drivers, downloaded the MySQL JDBC driver, and copied it into Pentaho BI Server and PRD.

We also created a JDBC connection with our sakila database and wrote an SQL query to obtain data to fill our report. We learned how to modify certain sections and objects of our report; among these modifications, we configured **Details Header** and **Details Footer** sections to be repeated on every page.

We discussed the most commonly used aggregation functions and created a formula to use a function to modify the style of an object. We also explained how to use and apply an encoding charset to our report.

Finally, in order to strengthen the acquired knowledge we proposed the creation of a new report from the ground up.

In the next chapter we will explain how to create **Groups** in our reports.

6
Adding Groups

In this chapter, we will use the report we created in the previous chapter and configure it to work with groups.

Through the use of groups, we will be able to group our information according to several criteria and thereby provide the end user a more clearer view of their data. Groups are a feature commonly used in many reports.

The topics that will be covered in this chapter are as follows:

- Modifying the query in our data set as well as the layout of our report.
- Discussing the hierarchy of positioning objects within different sections, and enabling an object to go up or down within the hierarchy level.
- Generating a group for each country value. We will also take a look at how we can enforce each group to start on a new page.
- Modifying the functions so that they perform their calculations based on the values present in each group.

As an extra, we will invite you to create your own report from the ground up, as well as give you a series of tips to assist you in its creation.

Starting practice

We should now open the report created in the previous chapter (`03_Adding_Realtional_DS.prpt`) and save it with the following name: `05_Adding_Groups.prpt`. This report will serve as the base report we will be using throughout this chapter.

Time for action – modifying the SQL query

We will now modify the previously defined SQL query with the objective of getting a data set that is more suitable to working with groups.

1. Go to the **Data** panel (in the **Panel** tab). Within the **Data Sets** tree, we will right-click on the **JDBC: sakila db** node and select the **Edit Datasource...** option, as shown in the following screenshot:

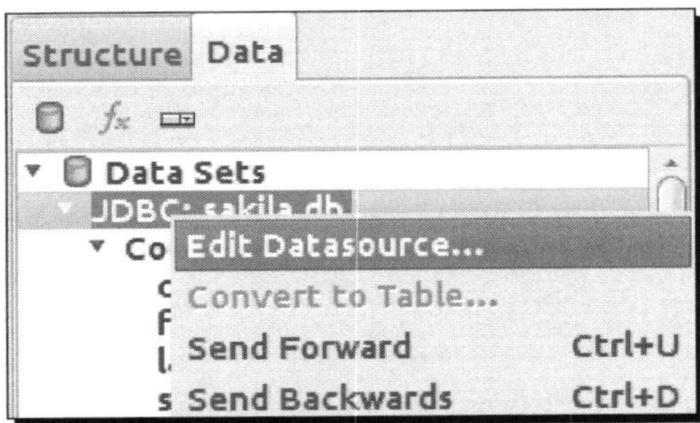

2. Just as in the previous chapter, we will be presented with the **Connections Editor** window. What we will do here is select the **sakila db** item within the **Connection** section; then, in the **Available Queries** section, we will select **CountryCustomerAmount**.
3. Now, in the **Query** section, we will select the SQL query written there and delete it and then replace it with the following code:

```
SELECT country.country_id, country.country, customer.first_name,
customer.last_name, SUM(payment.amount) sum_amount
FROM payment
INNER JOIN customer ON customer.customer_id=payment.customer_id
INNER JOIN address ON address.address_id=customer.address_id
INNER JOIN city ON city.city_id=address.city_id
INNER JOIN country ON country.country_id=city.country_id
WHERE country.country_id IN (20,24,29,34,48,67,74)
GROUP BY payment.customer_id
ORDER BY country.country, customer.first_name
```

4. The following screenshot shows what we have just done:

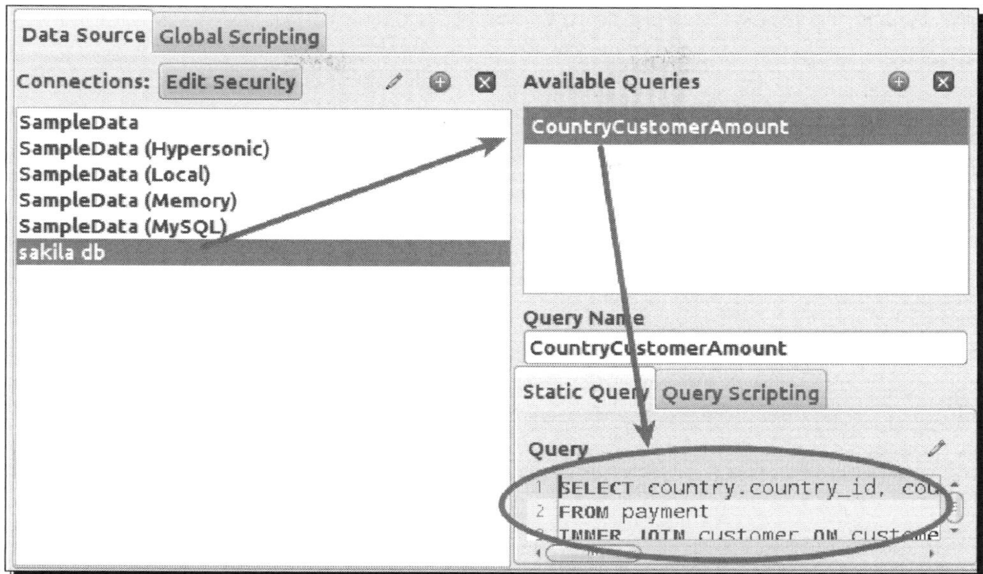

What just happened?

We edited the **CountryCustomerAmount** data set and modified its SQL query so that the obtained data can be used in the creation of a report that uses groups.

Time for action – configuring the layout

We will now modify the layout of our report so that it looks like the following:

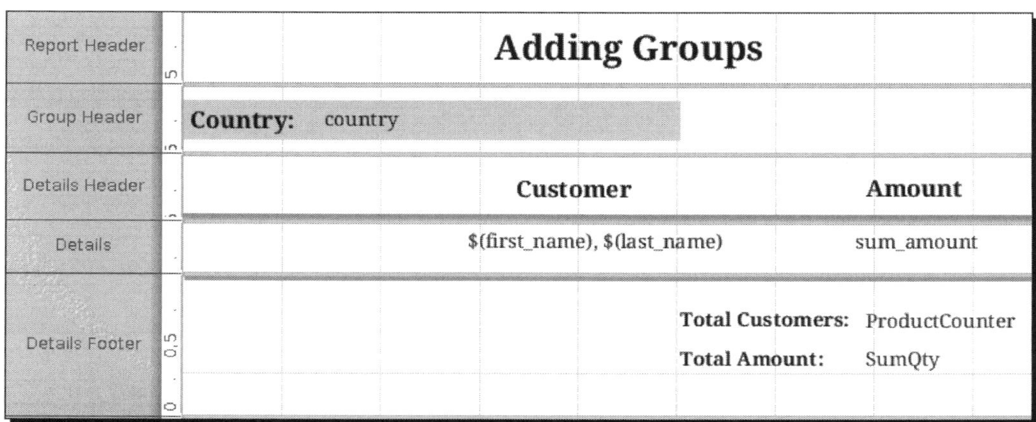

We will modify the **Report Header**, **Group Header**, **Details Header**, **Details**, and **Details Footer** sections.

1. In the **Report Header** section, we will insert a label to serve as the title, containing the text `Adding Groups`.
2. In the **Group Header** section, we will delete the label we were previously using as the title and put a label containing the text `Country:`. We will also diminish this object's length and place a text field to its right. We will set the **Attributes.field** value of this newly added text field to **country**. In PRD, overlapping objects might not be shown correctly in the final report; this is why we adjusted the label's length. When an overlap between objects exists, PRD colors them red to alert us. However, there are some objects that can overlap, such as rectangle, ellipse, horizontal line, and vertical line.
3. We will now add a rectangle to the **Group Header** section. We do this by using its icon, which is shown in the following screenshot:

4. We then modify its size and position so that it looks like the following:

5. We will configure this rectangle in the following way:
   - **Style.bg-color** = `#fcce9f`
   - **Style.text-color** = `#fcce9f`
6. As we can see, by assigning a background color to the **rectangle**, the other two objects cannot be displayed in the work area. This is because PRD handles objects in a layered fashion, and every time a new object is added, it is added to the top layer by default. If we go to the **Report** tree structure (in the **Structure** tab), we will be able to see, in the **Group Header** node, what the layer hierarchy of this section looks like.

   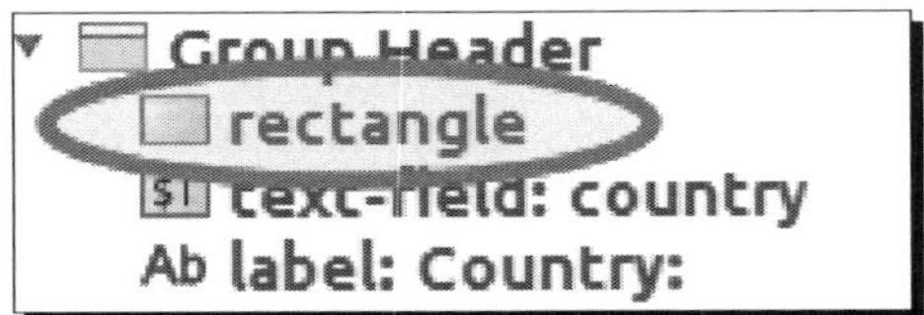

   What we need to do is move the rectangle down in this hierarchy until the aforementioned objects are visible once again.

7. In order to do this, we will select the **rectangle** object (whether on the report editor or in the **Structure** tab), right-click on it, and choose the **Send Backwards** option from the context menu (or press *Ctrl* + *D*). We should repeat this process until we obtain the desired result.

[To move an object up in the hierarchy, we can use the **Send Forward** option (or press *Ctrl* + *U*).]

8. We can now see how the **rectangle** object moved down the hierarchy until it was below the other two objects. The structure of your hierarchy should now look like the one shown in the following screenshot:

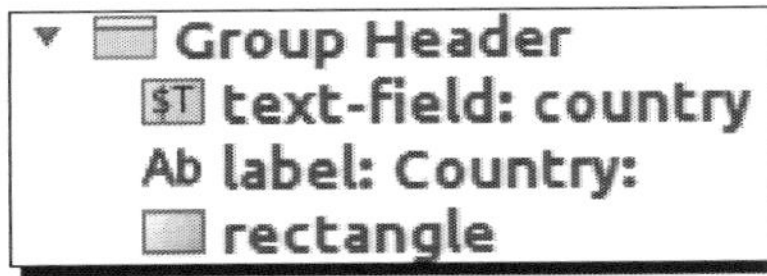

9. In the **Details Header** section, we will delete the label with the text **Country**.
10. In the **Details** section, we need to delete the **Country** text field as well as the first vertical line.
11. We will next configure the `RowBanding` function's color; as well as the color for the border bottom, from the **Details Header** section; and the border top, from the **Details Footer** section. For these last two objects, it is recommended that we use a color with a higher intensity than in the other cases; for example, `#fc7f03`.

What just happened?

We configured the general layout of our report. We placed a title in the **Report Header** section and then placed a label, a text field, and a rectangle in the **Group Header** section. We deleted a text field from the **Details Header** section, deleted a text field from the **Details** section, and changed a few colors as well.

Configuring the Group section

We will now configure the **Group** section. We are now going to modify our report so that it groups customers by country in an appropriate way. In order to do this, we will edit an attribute in the **Group** section.

Time for action – adding groups

If we preview our report, we will be able to see the following:

Adding Groups

Country: Canada

Customer	Amount
CURTIS, IRBY	167,62
DARRELL, POWER	91,75
DERRICK, BOURQUE	95,78
LORETTA, CARPENTER	93,78
TROY, QUIGLEY	144,7
JACKIE, LYNCH	93,75
LEON, BOSTIC	109,75
SAM, MCDUFFIE	117,76

However, if we compare these results with the ones obtained by MySQL, we will note that the PRD groups are not being created properly.

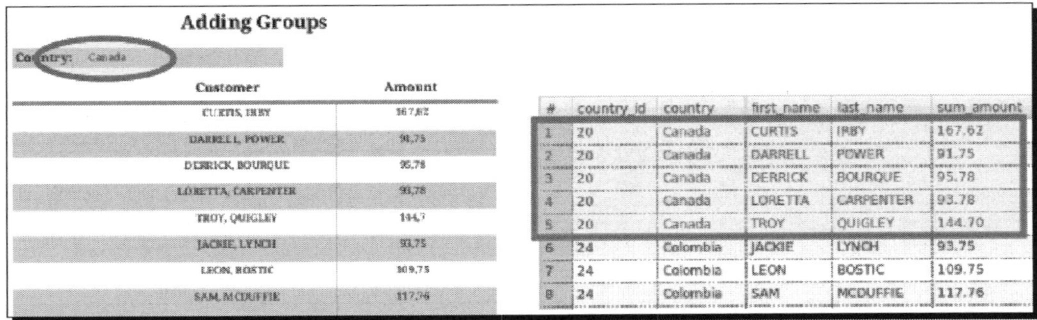

#	country_id	country	first_name	last_name	sum_amount
1	20	Canada	CURTIS	IRBY	167.62
2	20	Canada	DARRELL	POWER	91.75
3	20	Canada	DERRICK	BOURQUE	95.78
4	20	Canada	LORETTA	CARPENTER	93.78
5	20	Canada	TROY	QUIGLEY	144.70
6	24	Colombia	JACKIE	LYNCH	93.75
7	24	Colombia	LEON	BOSTIC	109.75
8	24	Colombia	SAM	MCDUFFIE	117.76

As we can see, the highlighted customers appearing in our report belong only to **Canada**; that is, our report is showing incorrect results.

In order for the groups to be correctly formed, we need to go to the **Structure** tab, navigate to **Master Report** | **Group**, select it, and modify the following:

- **Attributes.group** = `[country_id]`
- **Attributes.name** = `GroupCountry`

What we just did was indicated to PRD that the groups should be formed by these registries, which share the same `country_id` values. We could have put just `country` instead of `country_id`, but it is much more efficient to use fields of a numeric nature. With respect to `GroupCountry`, it is the name by which this group will be referenced in our report.

PRD supports adding one or more grouping criteria, but in our case we will be using only one. If, for example, we had to use the `city` field in addition to the `country` field in order to create the appropriate groups, we should specify both grouping criteria in the corresponding **Attributes.group** characteristic.

If we preview our report, we will see that the groups are correctly formed. For example, the first page looks like the following:

Adding Groups

Country: Canada

Customer	Amount
CURTIS, IRBY	167,62
DARRELL, POWER	91,75
DERRICK, BOURQUE	95,78
LORETTA, CARPENTER	93,78
TROY, QUIGLEY	144,7

Total Customers: 5

Total Amount: 593,63

And the second page like the following:

Country: Colombia

Customer	Amount
JACKIE, LYNCH	93,75
LEON, BOSTIC	109,75
SAM, MCDUFFIE	117,76
STACY, CUNNINGHAM	98,77
SYLVIA, ORTIZ	143,68
WANDA, PATTERSON	145,7

Total Customers: 11

Total Amount: 1.303,04

What just happened?

We modified the **Attributes.group** characteristic of the **Group** section so that it creates groups of customers according to their `country` fields.

Modifying functions

We will now modify the functions of our report so that they perform their calculations correctly, taking these newly created groups into account. We will also configure the **Group** section of our report so that every time the country changes, it continues on a new page.

Time for action – modifying functions and page breaks

Follow these steps to modify functions and page breaks:

1. If we pay attention to the values being reported by our report's functions, we will see that the calculations are not being correctly performed by the group. In order to fix this, we should make the following modification:
    - **Reset on Group Name** = `GroupCountry`

2. We can now perform a preview to see that the calculations are being performed correctly.
3. We will now configure our report so that each country begins on a new page. We will go to the **Structure** tab, navigate to **Master Report** | **Group**, and make the following modification:
   - **Style.pagebreak-after** = `true`

What just happened?

We configured the functions of our report to correctly perform their calculations on a per-group basis, and then configured the **Group** section so that each new country begins on a different page.

Learning more about groups

A basic requirement for creating groups is that the data set should be ordered according to the criteria that will be used to create the groups. This is why our SQL query contains the statement `ORDER BY country.country`.

If our data set were not ordered by `country`, we could end up with a data set like the following:

country_id	country	first_name
29	Egypt	ALFRED
48	Israel	CRYSTAL
20	Canada	CURTIS
20	Canada	DARRELL
74	Peru	DAVID
20	Canada	DERRICK
67	Netherlands	DUSTIN
29	Egypt	EMMA
29	Egypt	EVERETT
74	Peru	FREDDIE
48	Israel	GERALDINE

In this case, PRD would create the following groups:

country_id	country	first_name
29	Egypt	ALFRED
48	Israel	CRYSTAL
20	Canada	CURTIS
20	Canada	DARRELL
74	Peru	DAVID
20	Canada	DERRICK
67	Netherlands	DUSTIN
29	Egypt	EMMA
29	Egypt	EVERETT
74	Peru	FREDDIE
48	Israel	GERALDINE

This is because PRD creates a new group when the value of the grouping criteria changes.

PRD also provides a UI to manage groups. To access the UI, go to the **Structure** tab, right-click on the **Group** node, and select the **Edit Group...** option.

The following fields will appear:

- **Name**: The name of the group
- **Available Fields**: The fields we can use as grouping criteria
- **Selected Fields**: The fields currently being used as grouping criteria

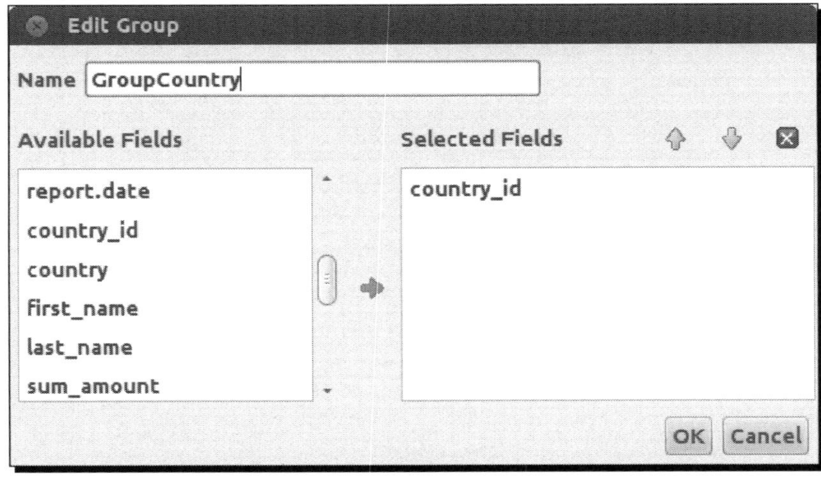

The buttons are used to move different grouping criteria up or down in the hierarchy.

If we need to create a group with more than one grouping criteria, for example, country and city, we should configure our group as follows:

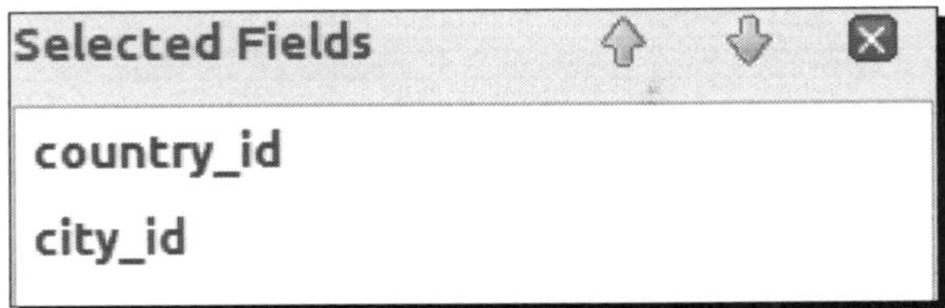

Have a go hero

Now that this chapter is finished, we will invite you to create your own report, in which you will be able to apply some of the things we have seen so far. The first page of the report we are inviting you to create should look like the following:

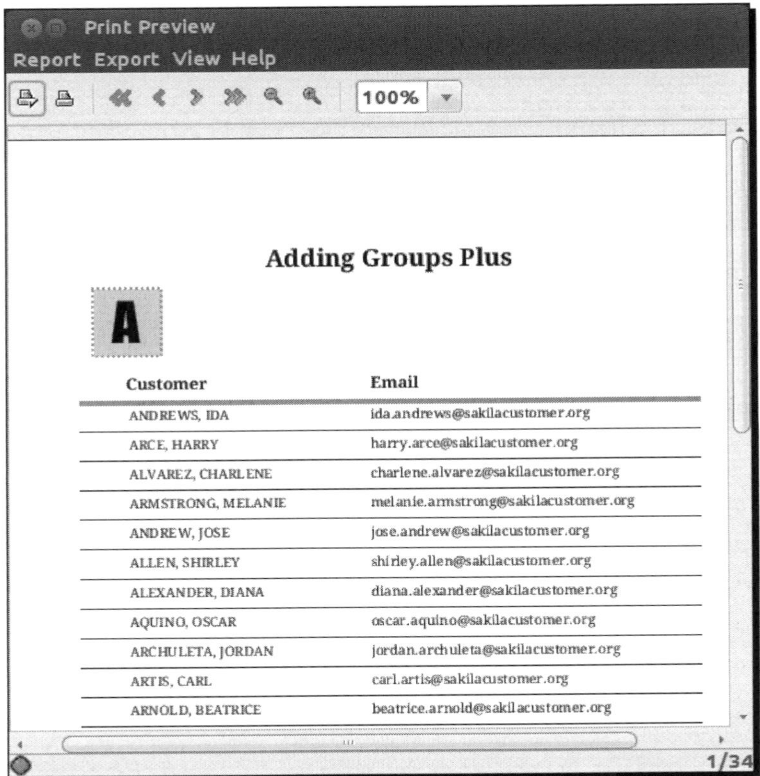

And the second page of the report should look like this:

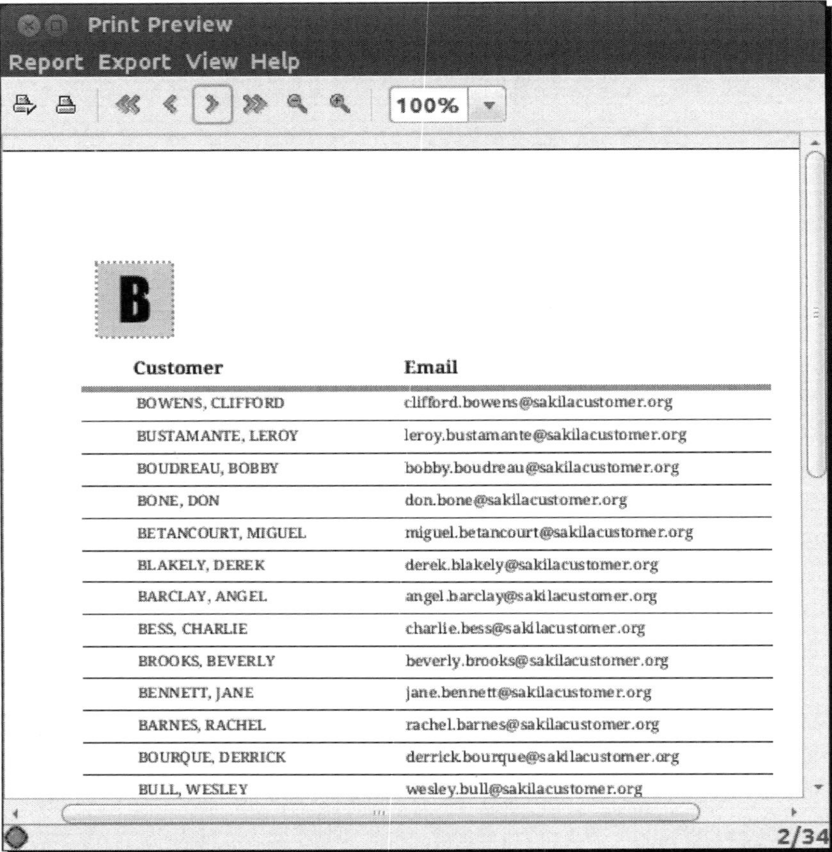

The steps you should be roughly following are as follows:

1. Create a new report and save it as the following: `06_Adding_Groups_Plus.prpt`.
2. Create a new JDBC data set and configure it to use the Sakila database.
3. The SQL query you should use is the following one:

```
SELECT LEFT(customer.last_name,1) as letter,
CONCAT(customer.last_name,', ',customer.first_name) as customer_
name,
LCASE(customer.email) as email
FROM customer
ORDER BY letter
```

4. Enable and configure the **Group Header** and **Group Footer** sections. This is to be repeated on each page.
5. Create the general layout of the report.
6. Configure the **Group** section of the report so that it groups customers according to their `letter` fields.
7. Configure the **Group** section so that each letter begins on a new page.

Pop Quiz – positioning hierarchy and groups

Q1. Which of the following affirmations are true?

1. When designing our report in PRD, if two or more objects overlap, they will always be colored red to indicate to us that we should separate them.
2. The **Send Backwards** option sends the selected object to the bottom of the positioning hierarchy.
3. It is possible to perform groupings on more than one criterion.
4. In order to have a function perform its calculations by group, we should place the name of the field on the **Reset on Group Name** field by which we wish the grouping to be done.

Summary

In this chapter, we created a copy of the report we used in the previous chapter and configured it to perform customer groupings according to the country to which they belong.

We modified the query of our data set so that we could obtain data in a way more easily suited for the group example. We then modified the layout of our report so that it applied to the one presented in this guide. During the recreation of this layout, we had to move an object downwards in the positioning hierarchy.

We configured the **Attributes.group** value of the **Group** section and created groups based on their `country_id` fields. We also configured the **Style.pagebreak-after** value of this group so that each new group begins on a different page.

We modified the **Reset on Group Name** value of the functions so that they perform their calculations by group.

Finally, in order to strengthen the knowledge acquired, we proposed the creation of a new report from the ground up.

In the next chapter, we will explain how to create parameters in our reports.

7
Adding Parameters

This chapter will be dedicated to parameters. Through the use of parameters, the final user will be able to interact with the report. A parameter is usually represented through a user interface component, which allows the selection or input of values.

Pentaho Report Designer (PRD) eases the task of parameter creation by giving us a simple and intuitive interface.

In this chapter:

- We will create both simple parameters and nested parameters
- We will make a parameter obtain its values through a data set
- We will discuss the different kinds of parameter visualization available, exposing the features of each one of them
- We will discuss how to make our SQL queries dynamically constructed according to the values the final user has provided through the use of parameters

As an extra, we will invite you to create your own report from the ground up, as well as give you a few tips to assist you in its creation.

Starting practice

In this chapter we will create a new report. We will then do the necessary changes in its layout for the final result as follows:

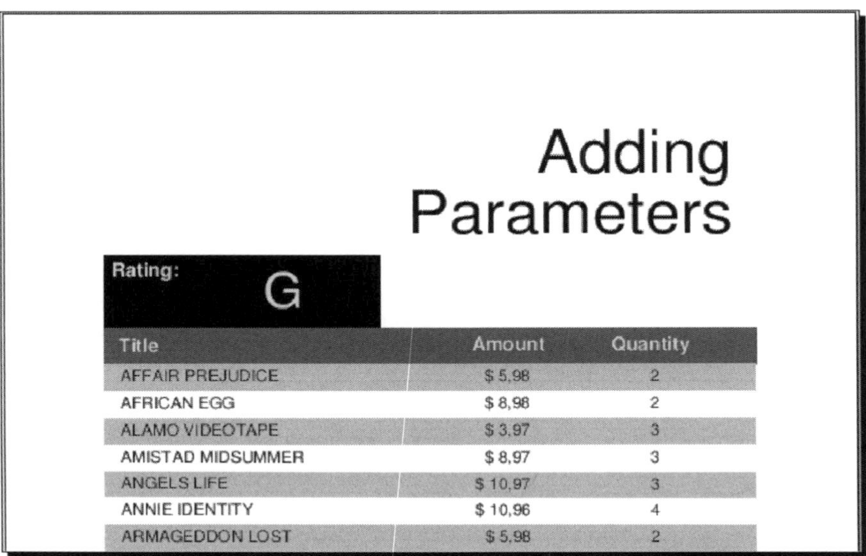

We are going to allow the end user to select the rating they want to analyze, as well as the year and month in which the films were rented.

Time for action – creating a new report

We will create a new report from scratch. In order to do this, we will need to create the report itself, then create a JDBC-type data set and establish its SQL query. Finally, we will create a general layout, which means we will need to add to our report a series of objects and configure them properly.

1. We will create a new report and save it under the name, `07_Adding_Parameters.prpt`.
2. We will create the following layout for our report:

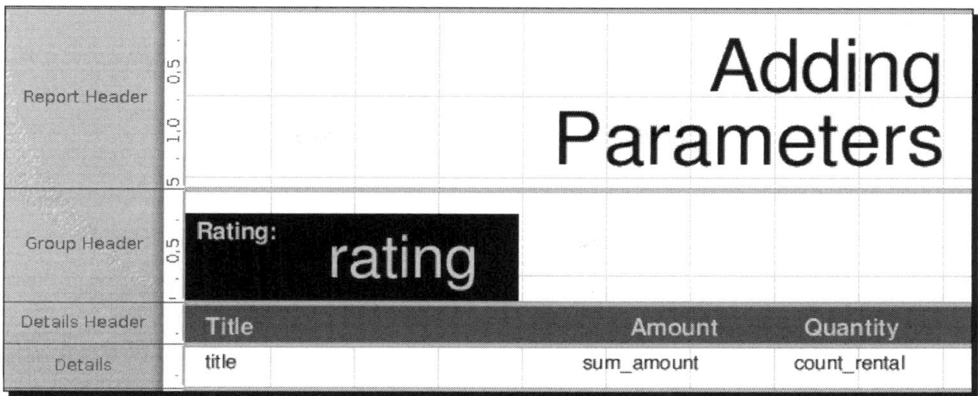

3. At this stage, we need to create a JDBC-type data set, establish the connection with our sakila database, and then create the following query:

```
SELECT film.rating, film.title,
SUM(payment.amount) AS sum_amount, COUNT(1)  AS count_rental
FROM payment
INNER JOIN rental ON rental.rental_id=payment.rental_id
INNER JOIN inventory ON inventory.inventory_id=rental.inventory_id
INNER JOIN film ON film.film_id=inventory.film_id
WHERE film.rating IN ('G','PG','PG-13','R','NC-17')
AND YEAR(payment.payment_date) = 2005
AND MONTH(payment_date) = 6
GROUP BY film.film_id
ORDER BY film.rating, film.title
```

   Initially, we will use the default values for `film.rating`, `YEAR(payment.payment_date)`, and `MONTH(payment_date)`. Later on, we will allow these values to be modified dynamically by the final user.

4. In the **Report Header** section, we will place and configure a label to serve as a title. We must configure the **Group** section so that each new group begins in a new page (**Style.pagebreak-after**).
5. In the **Group Header** section, we will enable and configure a label, a text field, and a rectangle.
6. In the **Details Header** section, we will enable and configure three labels.
7. In the **Details** section, we need to place and configure two text fields. We will also apply a **Row Banding** function to this section. We will configure the text field referencing the `sum_amount` field using the following:

   - **Attributes.format** = `$ #,##0.00;($ #,##0.00)`

What just happened?

We created a new report and then added and configured a JDBC-type data set to it. We also defined the layout proposed by this guide. To do so we had to configure the **Report Header**, **Group**, **Group Header**, **Details Header**, and **Details** sections.

Parameters

Parameters enable the final user to interact with the contents of the report, allowing the reports to present dynamically generated content and adapt to the needs of the user.

Pentaho Report Designer (**PRD**) allows the inclusion of parameters in its reports by means of a fairly nice UI. Parameters in PRD can be quite simple, such as the selection of a value from a list, or more complex, such as when nested parameters are created so that setting a value in one of them causes the modification of the values of others. This means that the data set obtained by the nested parameter depends on the values selected in another parameter. In the first case we could establish a list containing every year in which films were rented, and have the user select one of them:

In the second example, we could create two parameters so that one of them holds every country, and the other one holds every city available, and have them behave in a way such that when the user selects a country, the other parameter presents the cities belonging to the country previously selected:

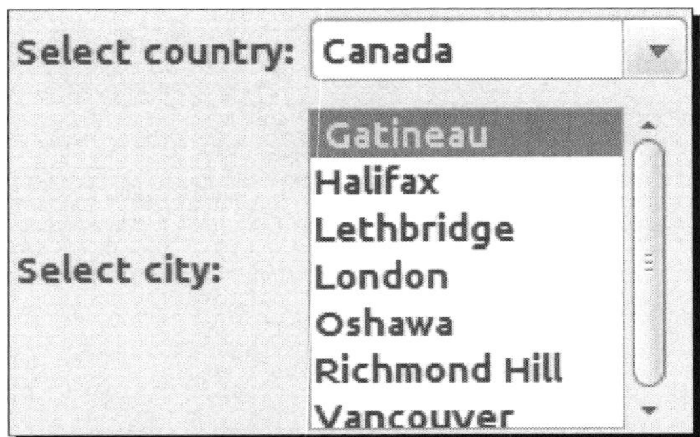

When nesting parameters, there is no limit as to how many hierarchical levels can be created.

At the time of adding parameters to our reports we can also use one single report and make it adapt to different use cases. For example, a production report grouped by the assembly line on which every manufactured product is present could be (and it is, in fact) too much information to present on a single report. In this case the addition of parameters to select the assembly line and/or the product type not only simplifies the report but also enables this report to be used by different users with different needs for information.

Another important point to consider is the possibility of creating reports that provide an analysis of more details and focus on the need for information of the current user.

By configuring our parameters on PRD, we are able to determine the way in which these will be presented to the final users. Next, we will explain each of these selectors or display types using as an example the film's rating list, whose values can be: `G`, `PG`, `PG-13`, `R`, or `NC-17`.

We will now look into the different display types available for use:

- **Dropdown**: This display type allows the selection of a single value from the list, and it is most commonly used for simple selections. It is used when the list to be shown is not too long.

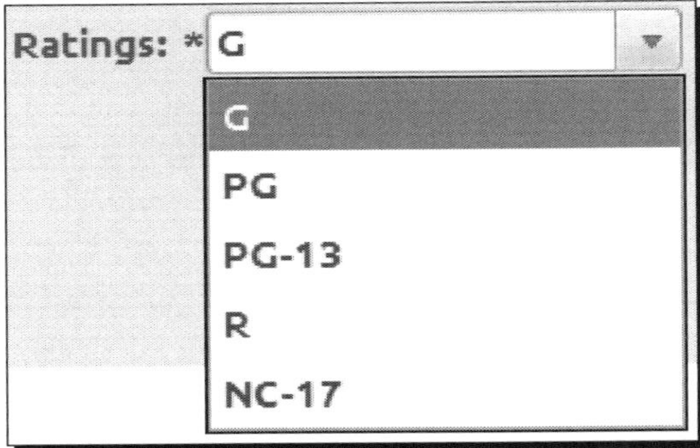

- **Single value list**: This display type also allows the selection of a single value from the list. In comparison to the previous selector (dropdown), this one uses more space but at the same time eases the search of values in long lists.

- **Multivalue list**: This display type allows the selection of one or more values from the list. It is not used much since the checkbox display type works in a similar way and is much more intuitive.

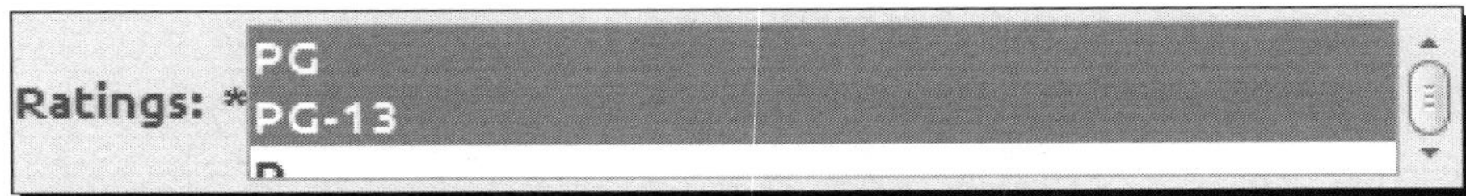

- **Radio button**: This display type allows the selection of a single value from the list. It is commonly used when the list of values is short and there is a need for visualizing every available option.

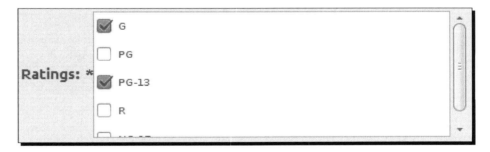

- **Checkbox**: This display type allows the selection of one or more values from the list and it is the most commonly used for multiple selections. It can be used to show both short and long lists.

- **Single selection button**: This display type allows for the selection of a single value from the list. It is used when the list is short and there is a need to keep every other value visible. As can be seen, it does not use too much screen space.

- **Multiselection button**: This display type is similar to Single Selection Button, but allows for the selection of one or more values.

- **Textbox**: This display type is commonly used when the final user wants to perform a search for a certain value, but does not know precisely what it is, or when the search cannot be predetermined. For example, this selector could be used to filter customers whose last names begin with the value present in the selector, or to show a report in which only the customers who have made purchases for a value greater than the one currently in the selector are present.

- **Text area**: This display type is similar to a textbox, but allows for the input of many characters. This is why horizontal and vertical scroll bars are present.

- **Date picker**: This display type is used so that the user can select a date from the Gregorian calendar.

If the [...] button is pressed, a quite useful interface for the selection of a date will pop up:

Time for action – adding parameters

We will create a new parameter so that the user can select the rating (or ratings) he or she wants to see in the report. In order to do so, we will configure a data set and then define and explain its properties. Among them we will find: **Name**, **Label**, **Value Type**, and **Display Type**.

Afterwards, we will modify our main data set, `RatingFilms`, so that it takes its values according to the recently created parameter.

1. Firstly, we will perform a preview on the report and explain how to properly present parameters to the user. We will add a parameter so that the user can select the rating (or ratings) he or she wants to analyze. We will go to the **Data** tab, select **Parameters**, right-click on it and select the **Add Parameter...** option, as shown in the following screenshot:

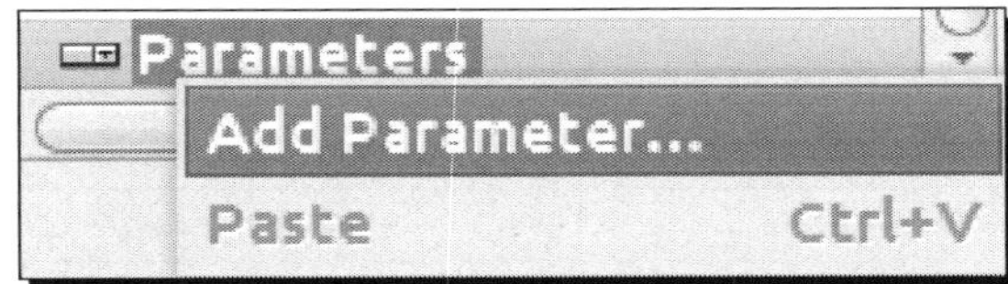

We will be presented with the following window, in which we will create and modify our parameters:

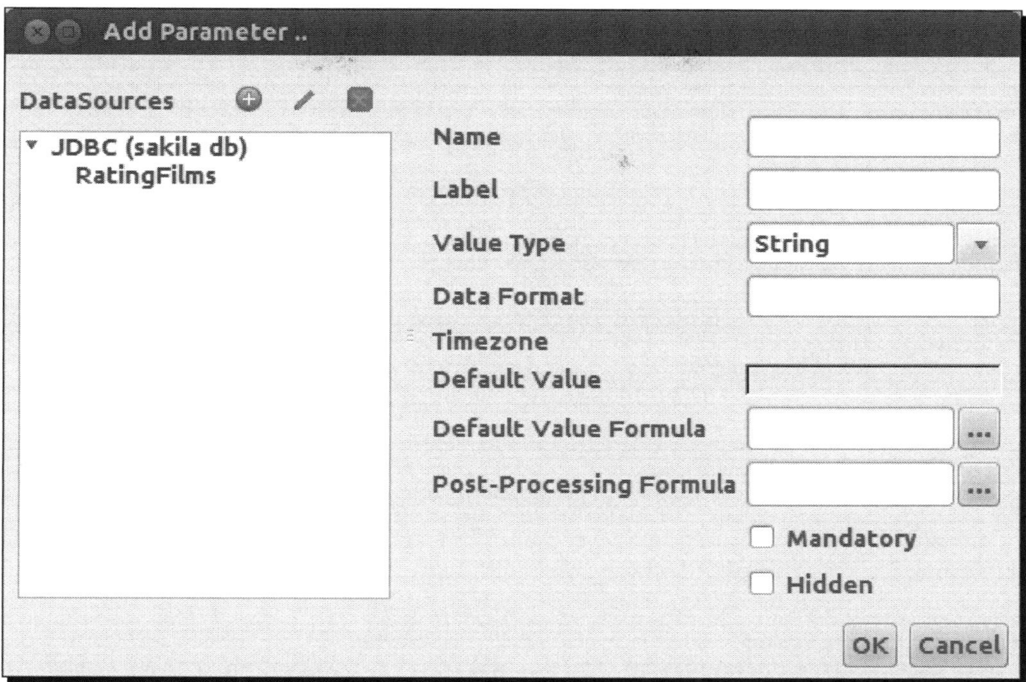

To the left, we find the data sets currently being used in our report. To the right, we see the parameters edition form.

2. We create a new data set so that it obtains the ratings list via a SQL query. On the right-hand side of the window, we will press the [+] button and then select the **JDBC** option:

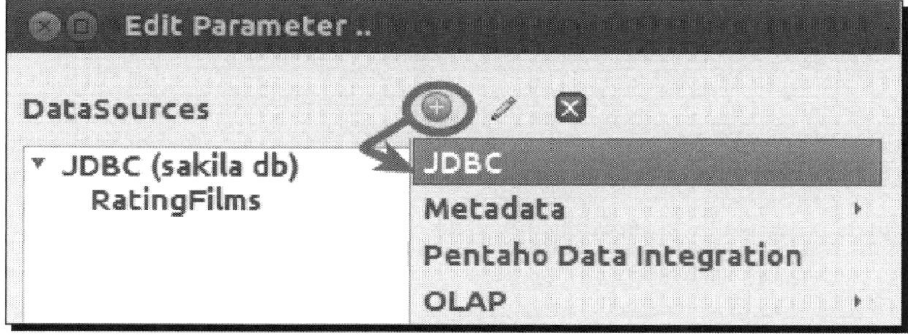

On the left-hand side, we will select the connection to our sakila database, and then create a new query (⊕) on which we will configure the following:

- **Query Name** = `ListOfRatings`
- **Query** = `SELECT DISTINCT film.rating FROM film ORDER BY 1`

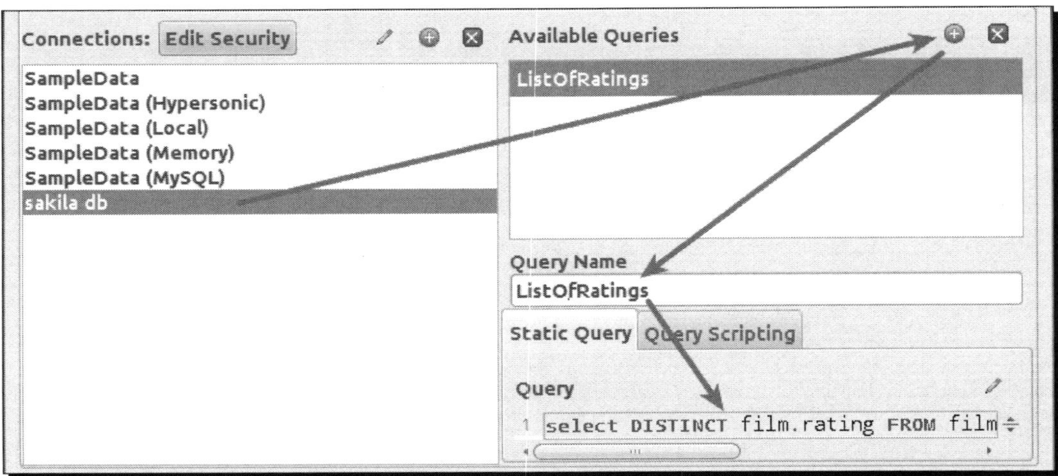

3. To continue, we will press the **OK** button. Now, based on the ratings list we will configure the parameter. On the left-hand side we will select the data set we just created (**ListOfRatings**), and then head to the right-hand side on which we will configure the following:

- **Name** = `SelectRating`: This is the name of the parameter
- **Label** = `Ratings`: This is the label that will be shown to the user
- **Value Type** = `String`: This is the type of value of the field with which we will be working
- **Mandatory** = `True`: This establishes whether it's optional, or not, for the user to select a value from the list before executing the current report.
- **Display Type** = `Multi Selection Button`: This is the way in which the list will be exposed to the user
- **Query** = `ListOfRatings`: This is the data set to be used
- **Value** = `rating`: This is the value that will be returned by the parameter
- **Display Name** = `rating`: This is the value to show to the final user

As we can observe, both **Value** and **Display Name** have the same value. Their use becomes important when the value we want to obtain is different from the value we want to show to the user. For example, suppose we have a list of films from which we want the user to select one. In this case we would have to set **Value** to the ID of the film, and **Display Name** to the title of the film. In this way, the user would select a film by its title, but we will get the ID of the selected film to use in our query.

4. To continue, we will press the **OK** button. What we will do now is modify the SQL query of our data set so that it obtains the ratings dynamically. We will head to the **Data** tab, select **RatingFilms**, right-click on it and then select the option **Edit Query...**:

We will modify the query so that it looks like the following:

```
SELECT film.rating, film.title,
SUM(payment.amount) AS sum_amount, COUNT(1)  AS count_rental
FROM payment
INNER JOIN rental ON rental.rental_id=payment.rental_id
INNER JOIN inventory ON inventory.inventory_id=rental.inventory_id
INNER JOIN film ON film.film_id=inventory.film_id
WHERE film.rating IN (${SelectRating})
AND YEAR(payment.payment_date) = 2005
AND MONTH(payment.payment_date) = 6
GROUP BY film.film_id
ORDER BY film.rating, film.title
```

What we did was replace the code `'G','PG','PG-13','R','NC-17'` with the code `${SelectRating}`, so that the condition of our query is adjusted to the values selected in the parameter we just created.

5. We will press **OK** to continue. If we perform a preview, we should see the following:

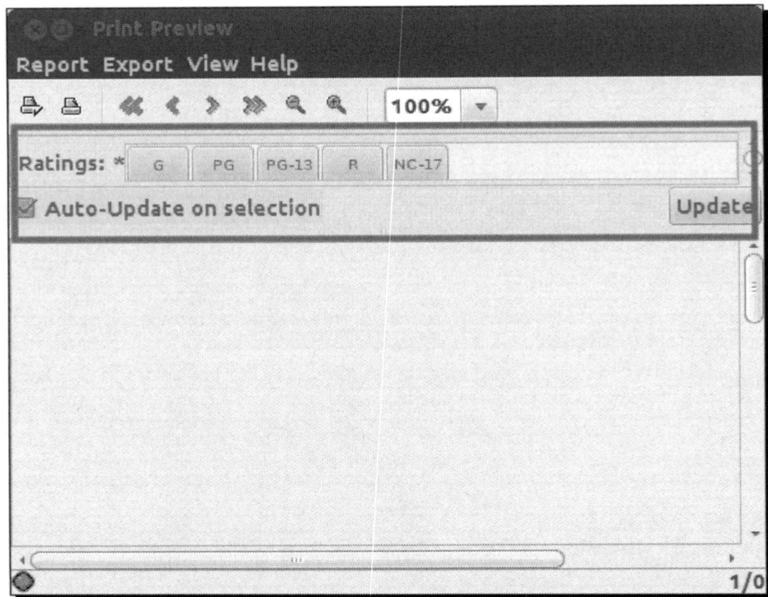

When we created the **SelectRating** parameter, we did not specify a default value. This is why no ratings are selected by default. To modify the default value of our parameter, we should either use the **Default Value** or **Default Value Formula** option.

Furthermore, when we created our parameter we configured it to be mandatory. This is why the report will not return any data until a value is selected. The * we can see the left of ratings hints about this behavior.

As can be seen in the following screenshot, PRD presents all our parameters in the upper section of the window. It also provides a few options:

- **Auto-Update on selection**: If this option is activated, any modification on the selected values will trigger a report recalculation, which is also known as live-update.
- **Update**: This button is used when **Auto-Update on selection** is disabled, and its function is to manually trigger the recalculation of our report with the current values selected in our Parameters.

We will now select a pair of ratings values, for example `G` and `PG`:

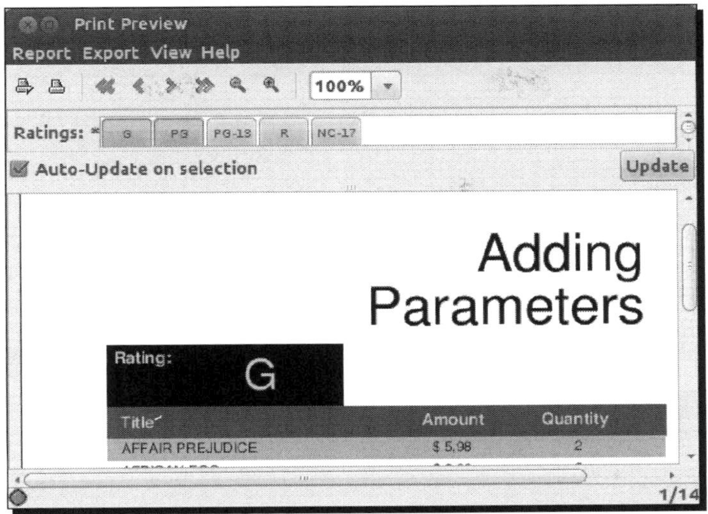

> To select more than one non-adjacent value, we need to hold the *Ctrl* key and then select the values. To select a series of adjacent values, we will usually select the first one, and then select the last one while holding the *Shift* key. Both techniques can be combined.

After performing such a selection, the value returned by our **SelectRating** parameter will be `'G','PG'`, generating a SQL query like this:

```
WHERE film.rating IN ('G','PG')
```

What just happened?

We created a parameter with the name **SelectRating** and defined its data set so that it obtains a list of every rating available from the sakila database. Then we configured the properties of **SelectRating** and among other things defined its **Name** and **Label** attributes, set it to **Mandatory**, chose the display type, and specified its **Value** and **Display Name** properties.

Later on we modified our data set so that the `RatingFilm` attributes takes into account the values selected by the user; that is, we replaced the static filter in our condition with the code `${SelectRating}`.

Finally, we performed a preview of our report and explained the way in which parameters are presented, as well as the options **Auto-Update on selection** and **Update**.

Time for action – creating nested parameters

We will create two new parameters. The first one will ask the user to select the year in which a film was rented, and the second one will ask the user to select the corresponding month.

Later on, we are going to nest these two parameters. The months in the second parameter will be shown according to the year selected in the first parameter. This way, the second parameter will only offer selection of those months in which there is relevant information present.

1. Finally, we will modify our main data set to take into account the values present in these two new parameters. We will create a parameter so that the final user can select the year in which films were rented, to be shown in the report. We will head to the **Data** tab, select **Parameters**, right-click on it, and select the **Add Parameter...** option.
2. On the left-hand side (**Datasource**), we will press the button to create the data set belonging to this new parameter. At this stage we will select, on the left-hand side of the window, the connection to the sakila database, create a new query (), and configure the following:
    - **Query Name** = `ListOfYears`
    - **Query** = `SELECT distinct YEAR(payment.payment_date) AS payment_year FROM payment ORDER BY 1`
3. We will press the **OK** button to continue. Now, on the left-hand side, we will select the data set we just created (**ListOfYears**), head to the right-hand side, and configure the following:
    - **Name** = `SelectYear`
    - **Label** = `Year:`
    - **Value Type** = `Number`
    - **Mandatory** = `True`
    - **Display Type** = `Drop Down`
    - **Query** = `ListOfYears`
    - **Value** = `payment_year`
    - **Display Name** = `payment_year`
4. We will press the **OK** button to continue. We will now create another parameter so that the final user can select a month in which films were rented to be present in the report. We will also configure this new parameter to receive the value the user has chosen in the previous parameter (`SelectYear`).

5. We will head to the **Data** tab, select **Parameters**, right-click on it, and select the **Add Parameter...** option.

6. On the left-hand side (**Datasource**), we will press the [+] button to create the data set belonging to our new parameter. Once there, we will select, on the left-hand side, the connection to the sakila database, create a new query ([+]), and configure the following:

   - **Query Name** = `ListOfMonths`
   - **Query** = `SELECT distinct MONTH(payment.payment_date) AS payment_month_number, DATE_FORMAT(payment.payment_date,'%M') AS payment_month_string FROM payment WHERE YEAR(payment.payment_date) = ${SelectYear} ORDER BY 1`

   This query will take into account the present value of the **SelectYear** parameter; that is why the code `WHERE YEAR(payment.payment_date) = ${SelectYear}` is included, and returns a list of months in which payments have been made. To obtain the number of the month in which the payments were done, the following code was used: `MONTH(payment.payment_date)`. To obtain the name of the month we use this code: `DATE_FORMAT(payment.payment_date,'%M')`. Internally, we will use the number of the month. The name of the month will be used to show the final user the corresponding options.

7. To continue, we will press **OK**.

8. On the left-hand side we will select the data set we just created (**ListOfMonths**). We will then head to the right-hand side and configure the following:

   - **Name** = `SelectMonth`
   - **Label** = `Month:`
   - **Value Type** = `Number`
   - **Mandatory** = `True`
   - **Display Type** = `Drop Down`
   - **Query** = `ListOfMonths`
   - **Value** = `payment_month_number`
   - **Display Name** = `payment_month_string`

9. We will now press the **OK** button to continue. Next, we will modify the SQL query of our data set to take into account the values for year and month as selected by the final user. To do this, we will head to the **Data** tab, select `RatingFilms`, right-click on in it, and then select the **Edit Query...** option.

We will modify the query to look like the following:

```
SELECT film.rating, film.title,
SUM(payment.amount) AS sum_amount, COUNT(1)  AS count_rental
FROM payment
INNER JOIN rental ON rental.rental_id=payment.rental_id
INNER JOIN inventory ON inventory.inventory_id=rental.inventory_id
INNER JOIN film ON film.film_id=inventory.film_id
WHERE film.rating IN (${SelectRating})
AND YEAR(payment.payment_date) = ${SelectYear}
AND MONTH(payment.payment_date) = ${SelectMonth}
GROUP BY film.film_id
ORDER BY film.rating, film.title
```

What we just did was replace the code `2005` with the code `${SelectYear}`, as well as the `6` code for `${SelectMonth}`.

10. We will press **OK** to continue. If we perform a preview, we will see something like this:

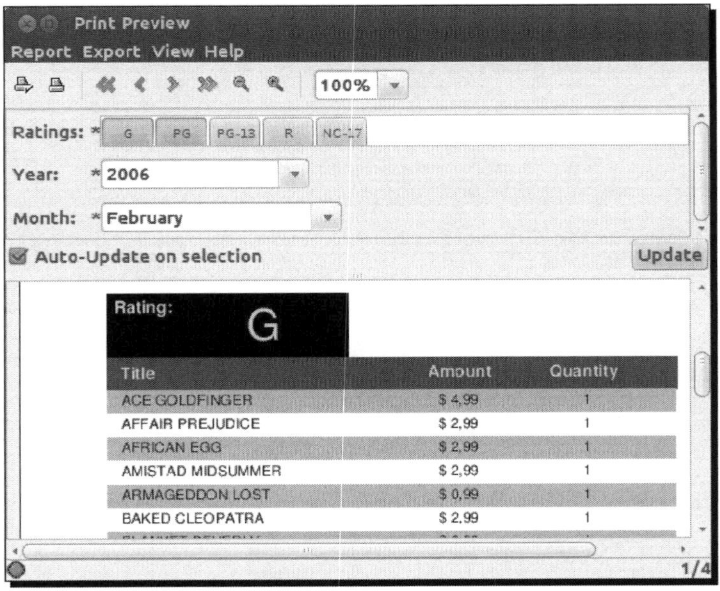

What just happened?

We created the **ListOfYears** parameter so that the final user can select the year he or she wishes to analyze. Later on, we created the **ListOfMonths** parameter and configured it so that the months' list to be shown depends on the year previously selected by the user. Finally, we modified the SQL query of the data set belonging to `RatingFilms`, so that it takes into account the values currently selected in the mentioned parameters.

Have a go hero

Now that we have concluded this chapter, we will invite you to create your own report. By doing so you will be able to apply some of the things we have learned so far. The proposed report should look like this:

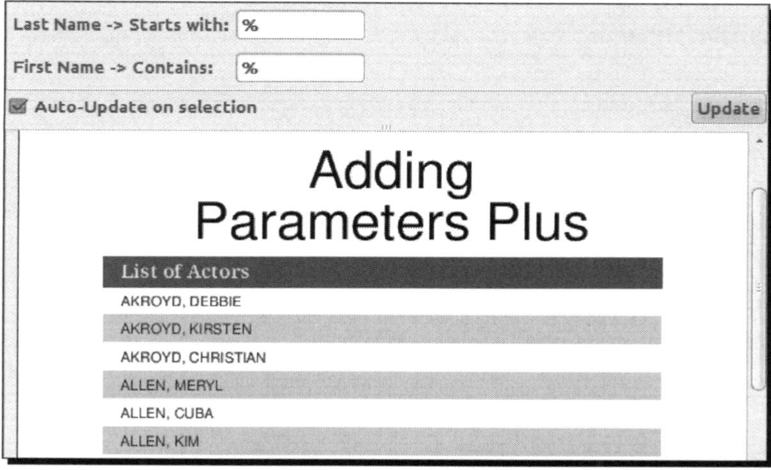

The steps you should be following are as follows:

1. Create a new report and save it under the name `08_Adding_Parameters_Plus.prpt`.
2. Create a new JDBC-type data set and configure it to use the sakila database.
3. Use the following SQL query:

```
SELECT first_name, last_name, concat(last_name, ', ', first_name)
AS full_name
FROM actor
ORDER BY last_name
```

4. Create the general layout for the report (label, text field, rectangle, and so on).

5. Create a new parameter and configure it in the following way:
   - **Name** = `SelectLastName`
   - **Label** = `Last Name -> Starts with:`
   - **Value Type** = `String`
   - **Default Value** = `%`
   - **Display Type** = `Text Box`
6. Create a second parameter with the following configuration:
   - **Name** = `SelectFirstName`
   - **Label** = `First Name -> Contains:`
   - **Value Type** = `String`
   - **Default Value** = `%`
   - **Display Type** = `Text Box`
7. Modify the SQL query so that it uses these parameters.

Pop quiz – format and parameters

Q1. Which of the following affirmations are true?

1. When configuring the format of a number field or date field, among the default options, we will only find those available that are related to the type of the data.
2. Parameters allow the user to interact with the contents of the report.
3. When creating nested parameters, PRD only allows hierarchies that are two-level deep.
4. If the parameter must show a long list for a simple selection, the best option is to use a **dropdown** display type.
5. If the parameter shows a short list for a simple selection, and it is desired to visualize every option available, the best option is to use a **Single value list** display type.
6. If the parameter shows a short list for multiple selections, and it is desired to utilize as little screen space as possible, a good option would be to use a **Multiselection button** display type.
7. When adding a new parameter, it is mandatory to always use a data set.

Summary

We created a report from scratch and configured it so that its layout matches the one proposed in this guide. We also added and configured the objects needed (label, text field, and so on), and set up a JDBC-type data set.

We explained what a parameter is and what it allows us to do. We discussed different types of parameters and their typical uses. We mentioned and explained the main features of every display type available.

We added to our report a simple parameter, then configured its data set and its main properties. Later on we modified the main data set so that it receives the value currently present in the parameter, thus creating a dynamic data set.

Next, we created two parameters so that the final user could select the year and month on which to perform an analysis. The month parameter was nested with the year parameter so that its values depend on the year selected by the user.

As done previously, we modified the main data set so that it takes into account the values present in these two parameters.

Finally, as a way to strengthen the acquired knowledge, we proposed the creation of a new report from scratch.

In the next chapter we will explain how to create formulas in our reports.

8
Using Formulas in Our Reports

In this chapter, we will talk about formulas. We will explain in detail how to create them and use them. As in previous chapters, we will use a practical example to guide us as we explain how to work with formulas, creating general-use formulas that we can use as an object and specific-use formulas that we can apply to our objects' styles and attributes. We will see the full potential that formulas offer in our reports, and we will create formulas that can be manipulated by the parameters that end users select.

By the end of the practical example, we will see how the combination of formulas and parameters opens up new horizons for the creation and personalization of reports and allows us great flexibility in design.

In this chapter we will do the following:

- Create a copy of the previous report, adapt to its layout, and give our parameters default values
- Create a formula that makes a row-by-row calculation and later add it to the Details section
- Configure the background color of one of our report's objects using a formula
- Create two new parameters so that the end user can choose the evaluation criteria of this formula

At the end of the chapter, we propose that you make some modifications to the report created in this chapter.

Starting practice

In this chapter, we will create a copy of the report created in the previous chapter, then we will do the necessary changes in its layout; the final result is as follows:

Using Formulas

Rating: G

	Title	Amount	Quantity	Total
□	AFFAIR PREJUDICE	$ 7,98	2	$ 15,96
■	AFRICAN EGG	$ 3,99	1	$ 3,99
□	ALAMO VIDEOTAPE	$ 4,98	2	$ 9,96
■	ANGELS LIFE	$ 15,98	2	$ 31,96
■	ANNIE IDENTITY	$ 8,97	3	$ 26,91
■	ARMAGEDDON LOST	$ 3,99	1	$ 3,99
□	ATLANTIS CAUSE	$ 5,98	2	$ 11,96
■	AUTUMN CROW	$ 9,99	1	$ 9,99
■	BAKED CLEOPATRA	$ 2,99	1	$ 2,99
■	BALLROOM MOCKINGBIRD	$ 0,99	1	$ 0,99

As we can observe in the previous screenshot, the rectangle that is to the left of each title changes color. We'll see how to do this, and much more, shortly.

Time for action – making a copy of the previous report

In this chapter, we will use the report we created earlier. To do so, we will open it and save it with the name `09_Using_Formulas.prpt`. Then we will modify its layout to fit this chapter. Finally, we will establish default values for our parameters. The steps for making a copy of the previous report are as follows:

1. We open the report `07_Adding_Parameters.prpt` that we created in the previous chapter. Next, we create a copy by going to **File | Save As...** and saving it with the name `09_Using_Formulas.prpt`.
2. We will modify our report so that it looks like the following screenshot:

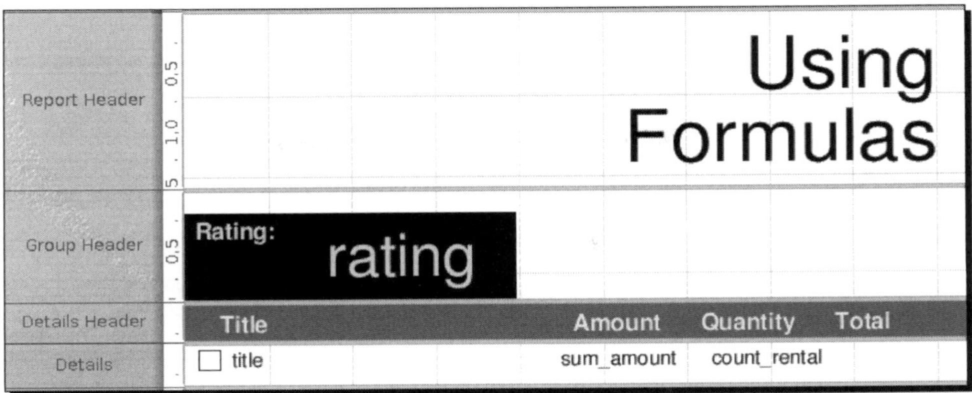

3. As you can see, we have just added a rectangle in the **Details** section, a label (**Total**) in the **Details Header** section, and we have modified the name of the label found in the **Report Header** section. To easily differentiate this report from the one used in the previous chapter, we have also modified its colors to grayscale. Later in this chapter, we will make the color of the rectangle vary according to the formula, so it is important that the rest of the report does not have too many colors so the results are easy for the end user to see.
4. We will establish default values in our parameters so we can preview the report without delays caused by having to choose the values for ratings, year, and month.
5. We go to the **Data** tab, select the **SelectRating** parameter, right-click on it, and choose the **Edit Parameter...** option:

6. In **Default Value**, we type the value `[G]`:

7. Next, we click on **OK** to continue. We should do something similar for **SelectYear** and **SelectMonth**:
   - For **SelectYear**, the **Default Value** will be `2005`.
   - For **SelectMonth**, the **Default Value** will be `5`. Remember that the selector shows the names of the months, but internally the months' numbers are used; so, `5` represents `May`.

What just happened?

We created a copy of the report `07_Adding_Parameters.prpt` and saved it with the name `09_Using_Formulas.prpt`. We changed the layout of the report, adding new objects and changing the colors. Then we established default values for the parameters **SelectRating**, **SelectYear**, and **SelectMonth**.

Formulas

To manage formulas, PRD implements the open standard **OpenFormula**. According to OpenFormula's specifications:

> *"OpenFormula is an open format for exchanging recalculated formulas between office application implementations, particularly for spreadsheets. OpenFormula defines the types, syntax, and semantics for calculated formulas, including many predefined functions and operations, so that formulas can be exchanged between applications and produce substantively equal outputs when recalculated with equal inputs. Both closed and open source software can implement OpenFormula."*

For more information on OpenFormula, refer to the following links:

- Wikipedia: `http://en.wikipedia.org/wiki/OpenFormula`
- Specifications: `https://www.oasis-open.org/committees/download.php/16826/openformula-spec-20060221.html`
- Web: `http://www.openformula.org/`
- Pentaho wiki: `http://wiki.pentaho.com/display/Reporting/Formula+Expressions`

Formulas are used for greatly varied purposes, and their use depends on the result one wants to obtain. Formulas let us carry out simple and complex calculations based on fixed and variable values and include predefined functions that let us work with text, databases, date and time, let us make calculations, and also include general information functions and user-defined functions. They also use logical operators (AND, OR, and so on) and comparative operators (>, <, and so on).

Creating formulas

There are two ways to create formulas:

- By creating a new **function** and by going to **Common** | **Open Formula**
- By pressing the ⊕ button in a section's / an object's **Style** or **Attributes** tab, or to configure some feature

In the report we are creating in this chapter, we will create formulas using both methods.

Using the first method, general-use formulas can be created. That is, the result will be an object that can either be included directly in our report or used as a value in another function, style, or attribute. We can create objects that make calculations at a general level to be included in sections that include **Report Header**, **Group Footer**, and so on, or we can make calculations to be included in the **Details** section. In this last case, the formula will make its calculation row by row. With this last example, we can make an important differentiation with respect to aggregate functions as they usually can only calculate totals and subtotals.

Using the second method, we create specific-use functions that affect the value of the style or attribute of an individual object. The way to use these functions is simple. Just choose the value you want to modify in the **Style** and **Attributes** tabs and click on the button that appears on their right. In this way, you can create formulas that dynamically assign values to an object's color, position, width, length, format, visibility, and so on. Using this technique, stoplights can be created by assigning different values to an object according to a calculation, progress bars can be created by changing an object's length, and dynamic images can be placed in the report using the result of a formula to calculate the image's path.

As we have seen in the examples, using formulas in our reports gives us great flexibility in applying styles and attributes to objects and to the report itself, as well as the possibility of creating our own objects based on complex calculations. By using formulas correctly, you will be able to give life to your reports and adapt them to changing contexts. For example, depending on which user executes the report, a certain image can appear in the **Report Header** section, or graphics and subreports can be hidden if the user does not have sufficient permissions.

In the following chapters, we will see how to let PRD know which user is executing the report.

The formula editor

The formula editor has a very intuitive and easy-to-use UI that in addition to guiding us in creating formulas, tells us, whenever possible, the value that the formula will return. In the following screenshot, you can see the formula editor:

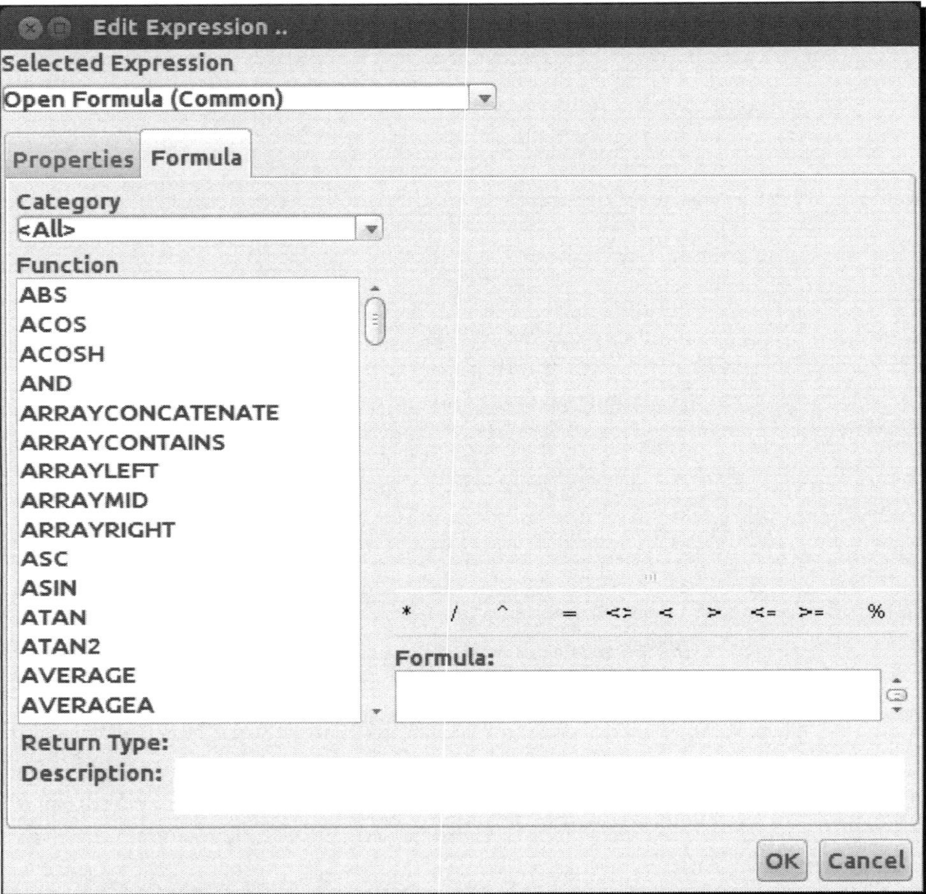

We will explain its layout with an example. Let's suppose that we added a new label and we want to create a formula that returns the value of **Attributes.Value**. For this purpose, we do the following:

- Select the option to the right of **Attributes.Value**. This will open the formula editor. In the upper-left corner, there is a selector where we can specify the category of functions that we want to see. Below this, we find a list of the functions that we can use to create our own formulas. In the lower-left section, we can see more information about the selected function; that is, the type of value that it will return and a general description:

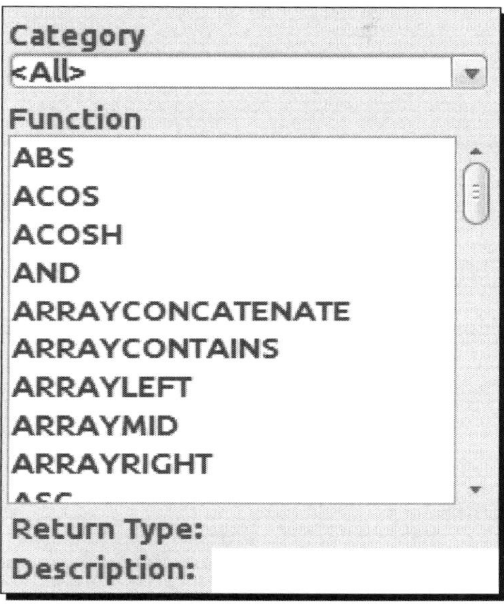

- We choose the **CONCATENATE** function by double-clicking on it, and in the lower-right section, we can see the formula (**Formula:**) that we will use. We type in `=CONCATENATE(Any)`, and an assistant will open in the upper-right section that will guide us in entering the values we want to concatenate.

We could complete the **CONCATENATE** function by adding some fixed values and some variables; take the following example:

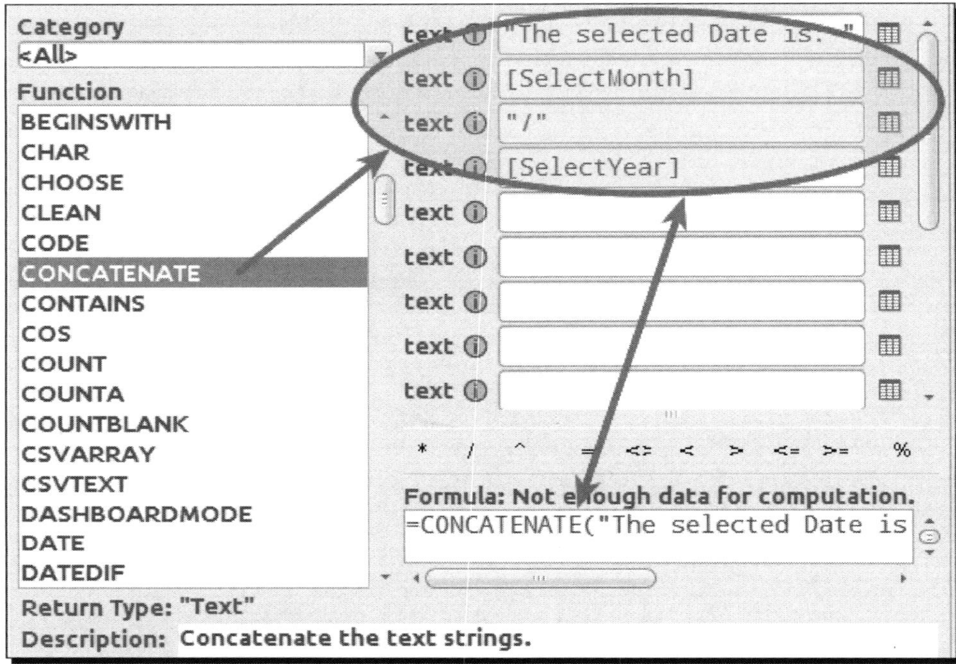

If there is an error in the text of the formula, text will appear to warn us. Otherwise, the formula editor will try to show us the result that our formula will return. When it is not possible to visualize the result that a formula will return, this is usually because the values used are calculated during the execution of the report.

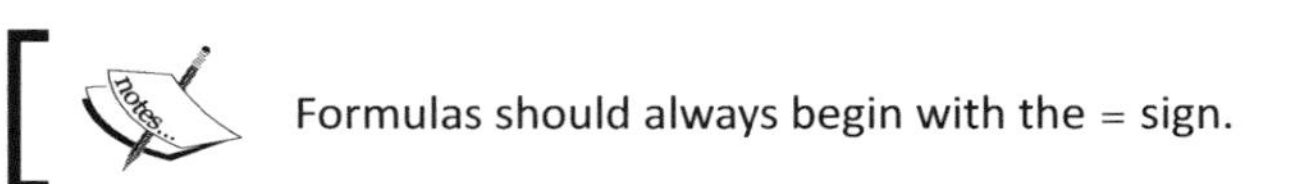

Formulas should always begin with the = sign.

Initially, one tends to use the help that the formula editor provides, but later, with more practice, it will become evident that it is much faster to type the formula directly. Also, if you need to enter complex formulas or add various functions with logical operators, the formula editor will not be of use.

Time for action – creating a new formula

1. We will use the formula editor to create a new formula that multiplies the Amount and Quantity. Then we will place it in the **Details** section so it makes its calculation row by row. Finally, we will change the type of object for the Amount and change the format in which the numbers are presented. We will create a formula to make a calculation based on the Amount and Quantity of each of the rows and place this value under the label **Total**. We choose the **Data** tab, right-click on **Functions**, and choose the **Add Functions...** option:

2. In the new window, we go to **Common** | **Open Formula** and click on **OK**.

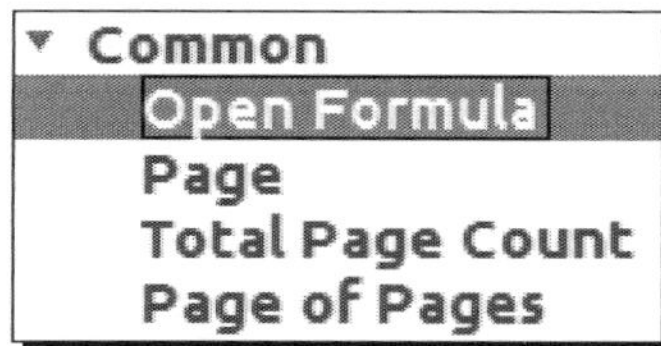

3. We will configure the formula we just created. First, we change its name:

- **Function Name** = `FormulaTotal`

4. Next, we specify the calculation that this formula will make. We press the [...] button to the right of the formula. This will open the formula editor.

5. In the lower-right portion of the formula editor, we see only the = sign where it says **Formula:**.

6. The calculation that we want to make is a multiplication of the `sum_amount` and `count_rental` fields. To choose the `sum_amount` field, we press the button and choose **[sum_amount]**.

Let's see how our formula is coming along:

7. Next, we add the multiplication sign by either typing it from the keyboard or pressing the [*] button.

8. Finally, we press the button again, but this time we choose **count_rental**.

   Our formula should look like this:

   ```
   =[sum_amount]*[count_rental]
   ```

   Done! We have created our first formula.

9. When you add a field to the formula, use the following nomenclature:

   `[field_name]`

   Now we press **OK** to continue. We add the recently created formula (**FormulaTotal**) to the **Details** section under the **Total** label:

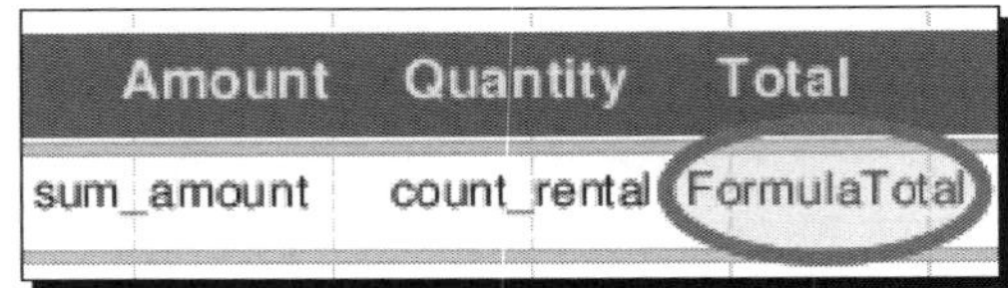

   If we choose **FormulaTotal** and look at **Attributes.type**, we see that it is a **Text-field** type object; this means we cannot apply the same format to it as we did in the previous chapter with **sum_amount**.

> Remember that what we did with **sum_amount** was configure its **Attributes.format** attribute with the value `$ #,##0.00;($ #,##0.00)`. We were able to do this because **sum_amount** is a **Number-field** type object.

10. Next, we will convert the **FormulaTotal** object to Number-field. To do so, we select **FormulaTotal**, and in the upper menu, we choose **number-field** by going to **Format** | **Morph** |.

11. Next, we configure the following:

    - **Attributes.format** = `$ #,##0.00;($ #,##0.00)`

> Another way to do this is by adding a Number-field object to our report and assigning the value `[FormulaTotal]` to its **Attributes.field** attribute, and then configuring the desired format in **Attributes.format**.

What just happened?

We created a new formula. We did it by creating a function and then by going to **Common** | **Open Formula**. Next, we used the formula editor UI to create an expression that multiplies the fields `Amount` and `Quantity`. Finally, we added our formula to the **Details** section, so it will make its calculation row by row.

Time for action – styles with formulas

We will configure the rectangle's **Style.bg-color** property, which we have previously placed in the **Details** section, so that its color will be defined based on a row-by-row evaluation of the **sum_amount** field. We will use the formula editor and the `IF` function to do so. Next, we will create two parameters so that the final user can establish the conditions based on which the rectangle will be colored. What we will do now is create a formula so that the background color of the rectangle we added earlier changes according to certain values.

1. We select **Rectangle**, and in the **Style** tab, press the ⊕ button found on the right of **bg-color**:

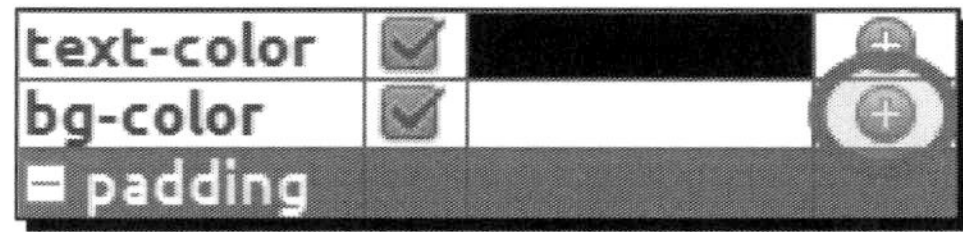

2. This will open the formula editor. In **Formula:**, we type the following:

```
=IF([sum_amount]<4;"#990000";IF([sum_
amount]<6;"#cccc00";"#66cc00"))
```

3. Next, we click on **OK** to continue.

We will explain each part of this calculation, but first we will talk a bit about the function **IF**. The `IF` function receives the following three parameters that are separated by semicolons (`;`):

- The first is a logical expression that will return a true or false value. A comparison is often placed here, for example `[sum_amount]<4`, where the result of the comparison will return `true` if `[sum_amount]` is less than (<) `4`, else it will return `false`.
- The second value is what the function will return when the first value is true.
- The third value is what the function will return when the first value is false.

So the IF function could be explained as follows:

- If sum_amount is less than 4 then the color will be red (#990000); else evaluate what to do according to the second IF function)

And the second IF function can be explained as follows:

- IF([sum_amount] is less than 6?; color yellow (#cccc00); color green (#66cc00)

We can see how our report is coming along by previewing the following screenshot:

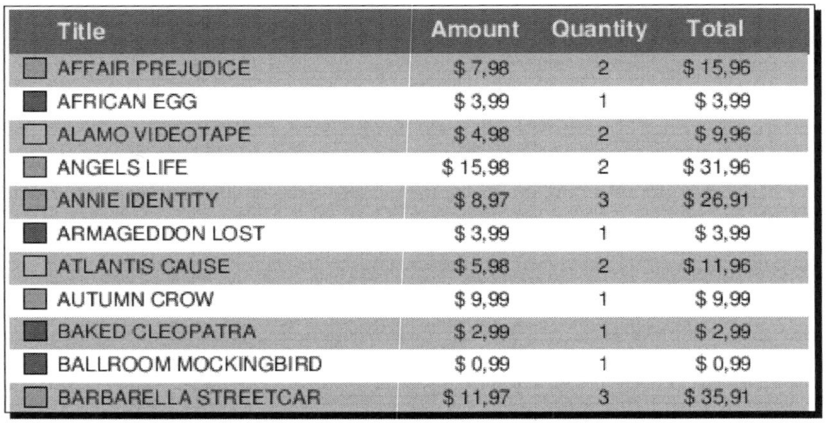

Title	Amount	Quantity	Total
AFFAIR PREJUDICE	$ 7,98	2	$ 15,96
AFRICAN EGG	$ 3,99	1	$ 3,99
ALAMO VIDEOTAPE	$ 4,98	2	$ 9,96
ANGELS LIFE	$ 15,98	2	$ 31,96
ANNIE IDENTITY	$ 8,97	3	$ 26,91
ARMAGEDDON LOST	$ 3,99	1	$ 3,99
ATLANTIS CAUSE	$ 5,98	2	$ 11,96
AUTUMN CROW	$ 9,99	1	$ 9,99
BAKED CLEOPATRA	$ 2,99	1	$ 2,99
BALLROOM MOCKINGBIRD	$ 0,99	1	$ 0,99
BARBARELLA STREETCAR	$ 11,97	3	$ 35,91

The limit values that we have chosen in making the previous formula are totally arbitrary. What we will do now is create two parameters so that the end user can define the value of these limits.

The first parameter will collect the value that will be used to divide the bottom range from the middle, and the second parameter will divide the middle from the top.

Next, we will create the first parameter:

- **Name** = SelectFirstThreshold
- **Label** = First Threshold:
- **Value Type** = Number
- **Default Value** = 4
- **Display Type** = Text Box

Now we will create the second parameter:

- **Name** = `SelectSecondThreshold`
- **Label** = `Second Threshold:`
- **Value Type** = `Number`
- **Default Value** = `6`
- **Display Type** = `Text Box`

In the formula that we have just applied to **Style.bg-color** of the rectangle, we will modify the calculation as follows:

```
=IF([sum_amount]<[SelectFirstThreshold];"#990000";IF([sum_amount]
<[SelectSecondThreshold];"#cccc00";"#66cc00"))
```

If we preview the report and modify the values of the parameters `SelectFirstThreshold` and `SelectSecondThreshold`, we will see how the background color of the rectangle varies.

Lastly, we will change the order the parameters appear in so that the two new parameters are in the top part of the list of selectors when we execute our report.

We go to the **Data** tab, select the **SelectFirstThreshold** parameter, right-click on it, and choose the **Send Forward** option. This will make the chosen parameter move up one level in the hierarchy. We should repeat this procedure until **SelectFirstThreshold** is first in the list.

Then we will use the same procedure to position **SelectSecondThreshold** second in the list.

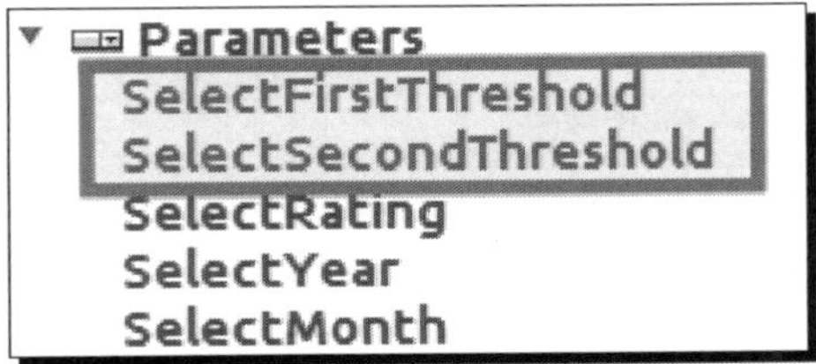

If we preview our report, we can see the changes we have made:

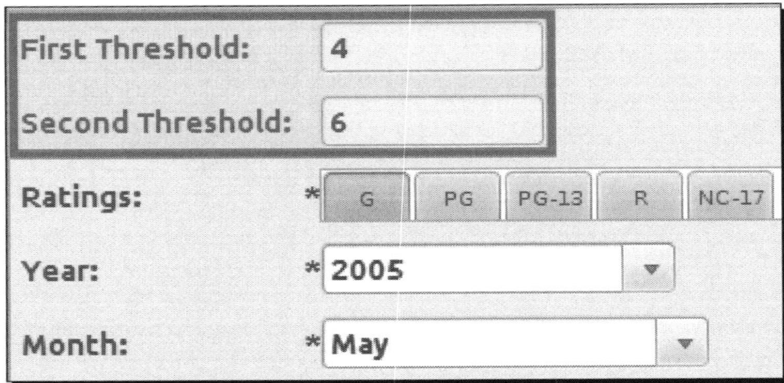

What just happened?

We created a new formula to calculate our rectangle's **Style.bg-color** property according to the value of the **sum_amount** field in each row. We used the `IF` function to do so, which was explained in detail through the example. Later we created the parameters `SelectFirstThreshold` and `SelectSecondThreshold` so that the end user is able to choose the values of the limits used by the formula to calculate the color of our rectangle. Lastly, we placed these two new parameters at the top of the selector list.

Have a go hero

Next, to sharpen the skills we have learned, we will modify the report created in this chapter and adapt it to meet new requirements.

The report that we propose, which you have to create, will have an image with a stoplight in the **Group Footer** section, and the following screenshot will be shown at the end of each group, in this case at the end of the analysis of the films of each rating. Let's see the last page of the rating `G`:

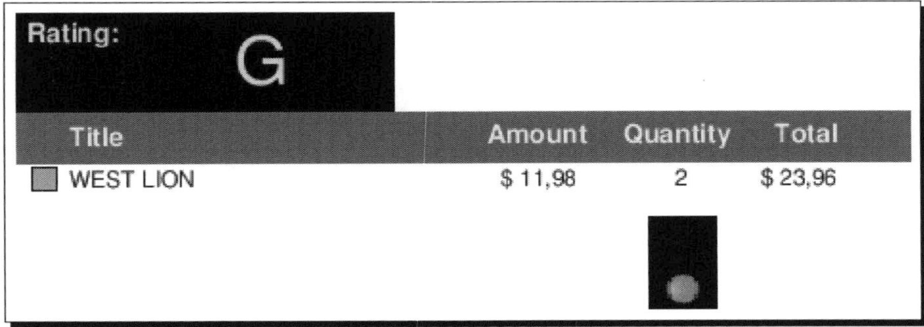

The steps you should follow, broadly speaking, are as follows:

1. Create a copy of the `09_Using_Formulas.prpt` report and save it with the name `10_Using_Formulas_Plus.prpt`.
2. Create a function of the type **Running | Average (Running)** and configure it as follows:
   - **Function Name** = `AvgAmount`
   - **Field Name** = `sum_amount`
   - **Reset On Group Name** = `RatingGroup`

If you are using Windows, you should use the backslash instead of the forward slash to separate folders; that is, you should use \ instead of /.

This formula will insert the path corresponding to an image based on a comparison made to the average of **sum_amount** (function `AvgAmount`). This formula can be explained as follows:

- If `[AvgAmount]` is less than `[SelectFirstThreshold]`, then insert a red stoplight (`traffic_red.png`); else if `[sum_amount]` is less than `[SelectSecondThreshold]`, then insert a yellow stoplight (`traffic_yellow.png`), and insert a green stoplight (`traffic_green.png`)

Pop quiz – formulas

Q1. Which of the following statements is true?

1. If we enter a value in a parameter's **Default Value** field, while the report is being executed, this value will always appear to be selected.
2. PRD implements OpenDocument to manage formulas.
3. The formula editor includes functions for making mathematical calculations but does not include functions for making statistical calculations.
4. There are two ways to create formulas in PRD, one for general use and another for specific use.
5. To create a formula in PRD, you just drag this object from the insertable objects' area.
6. The formula editor is a wizard that will help us to create our formulas step by step.

Summary

We opened a report created in the previous chapter, we saved it with another name, and we modified its layout to fit the necessities of the new exercise. We defined the default values for the parameters **SelectRating**, **SelectYear**, and **SelectMonth**.

We explained what formulas are, what they are used for, and the ways to use them. We also talked about the formula editor UI and used it in a practical example.

We created a formula named **FormulaTotal** and used the formula editor to enter the calculation that it will make. Then we included **FormulaTotal** in our report in the **Details** section.

We configured **Attributes.bg-color** for a rectangle that we added to our report so that its background color is determined by a formula.

Next, we created two parameters (`SelectFirstThreshold` and `SelectSecondThreshold`) so that the final user can input values that will intervene in the calculation of the formula that defines the background color of our rectangle.

Finally, so you could sharpen the skills learned, we proposed that you modify the report created in this chapter to show a stoplight.

In the next chapter, we will explain how to add charts in our reports.

9

Adding Charts

This chapter is dedicated to charts. We will talk about chart functions, good and bad practices of using charts, and how to create and configure our own charts among other topics.

By explaining each type of chart, we will be able to understand which chart to use for a particular need, and how to configure the chart so that its look and feel is what we want.

We will also see how charts allow us to show data from different perspectives and add value to our reports.

In this chapter we will perform the following operations:

- Create a new report, create its data set, and create two parameters
- Create and configure a pie chart
- Create and configure a bar chart

Finally, we propose that you modify a previous report and add a chart to it to give it greater capacity for analysis.

Starting practice

In this chapter, we will create a new report and configure the data set, labels, parameters, and so on, but most importantly we will create and configure two charts. When we finish the exercises, we will have a report that looks like this:

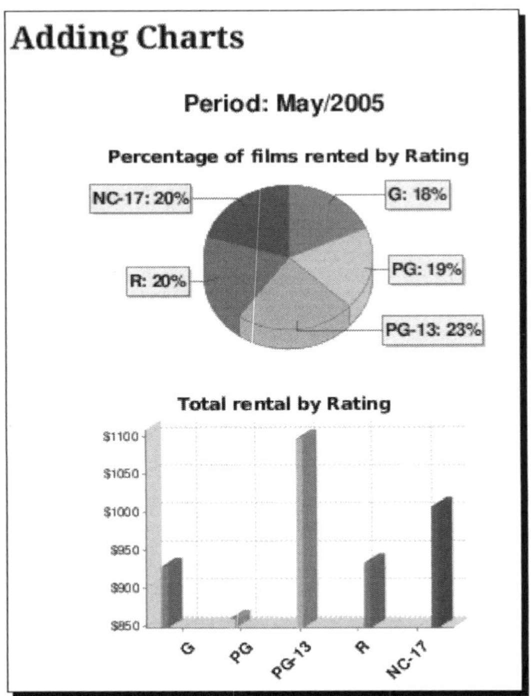

The upper half of the preceding chart is a **pie chart** and the bottom is a **bar chart**. Both charts use the main data set of our report as its data source.

We will learn about charts in PRD and then manipulate them.

Time for action – creating a new report

We will now create a new report that we will use in this chapter's exercises. We will create a JDBC data set that connects to the Sakila database, and we will establish its SQL query. Next, we will create two parameters to choose the year and month for which we want data, and finally we will add the `Message` object to show the period under analysis.

1. We will create a new report and save it with the name `11_Adding_Charts.prpt`.

2. We will create a JDBC data set and configure it as follows:

   - **Connections** = `sakila db`
   - **Query Name** = `Ratings`
   - **Query** =

```
SELECT film.rating, SUM(payment.amount) sum_amount,
count(1) count_rental
FROM payment
INNER JOIN rental ON rental.rental_id=payment.rental_id
INNER JOIN inventory ON inventory.inventory_id=rental.
inventory_id
INNER JOIN film ON film.film_id=inventory.film_id
WHERE YEAR(payment.payment_date)=${SelectYear}
AND MONTH(payment_date) = ${SelectMonth}
GROUP BY film.rating
```

3. We will create two parameters. The first is `SelectYear` and the second is `SelectMonth`. We will create them and establish a default value, as we did in the previous chapter.

4. We put an object, `Message`, in the **Report Header** section to show us the values that have been chosen as parameters. By doing so, the period under analysis can be seen when we export the report in different formats. We configure the message as follows:

   - **Attributes.value** = `=CONCATENATE("Period: ";IF([SelectMonth]=1; "January"; IF([SelectMonth]=2; "February"; IF([SelectMonth]=3; "March"; IF([SelectMonth]=4; "April"; IF([SelectMonth]=5; "May"; IF([SelectMonth]=6; "June"; IF([SelectMonth]=7; "July"; IF([SelectMonth]=8; "August"; IF([SelectMonth]=9; "September"; IF([SelectMonth]=10; "October"; IF([SelectMonth]=11; "November"; "December")))))))))));"/";[SelectYear])`

What just happened?

We created a new report and named it `11_Adding_Charts.prpt`. We created a JDBC data set and configured its connection and SQL query. We created and configured the `SelectYear` and `SelectMonth` parameters. Also, we added and configured a `Message` object to show the time period chosen by the end user. We also saw a small preview of the report that we will create by the end of the chapter.

Charts

PRD uses **JFreeChart** to manage charts. JFreeChart is a Java library that lets us create many types of high-quality charts. It also allows the charts to be highly customizable. The license that JFreeChart uses is the **GNU LGPL**, which allows proprietary software to use this library.

For more information on JFreeChart, please refer to:

- Wikipedia: `http://en.wikipedia.org/wiki/JFreeChart`
- Official site: `http://www.jfree.org/jfreechart/`

Charts give life to our reports and make them more than simple flat reports, giving them another dimension. Regarding this, *Thomas Morgner*, the Architect of PRD, said:

> *"Reporting without charting is like zombies without the inevitable hunt for fresh brains. You can do it, yes, but it is sure not fun."*

Earlier most reporting software were not prepared to include charts, and the software that allowed charts presented serious limitations in their configuration. As such, most reports were just lists. Later, with the advent of new technology and software growth, including a chart in a report was no longer rare. Reports began to be overpopulated with charts, colors, and more colors. Continuing *Thomas Morgner's* analogy, we could say that the panorama became a zombie apocalypse but with no teeth.

That is, given the possibility of simply adding charts to our reports, when it had been difficult in prior years, many reports were created with an overpopulation of charts. Charts were placed in reports simply because it was possible, or perhaps because it was popular at the time. A problem comes up when the chart does not fulfill a specific function in the report but instead makes it difficult to read the data, distracts attention from more critical information, and creates a visual contamination as well as increasing the report's size. This reminds us of the now—fortunately—forgotten HTML tag, `<BLINK>`.

Returning to the undead, we think that a zombie *that isn't very hungry* is much better than one *without teeth*.

If we're going to include charts in our reports, we should be clear about the function they will serve and whether they are necessary. We should also know what type of chart will best present the information we want to display. It is also best to configure the charts to control the quantity and type of additional information to be displayed, for example, whether or not to include tags, titles, subtitles, legends, colors, effects, behavior, and so on.

A good chart will show us summarized information about the data we are analyzing, will tell us at a glance the situation of our data, will give a different perspective of the analysis, and so on.

Creating and configuring charts

To add a chart to our report, we just drag-and-drop the object `Chart` to the section desired.

Next, to configure it, we double-click on it. This will open a window such as the following one, where we have marked the three principal parts:

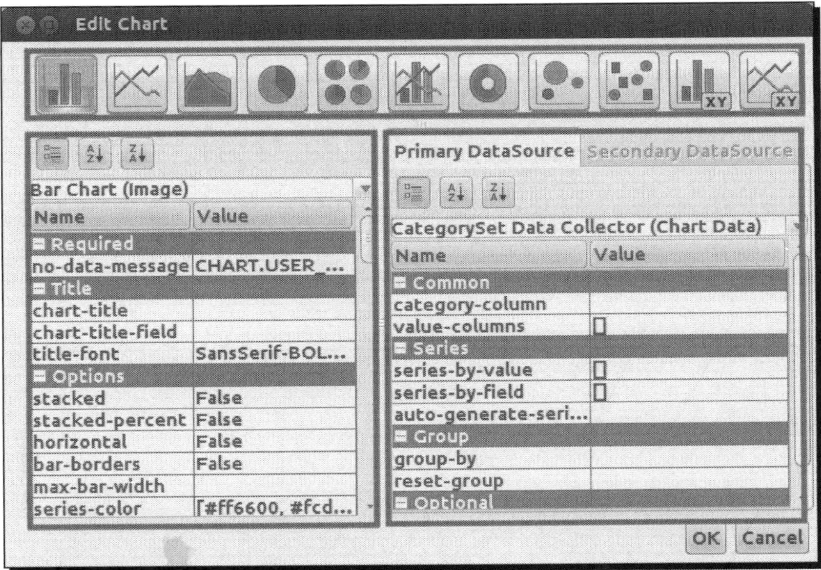

Each of these parts fulfills a specific task in configuring our charts:

- The *upper* part is where we choose the type of chart. As we can see, each chart is represented by a small icon.
- The part to the *right* is where we specify the data sources to use and the fields to include.
- The part to the *left* is where we configure the chart's details.

Based on the type of chart chosen, the options presented in the parts to the left and right will vary.

We can see that, just like in Style and Attributes, the characteristics to be defined in the parts to the left and right are grouped according to categories based on their function.

Types of charts

PRD includes a great variety of types of charts. They are as mentioned in the following sections.

The bar chart

The following is the icon for bar charts:

If we open the report found in `[PRD_HOME]/samples/Charts/Bar Chart.prpt`, we will see an example of this type of report:

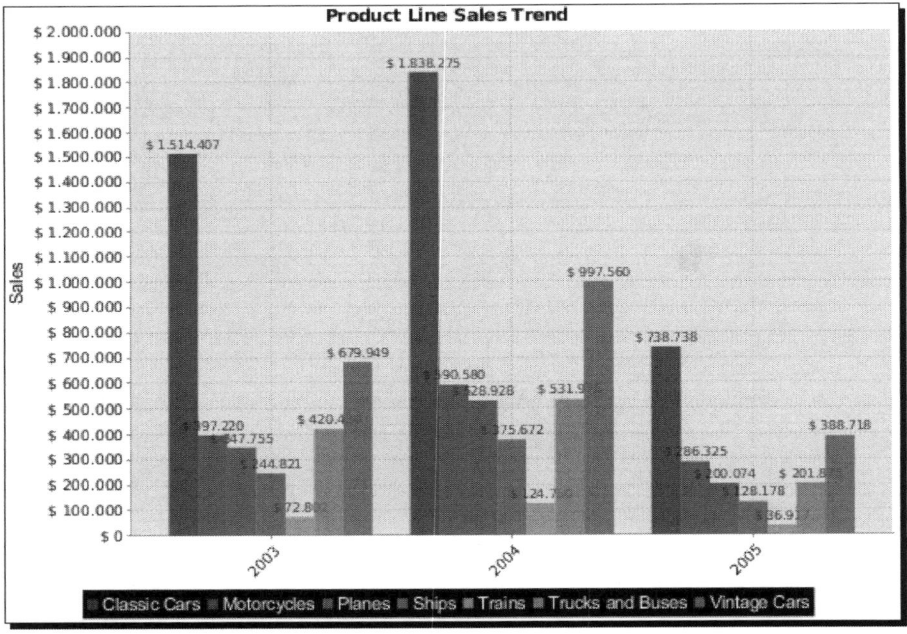

In this type of chart, values are represented as vertical bars of different heights, which lets us make a rapid analysis by comparing the different bars' heights. On one axis (usually the y axis or vertical axis), we find the numerical values that the bars can take, and on the other axis (usually the x axis or the horizontal axis), we find the bars representing the items under analysis.

The previous example shows the sales for each product line in each year. The y axis shows the sales and the *x* axis the product line (**Classic Cars**, **Motorcycles**, and so on) grouped by year (2003, 2004, and so on).

This type of chart uses only one data source.

If we double-click on the object `Chart`, we see to the right how it was configured:

- **value-columns** = `[SALES]`: This is the value that will be shown on the y axis
- **series-by-field** = `[PRODUCTLINE]`: This is the item under analysis
- **category-column** = `YEAR_ID`: This is the category by which the items will be grouped

It is best practice, when using charts, to have a category that represents items whose value is below a determined limit. That way, if there are many items but with very low values, instead of having them take up a lot of space in our chart, they can belong to another category with the name `Others`. This should be done when creating the data source that the chart will use.

Suppose we want this chart to show stacked bars. All we have to do is double-click on the object `Chart` in the report and configure the following on the left-hand side:

- **stacked** = `True`

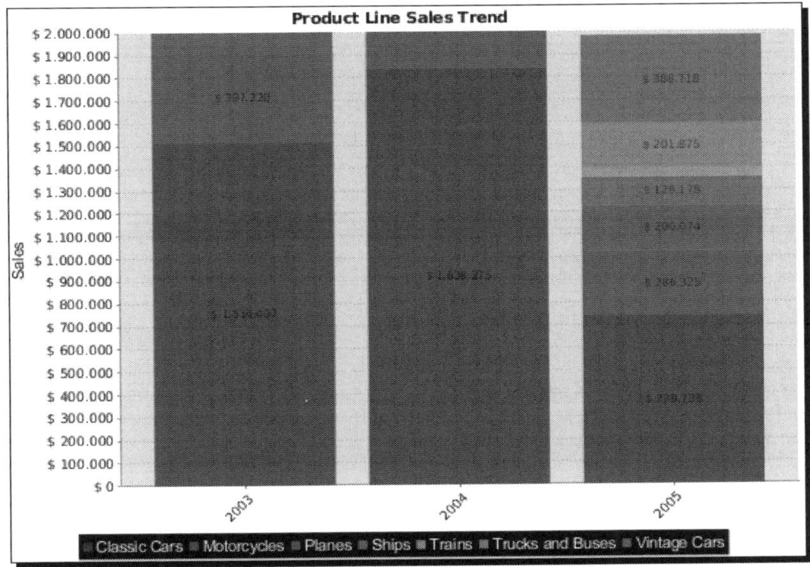

If we want the chart to show the bars horizontally, all we have to do is modify the following:

- **horizontal** = `True`

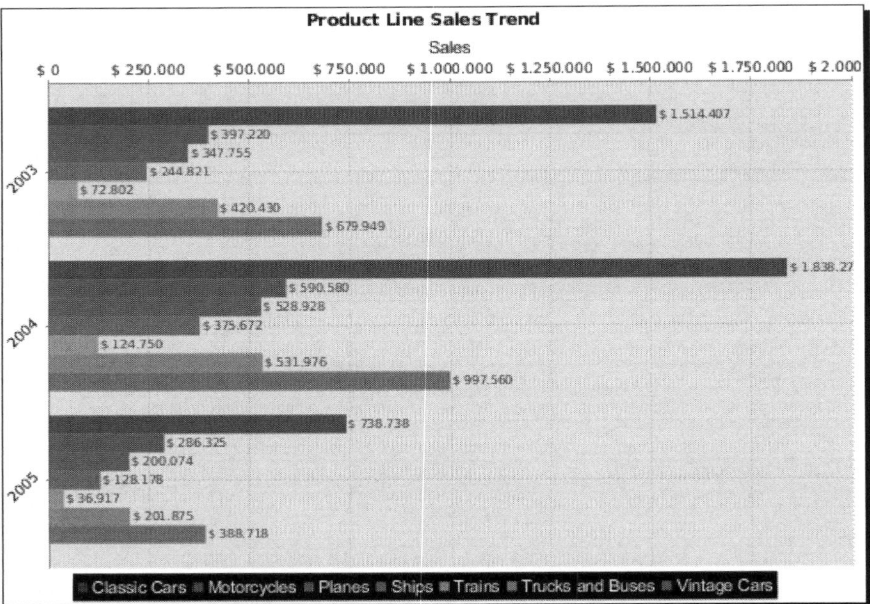

The line chart

The following is the icon for line charts:

If we open the report found in `[PRD_HOME]/samples/Charts/Line Chart.prpt`, we will see an example of this type of report:

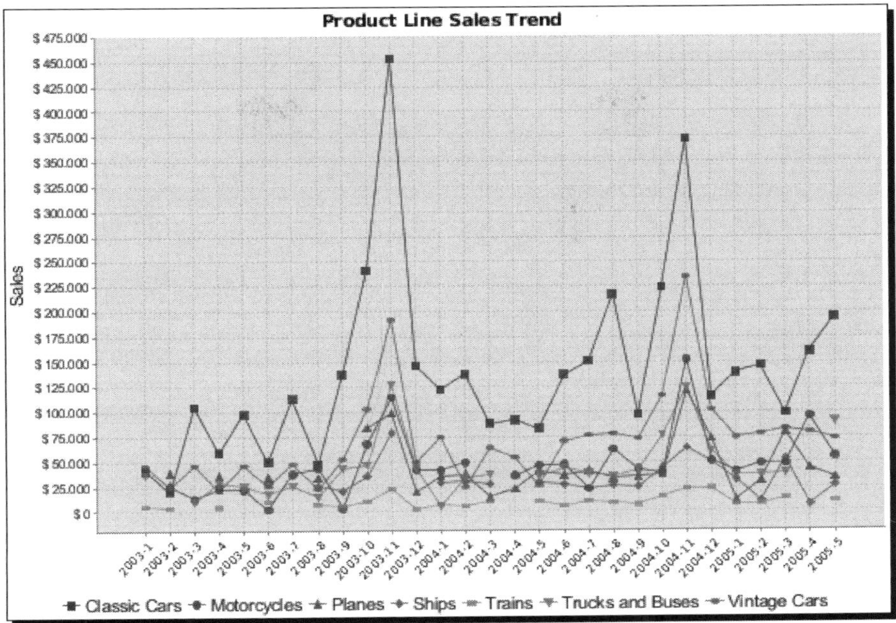

In this type of chart, we have the values to be analyzed on one axis (usually the y axis), and on the other axis (usually the x axis), time periods. Here the values of different items in each period of time are marked as a point, and a line is drawn between the successive points.

In the example we just saw, Sales are shown for each Product Line in a time period. The y axis shows the Sales, where each line in the chart represents a Product Line (**Classic Cars**, **Motorcycles**, and so on), and the x axis shows a time period indicated by year and month (2003-01, 2003-02, and so on).

This type of chart uses only one data source.

If we double-click on the object `Chart`, we see to the right how it was configured:

- **value-columns** = `[SALES]`: This is the value that will be shown on the y axis
- **series-by-field** = `[PRODUCTLINE]`: This is the item under analysis
- **category-column** = `NewDate`: This is the time period expressed in year and month

As the time period under analysis was long and needed many labels on the x axis, these were configured to be slanted:

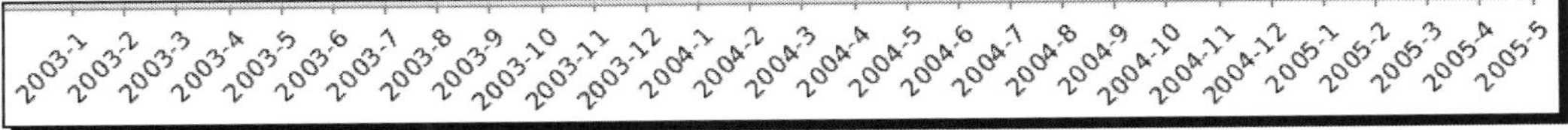

This was done as follows:

- **x-axis-label-rotation** = `45.0`

Here we can also see that the lines were configured to be semitransparent. This is done by reducing the value of **plot-fg-alpha**. The values that this characteristic can have go from `0` (totally transparent) to `1` (opaque).

The area chart

The following is the icon for area charts:

If we open the report found in `[PRD_HOME]/samples/Charts/Area Chart.prpt`, we will see an example of this type of report:

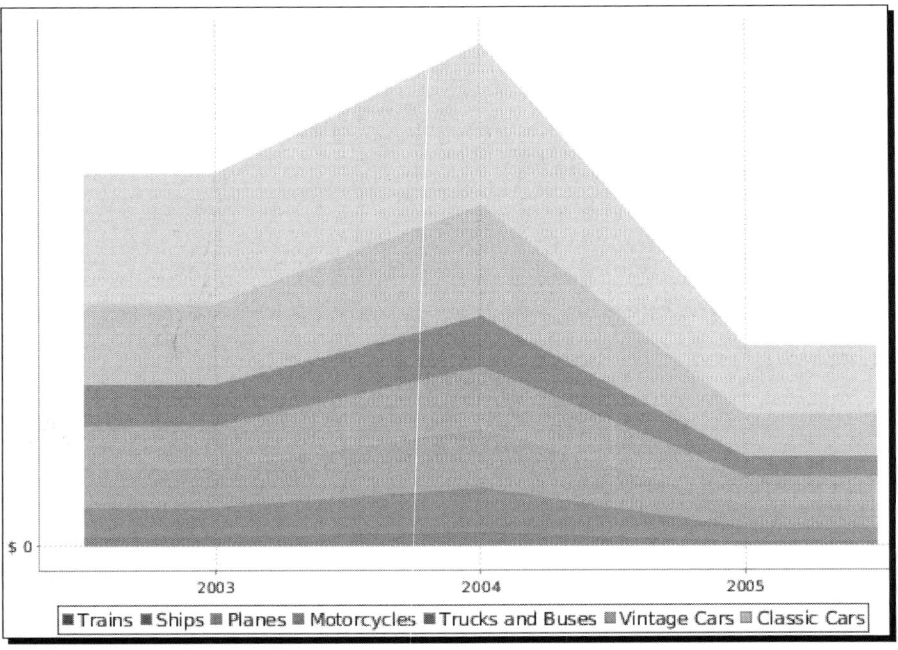

This type of chart is similar to a line chart. The difference is that in the area chart, the area under the line is colored to indicate the evolution of the values. In this example, the areas have been configured to stack on each other to avoid superimposing the areas of each item.

This type of chart uses only one data source.

> If you do not want the areas to stack, there is a way to make the areas not cover each other:
>
> - Make them somewhat transparent by modifying the value of **plot-fg-alpha**
> - In **serie-color**, choose a collection of colors that are very different from each other
> - In **lot-bg-color**, choose a dark color, for example, dark gray

If we want our report to show the value of each angle on the edge of each area, we just configure the following:

- **show-item-labels** = `Show Labels`

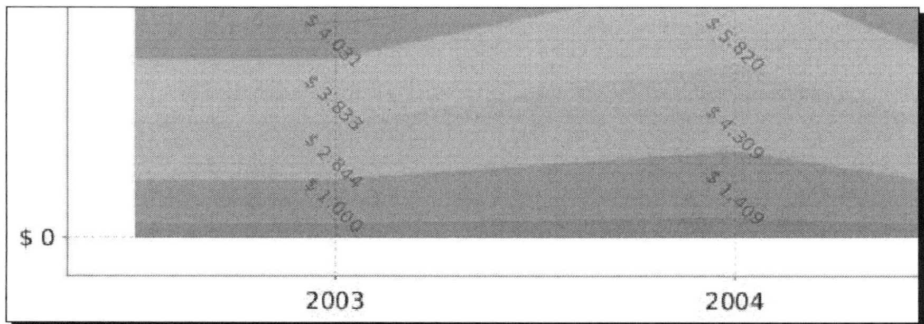

We can see that the values are not shown on the y axis. This is because the interval that has been defined for the y axis values is very large. As the areas are stacked, the value (height) of each new item is calculated starting from the value (height) of the previous item. So in this case, the label on the y axis is unnecessary and would be confusing. To modify the interval for the y axis, modify **y-tick-interval**.

If we double-click on the object `Chart`, we will see to the right-hand side how it is configured. This example shares the same configuration as the example for the bar chart.

The pie chart

The following is the icon for pie charts:

If we open the report found in `[PRD_HOME]/samples/Charts/Pie.prpt`, we will see an example of this type of report:

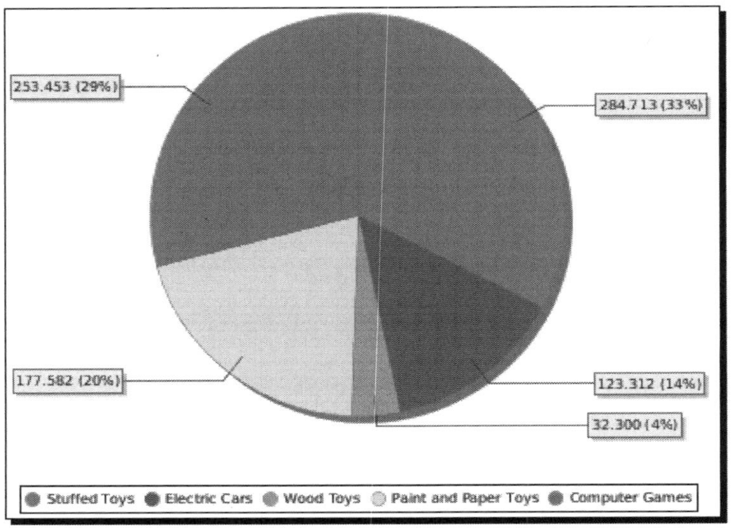

In this type of chart, the values of the items are represented as portions of a pie. In this case, the circle shows the sales values of a series of products (**Stuffed Toys**, **Electric Cars**, and so on).

A pie chart uses only one data source.

If we double-click on the object `Chart`, we see to the right how it was configured:

- **value-columns** = `Sales`
- **series-by-field** = `[Product]`

As you can see, each portion of the pie is labeled with its Sales value and the percentage that this represents of the total pie. This is due to the following configuration:

- **label-format** = `{1} ({2})`

`{0}`, `{1}`, `{2}`, and `{3}` are variables that return different values according to the type of chart; in this case:

- `{0}` returns the name of the item
- `{1}` returns the value of the item
- `{2}` returns the percentage of the total that the item represents
- `{3}` returns the sum of the values of all items

These variables can be combined with text to obtain a desired result.

If we remove the legend box present in the lower part of the chart (**show-legend** = `False`), we could configure `label-format` as follows:

- **label-format** = `Product: {0} - Sales {1}`

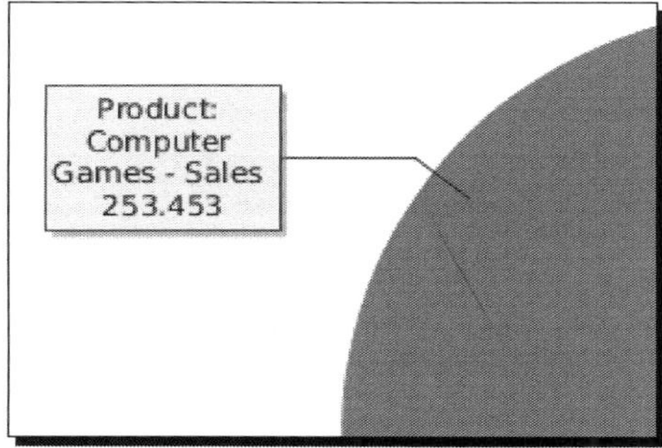

The multipie chart

The following is the icon for multipie charts:

If we open the report found in `[PRD_HOME]/samples/Charts/Multi Pie Chart.prpt`, we will see an example of this type of report:

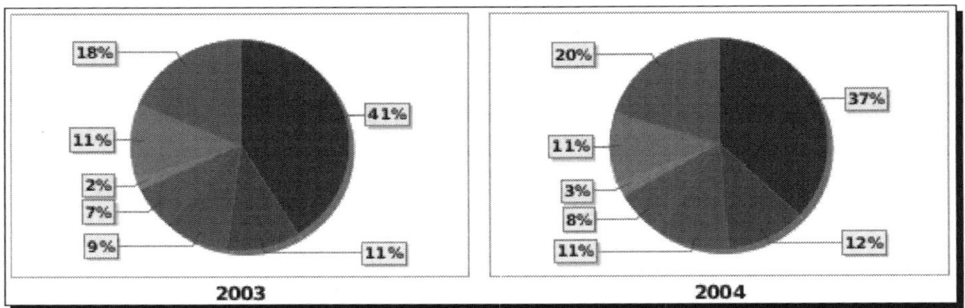

Multipie charts present a pie chart for each new element of a series (**series-by-field**). In this case, the series represent the years (2003, 2004, and so on).

This type of chart uses only one data source.

The barline chart

The following is the icon for barline charts:

If we open the report found in `[PRD_HOME]/samples/Charts/Bar Line Chart.prpt`, we will see an example of this type of report:

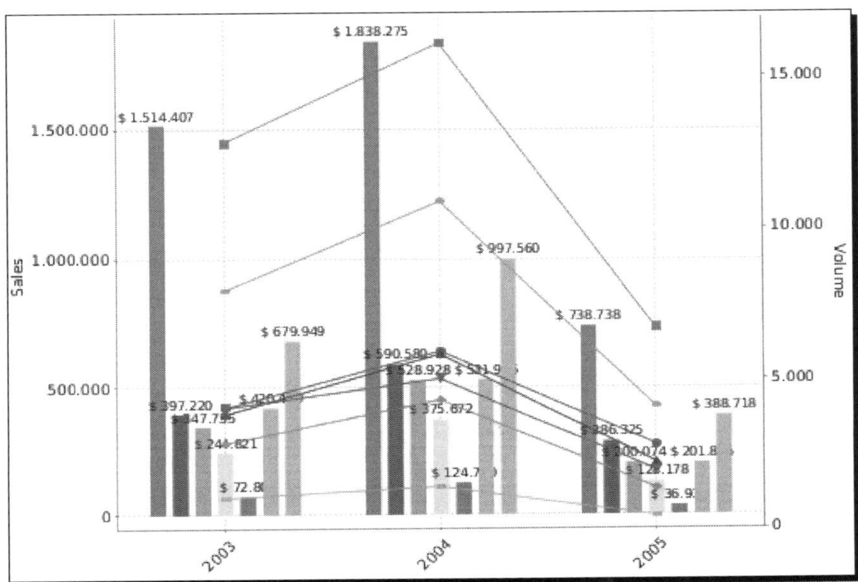

This type of chart combines the bar chart and the line chart and has individual configurations for a bar chart (**Bar Options**) and for a line chart (**Line Options**). In this case, the items represent the Product Line (**Classic Cars**, **Motorcycles**, and so on) and are grouped by year (2003, 2004, and so on). The bars represent the sales and their scale is on the left, while the lines represent the volume and their scale is on the right.

If we double-click on the object `Chart`, we will see to the right that the **Secondary DataSource** tab is now available. This implies that this type of chart has two data sources:

- **Primary DataSource**: This is used in a bar chart and is configured as follows:
    - **category-column** = `YEAR_ID`
    - **value-columns** = `[SALES]`
    - **series-by-field** = `[PRODUCTLINE]`
- **Secondary DataSource**: This is used in a line chart and is configured as follows:
    - **category-column** = `YEAR_ID`
    - **value-columns** = `[VOLUME]`
    - **series-by-field** = `[PRODUCTLINE]`

The scale to the left (vertical axis in this case) can be configured by editing the characteristics of **Y-Axis**, while the scale to the right can be configured by editing the characteristics of **Y2-Axis**.

We said that it uses two different data sources, but one data set should always be used.

The ring chart

The following is the icon for ring charts:

This type of chart is identical to a pie chart, except that a ring chart has a hole in the middle of the pie, making a ring.

To see an example of this report, we can open the pie chart found in `[PRD_HOME]/samples/Charts/Pie.prpt`, double-click on the object `Chart`, and choose the type of chart **Ring Chart**. If we pay attention, we will see that the only difference to a pie chart is that a ring chart has one more field, **section-depth**.

The ring chart will look like this:

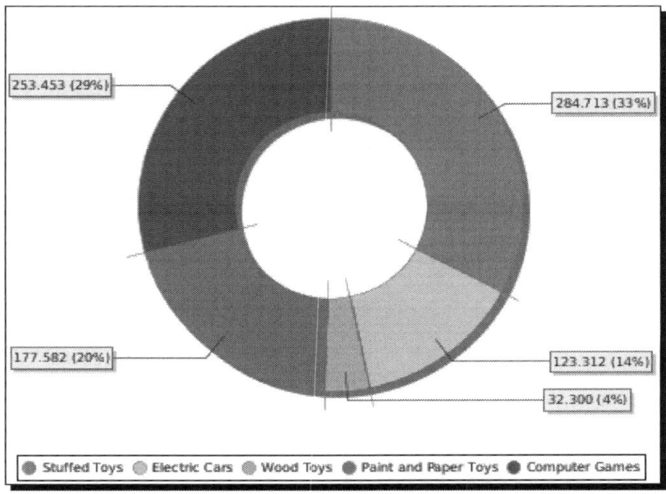

The bubble chart

The following is the icon for bubble charts:

If we open the report found in `[PRD_HOME]/samples/Charts/Bubble Chart by Line.prpt`, we will see an example of this type of report:

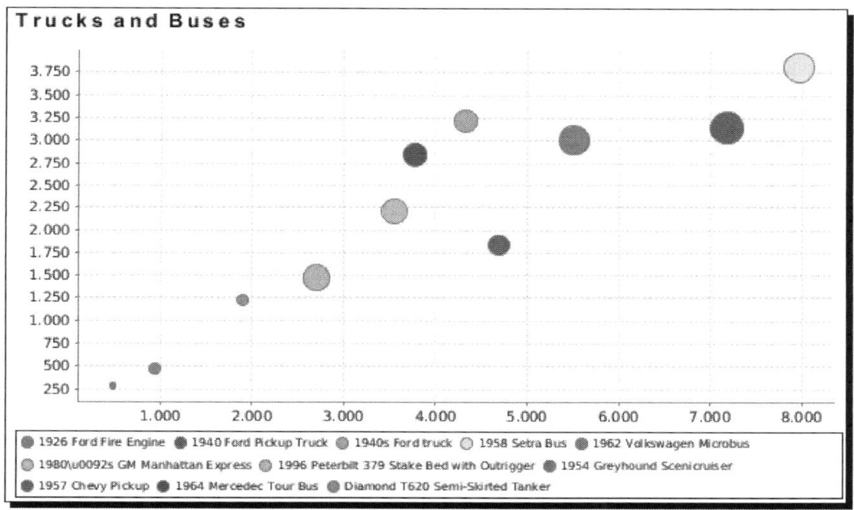

This type of chart presents data in three dimensions. The x and y axes represent the two different scales on which each point will be placed, and the z axis is represented by making each point larger. In this case, the points represent the Products, the y axis is the Cost, the x axis is the Sales, and the z axis (or dot size) represents the quantity ordered of this product.

For more information about bubble charts, go to `http://en.wikipedia.org/wiki/Bubble_chart`.

If we double-click on the object `Chart`, we see to the right how it was configured:

- **x-value-columns** = `[SALES]`
- **y-value-columns** = `[COST]`
- **z-value-columns** = `[QUANTITYORDERED]`
- **series-by-field** = `[PRODUCTNAME]`

We can see that **reset-group** has the value `Line`. `Line` is the **Attributes.name** value of **Master Report | Report Header | Group**.

A bubble chart uses only one data source.

The scatter-plot chart

The following is the icon for scatter-plot charts:

If we open the report found in `[PRD_HOME]/samples/Charts/Scatter XY Collector.prpt`, we will see an example of this type of report:

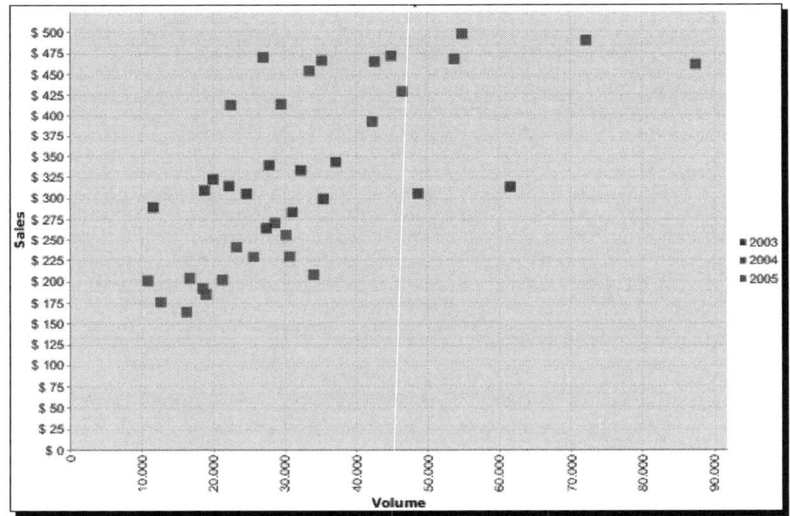

This type of chart is generally used to analyze the relation between two variables, to identify patterns, to detect values that don't follow the average, and to show the amount of dispersion that exists among data.

For more information about scatter plots, go to `http://en.wikipedia.org/wiki/Scatter_plot`.

The example report analyzes the dispersion of products by year taking into account the values **Sales** and **Volume**.

If we double-click on the object `Chart`, we see to the right how it was configured:

- **x-value-columns** = `[SALES]`
- **y-value-columns** = `[VOLUME]`
- **series-by-field** = `[YEAR_ID]`

This type of chart uses only one data source.

The XY bar chart

The following is the icon for XY bar charts:

If we open the report found in `[PRD_HOME]/samples/Charts/XY Bar Chart.prpt`, we will see an example of this type of report:

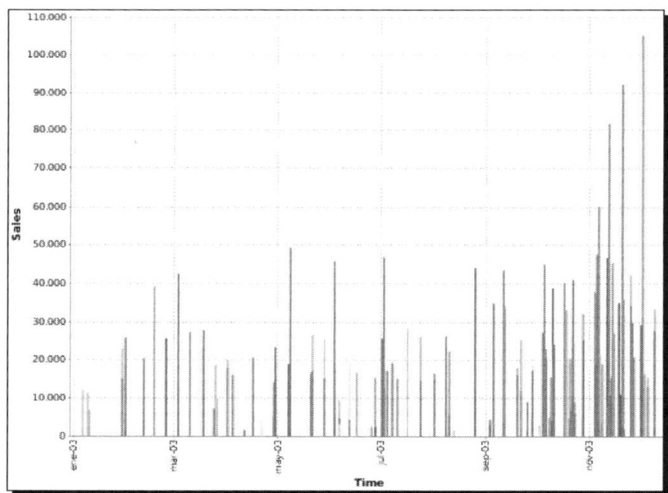

In an XY chart (XY bar chart, XY line chart, XY area chart, extended XY line chart, and XY area line chart), a time scale is usually placed on the x axis and the interval values on the y axis so comparisons can be made between times and values.

This chart uses bars and has only one data source.

The XY line chart

The following is the icon for XY line charts:

If we open the report found in `[PRD_HOME]/samples/Charts/XY Line Chart.prpt`, we will see an example of this type of report:

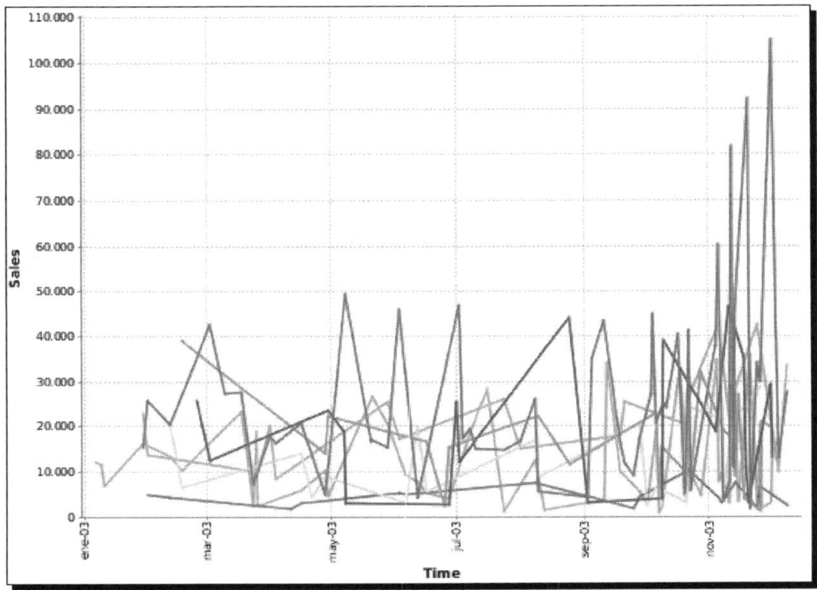

This is a type of XY chart that uses lines and has only one data source.

The XY area chart

The following is the icon for XY area charts:

If we open the report found in `[PRD_HOME]/samples/Charts/XY Area Chart.prpt`, we will see an example of this type of report:

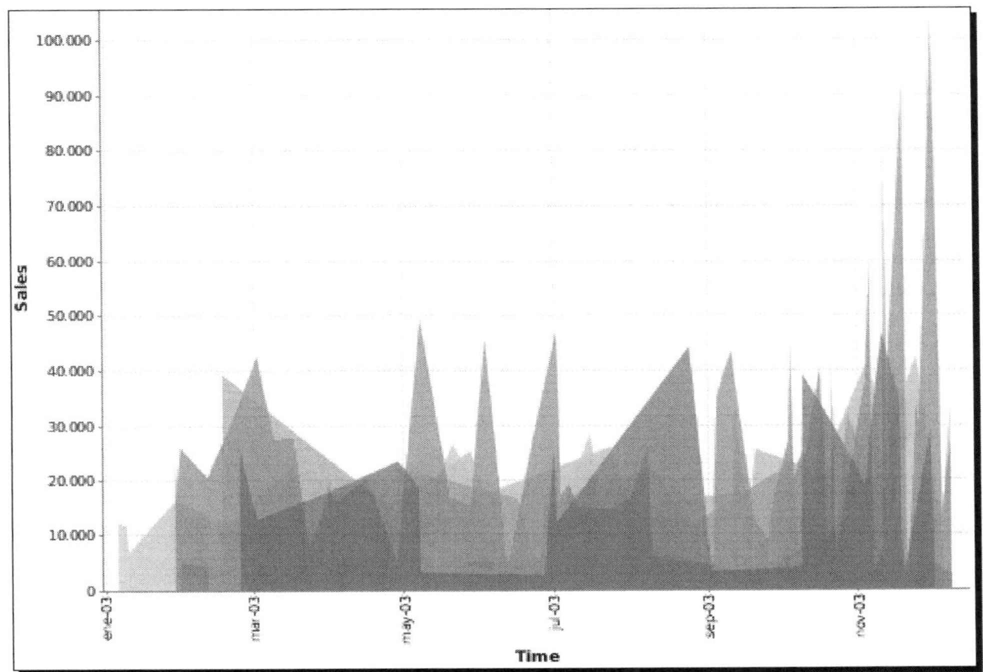

This is a type of XY chart that uses areas and has only one data source.

The extended XY line chart

The following is the icon for extended XY line charts:

This type of chart is similar to an XY line chart but offers more configuration options.

The waterfall chart

The following is the icon for waterfall charts:

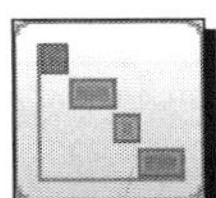

If we open the report found in `[PRD_HOME]/samples/Charts/Waterfall Legacy.prpt`, we will see an example of this type of report:

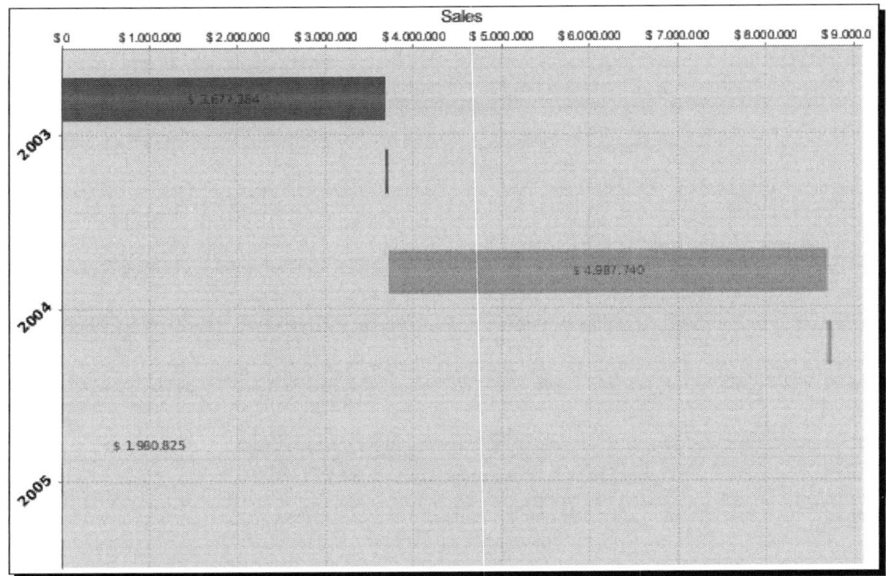

This type of chart is generally used to show increases and decreases in the values under analysis. The first and last values of the chart are represented with a common bar. From the second bar onward, the bars are positioned relative to the right edge of the first bar. If the second value represents a positive value, the bar grows to the right and is green; however, if the value is negative, the bar decreases to the left and is red.

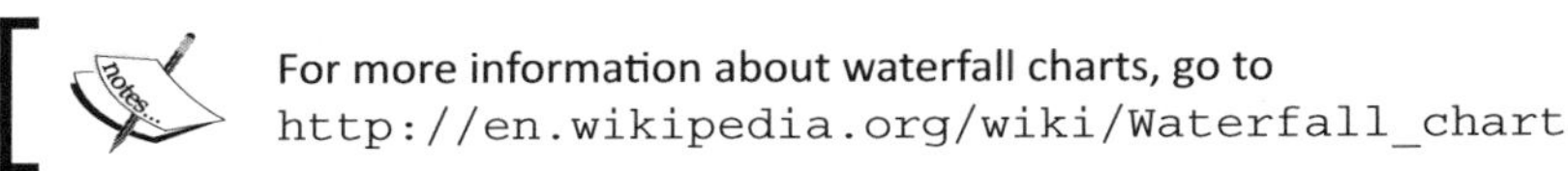

For more information about waterfall charts, go to `http://en.wikipedia.org/wiki/Waterfall_chart`.

The example report analyzes the sales and volume totals by Year (2003, 2004, and so on).

If we double-click on the object `Chart`, we see to the right how it was configured:

- **category-column** = `YEAR_ID`
- **value-columns** = `[SALES, VOLUME]` (this establishes the two fields to be analyzed)
- **series-by-value** = `[YEAR_ID]`

This type of chart uses only one data source.

The radar chart

The following is the icon for radar charts:

If we open the report found in `[PRD_HOME]/samples/Charts/Radar Chart.prpt`, we will see an example of this type of report:

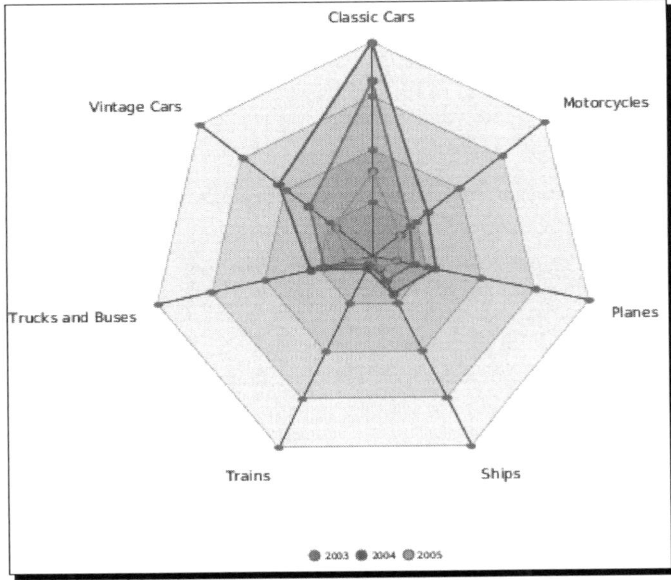

In this type of chart, the items under analysis are represented as a branch in the radar. In this case, the items are the values of the Product Line (**Classic Cars**, **Motorcycles**, and so on); the different series are represented by colored lines, in this case Year (2003, 2004, and so on); and the position where each colored line intersects the branch corresponding to each item is determined by the value under analysis, in this case Sales.

For more information about radar charts, go to `http://en.wikipedia.org/wiki/Radar_chart`.

If we double-click on the object `Chart`, we see to the right how it was configured:

- **value-columns** = `[SALES]`
- **series-by-field** = `[YEAR_ID]`
- **category-column** = `PRODUCTLINE`

This type of chart uses only one data source.

The XY area line chart

The following is the icon for XY area line charts:

If we open the report found in `[PRD_HOME]/samples/Charts/XY-Area-Line.prpt`, we will see an example of this type of report:

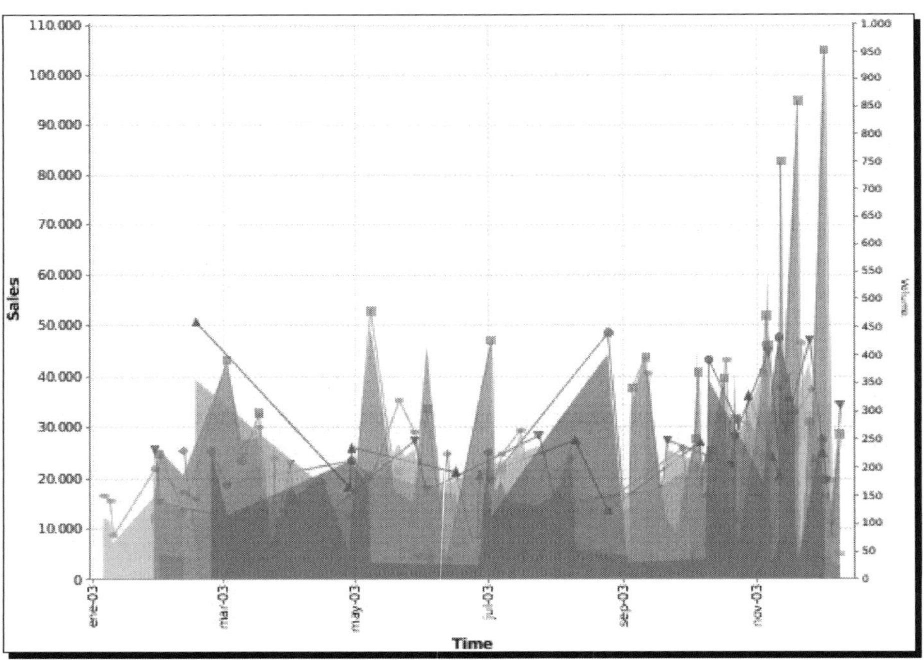

This is a type of XY chart that uses areas and lines and has two data sources.

Restarting practice

We have explained the basic theoretical concepts about charts; now let's continue the practice.

Time for action – creating a pie chart

We will add a pie chart to our report to display information about the movies rented. Then we will configure the type of chart we want to visualize, its data source, and other characteristics.

1. We will create a chart to display an analysis of the percentage of movies rented by rating. Add a chart to the **Report Header** section, dragging-and-dropping the ( ) `Chart ()` object.
2. Double-click on **Chart** to start configuring it.
3. In the upper part, choose the pie chart type:

4. In the right-hand part, configure the data source as follows:
   - **value-column** = `count_rental` (the value under analysis)
   - **series-by-field** = `[rating]` (the item to be represented as a portion of the pie)
5. In the left-hand part, configure the following:
   - **chart-title** = `Percentage of films rented by Rating`
   - **label-font** = `FreeSans-BOLD-14`
   - **label-format** = `{0}: {2}`
   - **3-D** = `True`
   - **show-legend** = `False`

6. Next, click on **OK** to continue. If we preview it, we will see this:

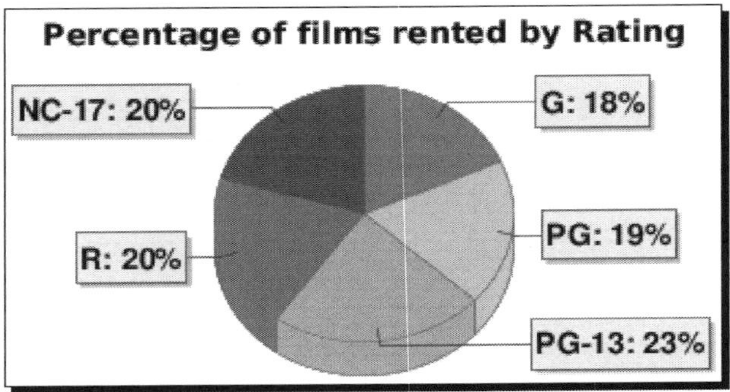

What just happened?

We added a `Chart` object to the **Report Header** section. Then we edited this object, making it a pie chart and configuring its data source to analyze the quantity of films rented by rating. We configured the title of the chart, changed the characteristics of the source of the labels that display information for each portion of the pie, gave the chart a 3D effect, and hid the chart's legend.

Time for action – creating a bar chart

We will add a bar chart to our report to display information about the movies rented. Then we will configure the type of chart we want to visualize, its data source, and other characteristics. We will create a chart to display an analysis of the total number of movies rented by rating.

1. Add a `Chart ()` object to the **Report Header** section under the pie chart.
2. Double-click on this new chart to start configuring it. In the *upper* part, choose the bar chart type:

3. In the right-hand part, configure the data source as follows:
    - **category-column** = `rating` (the item to be represented by the bars)
    - **value-columns** = `[sum_amount]` (the value under analysis)
    - **series-by-field** = `[rating]`

If we do not specify the **series-by-field** value, the chart will show us all the bars in the same color and by default place them in `Series 1`. By establishing the `rating` value, we make each column independent from the others, and as such, each will have a different color.

4. In the left-hand part, configure the following:
   - **chart-title** = `Total rental by Rating`
   - **3-D** = `True`
   - **label-font** = `FreeSans-BOLD-14`
   - **x-axis-label-rotation** = `45.0`
   - **y-font** = `FreeSans-PLAIN-10`
   - **y-tick-font** = `FreeSans-PLAIN-10`
   - **y-tick-fmt-str** = `$`
   - **show-legend** = `False`
5. Next, click on **OK** to continue. If we preview it, we will see this:

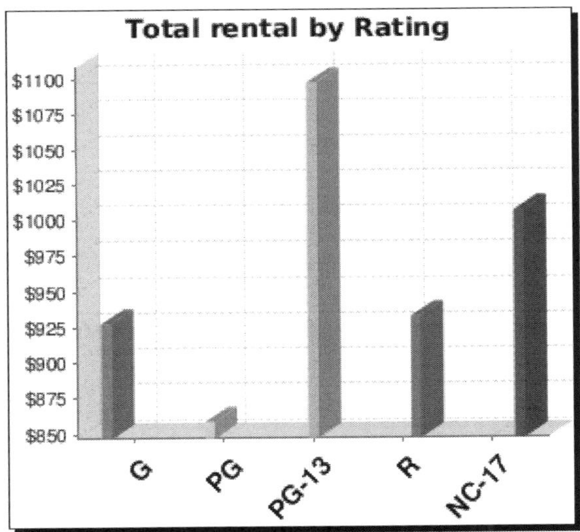

What just happened?

We added a `Chart` object to the **Report Header** section. Then we edited this object, making it a bar chart and configuring its data source to analyze the total number of films rented by rating. We configured the chart's title, gave the chart a 3D effect, changed the characteristics of the source of the labels that display information about each bar, rotated the x axis labels by 45 degrees, changed the source of the y axis labels, made the y axis values begin with the dollar sign, and hid the chart's legend.

The relationship between charts and report sections

Just like any other object, the behavior of a chart depends on the section of the report where it is added.

If we place a chart in a **Header** section (**Report Header**, **Details Header**, and so on) or a **Footer** section (**Report Footer**, **Details Footer**, and so on), the chart will be shown each time these sections are shown in the report. Usually they are shown once per page. In this case, `Chart` will have access to all the rows in the data set.

On the other hand, if we place a chart in the **Details** section, the chart will be shown once for each row in the section. Usually they are shown many times per page. In this case, the chart will only have access to the data of the row under analysis.

Have a go hero

Now we propose that you modify the report you have already made and add a ring chart to show the information from another perspective. A ring chart will be displayed for each new element in the group, in this case for each new country. The report should look like this:

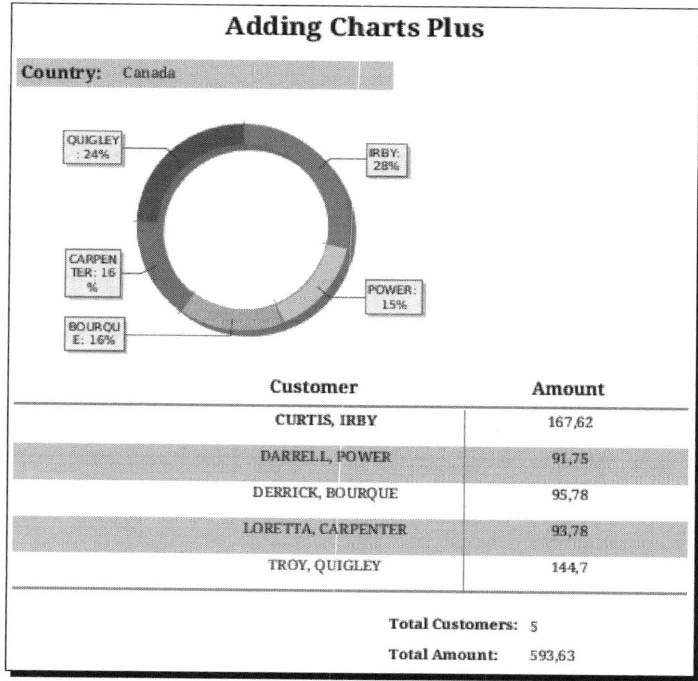

Adding Charts Plus

Country: Canada

Customer	Amount
CURTIS, IRBY	167,62
DARRELL, POWER	91,75
DERRICK, BOURQUE	95,78
LORETTA, CARPENTER	93,78
TROY, QUIGLEY	144,7

Total Customers: 5

Total Amount: 593,63

The steps you should follow, broadly speaking, are as follows:

1. Create a copy of the `05_Adding_Groups.prpt` report and save it with the name `12_Adding_Charts_Plus.prpt`.
2. Place a `Chart` object in the **Group Header** section:

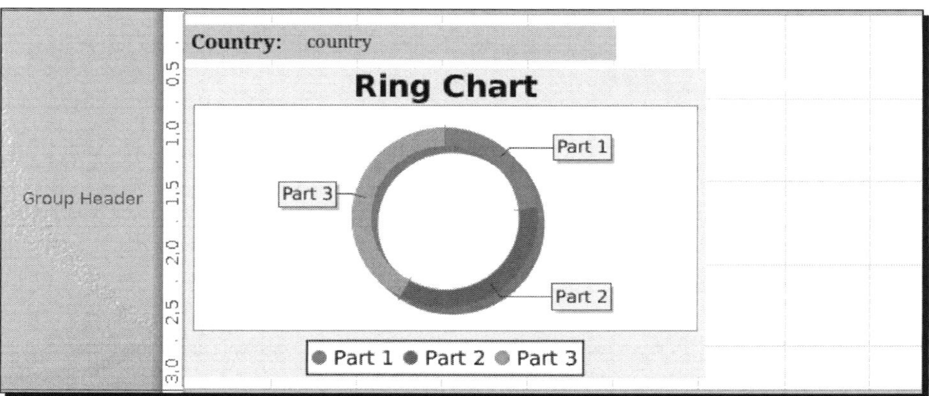

3. The chart will display the values of amount for each customer.

Pop quiz – charts

Q1. Which of the following statements are true?

1. JFreeChart is a Java library with a GNU LGPL license.
2. It is best practice to add charts to all our reports.
3. The more charts our reports contain, the more useful they will be.
4. If we want to easily see what percentage of the total each of our items represents, the best option to use is a bar chart.
5. If we need a chart to analyze three sets of variables for each item, a good option to use would be a bubble chart.
6. If we need to analyze a group of values and determine which of these do not follow normal behavior, a good option would be to use a scatter plot chart.
7. A waterfall chart shows bars similar to a bar chart, but with the difference that the waterfall chart uses the colors green and red to express positive and negative values respectively.

Summary

We created a report from scratch, and created and configured its data set. We created and established default values for two parameters: `SelectYear` and `SelectMonth`.

We explained each type of chart, its advantages, how to use it, how not to use it, and showed an example of each one of them. We talked about the chart editor UI and differentiated its three parts: where we choose the type of chart, where we configure the data sources, and where we configure the chart's behavior.

We added a pie chart to the **Report Header** section and then configured it to meet our needs.

We also added a bar chart to the **Report Header** section and configured it according to our needs.

Finally, we showed how the inclusion of charts in our reports influences them, and we proposed that you modify a previous report by adding a ring chart.

In the next chapter, we will explain how to add subreports in our reports.

10
Adding Subreports

This chapter is dedicated to Subreports. We will see what Subreports are and how they work and learn about their specific characteristics. We will also talk about the relation that exists between the main Report and its Subreports.

As we mix theory and practice, we will be able to appreciate the full potential of adding Subreports. We will be able to add information to our Reports in the form of tables, charts, and so on, whether this information is connected to our data set or not. This gives us an idea of the potential that Subreports provide.

In this chapter we will do the following:

- Create a new report, create its data set, and create a Parameter.
- Create two Subreports. The first Subreport will include a chart, and the second Subreport will include a table.
- Configure internal Parameters for both Subreports.
- Create data sets for both Subreports and configure them to use the values of the internal Parameters.
- Finally, we propose that you modify a previous report, and add a Subreport so you can apply what you have learned in this chapter.

Starting practice

In this chapter we will create a new report and modify it step-by-step so the final product looks like the following screenshot:

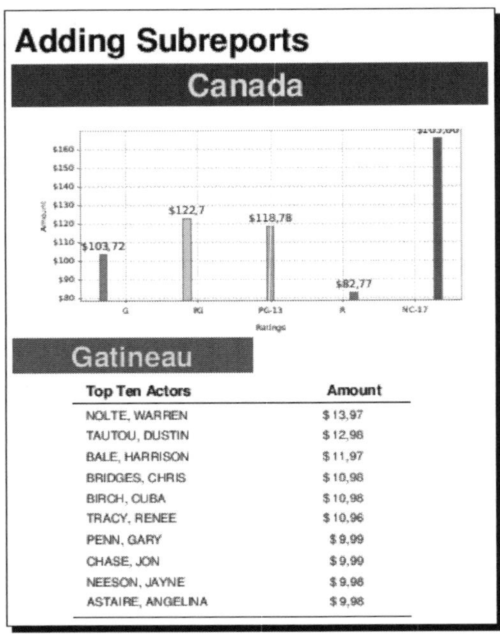

The data set that will be defined in the report will only return data about a country and a city. This is why the bar chart that we have placed in our report is actually inside a Subreport. The same thing happens with the table, **Top Ten Actors**. This information is in another Subreport.

In the following section, we will learn the "hows" and "whys" of this.

> One clarification about terminology before we begin: when we refer to Subreports themselves, we will use the term "Subreport", and when we refer to the insertable object [Sub], we will use the term "Sub-report".

Time for action – creating a new report

The following are the steps for creating a new report:

1. In the following section, we will create a new report that we will use in this chapter's exercises. We will create a JDBC data set that connects to the Sakila database, and we will establish its SQL query. Then we will create a Parameter to choose the country we want to analyze. Finally, we will adapt our report to the layout proposed in this guide. We create a new report and save it with the name, `13_Adding_Subreports.prpt`. We create a JDBC data set and configure it as follows:

    - **Connections** = `sakila db`
    - **Query name** = `CountryCity`
    - **Query** =

    ```
    SELECT DISTINCT country.country_id, country.country,
    city.city_id, city.city
    FROM country
    INNER JOIN city ON city.country_id = country.country_id
    INNER JOIN address ON address.city_id = city.city_id
    INNER JOIN customer ON customer.address_id =
    address.address_id
    INNER JOIN rental ON rental.customer_id =
    customer.customer_id
    WHERE country.country_id = ${SelectCountry}
    ORDER BY country.country
    ```

2. We create a new Parameter and its corresponding JDBC data set is as follows:

    - **Query Name** = `ListOfCountries`
    - **Query** =

    ```
    SELECT DISTINCT country.country_id, country.country
    FROM country
    WHERE country.country_id IN (20,24,29,34,48,67,74)
    ORDER BY country.country
    ```

    Now we configure the Parameter as follows:

    - **Name** = `SelectCountry`
    - **Label** = `Country:`
    - **Value Type** = `Number`
    - **Default Value** = `20`; this value is arbitrary and represents Canada
    - **Mandatory** = `True`

- **Display Type** = `Drop Down`
- **Value** = `country_id`
- **Display Name** = `country`

Now we will recreate the layout of the following image. After doing this, we will be ready to start the interesting part of this chapter, Subreports!

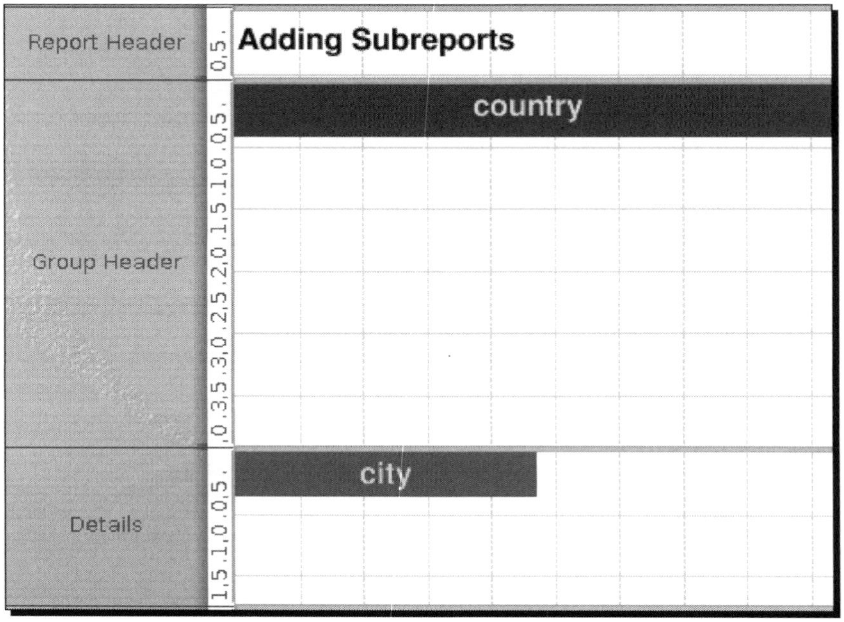

3. In the **Report Header** section, we place an **Attributes.value** label with the text `Adding Subreports`.
4. In the **Group Header** section, we place a rectangle and the field country, and configure their formats and colors. We expand the area of this section so it is similar to the layout presented earlier. This is where we will place our first Subreport.
5. In the **Details** section, we place a rectangle and the field `city`, and, as before, we configure their formats and colors. We should also expand the area of this section, as this is where we will add our second Subreport.
6. Finally, we go to the **Structure** tab, select the **Master Report**, go to **Group node**, and configure the following:

   - **Attributes.group** = `[country_id]`

What just happened?

We created a new report and named it `13_Adding_Subreports.prpt`. We created a JDBC data set and configured its connection and SQL query so that it returns the countries and cities where films have been rented. We created and configured the Parameter **SelectCountry**. The layout that our report should have was presented, and with this in mind, we took the necessary steps to adapt our report to the guide's requirements.

Subreports

Pentaho Report Designer (PRD) lets us add as many Subreports to our reports as necessary. This gives us a great hidden potential that we can use anytime.

Until now, we have seen that while various data sets can be defined in a report—for example, when we create Parameters—only one of them will be the principal data set that is, the one that contains the fields we will add to our report. Can you imagine what would happen if we could add two or more principal data sets to our reports? Imagine the quantity of related and unrelated information that our reports could display. Our report might look a lot like a dashboard.

With PRD we can move from internal manipulation of information (imagination) to reality by using Subreports.

Subreports in PRD

From a sci-fi point of view, we could say that by adding a Subreport to our main report, what we are doing is creating a portal to another report, just like in Stargate.

From a more formal perspective, we could say that a Subreport is a report within another report.

The layout, behavior, and use of a Subreport are similar to that of Reports. That is, we can configure its data set, add objects (label, textfield, chart, and so on), formulas, functions, and so on, but with the catch that we cannot add Parameters so that the end user chooses its values (the parameter values can be passed down from the main report to the Subreports).

PRD lets us add as many Subreports as we need to our reports, and also lets us add Subreports within Subreports.

The relation between Reports and Subreports

PRD lets Reports and Subreports interact by using the `import` and `export` Parameters. These are internal Parameters that give the Report the ability to send information to its Subreports and vice versa.

For example, if you want to add a Subreport to the section **Group Header** that will display detailed information about the item under analysis, the Report should send this information to the Subreport so that the data set returns the information for this value. It works similarly to the conventional Parameters that we have already looked at.

The relation between sections of the Report and Subreports

The behavior of a Subreport will vary notably depending on what section of the Report it is placed in. This is because the Subreport will be executed each time the section of the Report it is found in is executed. For example, if a Subreport is placed in the **Details** section, the Subreport will be executed once for each row. If the Subreport is placed in the **Group Header** section, and this section is present only at the beginning, the Subreport will be executed once at the beginning of each group.

If we complicate things a bit and propose an example in which the Report uses groups and the Group Header section is repeated only once at the beginning of each group and we place a Subreport in this section, the Subreport will be executed just once at the beginning of each group.

Depending on the type of information that we want to display, we should choose in which section of the Report to place our Subreports.

In the exercise that we do in this chapter, we include a Subreport in the **Report Header** section and another Subreport in the **Details** section. That way we can better understand their behavior.

Creating and configuring Subreports

To add a Subreport to our report, we just drag the Sub-report object (Sub) and drop it in any section of the work area.

When we do this, PRD will ask us if we want our report to be **Banded** or **Inline** as shown in the following screenshot:

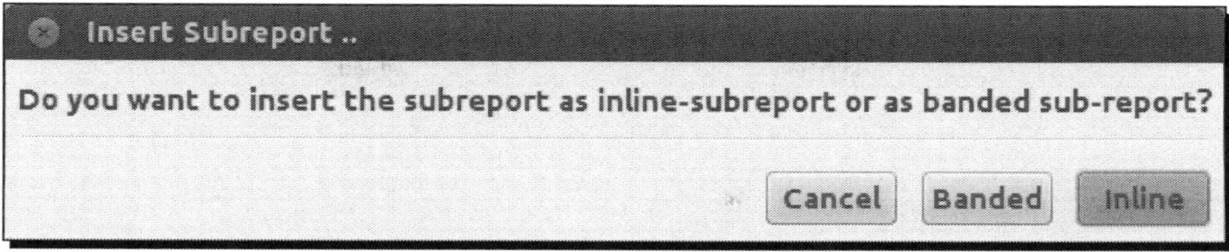

The following options refer to the position and anchoring of the Sub-report:

- If we choose the option **Banded**, the Sub-report will be as wide as our report, and we will not be able to modify its width but only its height. Its position will depend on the objects present in the section where we have placed the Sub-report. It will be placed at the end of all the section's objects, and we will not be able to modify its position.
- If we choose the option **Inline**, the position and size of the Sub-report will be totally configurable but is more resource intensive.

After choosing one of these options, PRD will ask us if we want the new Subreport to use one of the data sets in the main report. Next, a new tab will open where we can begin to configure our Subreport as shown in the following screenshot:

We can see that in the **Structure** tab, the main node is named **sub-report** as shown in the following screenshot:

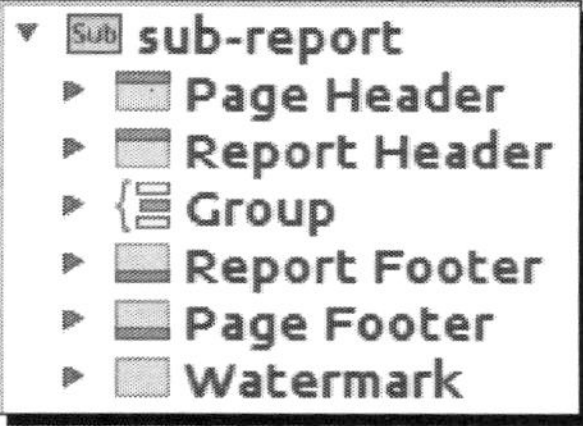

Opening and closing Subreports

Once we have added a Sub-report to our report, we can access the sub-report by double-clicking on the object in question. This will take us to the Subreport and open the tab if it is not already open. We can close the Subreport tab at any time without losing the changes made.

Restarting practice

Now that we have explained the basic theoretical concepts related to Subreports, we will put these concepts into practice.

Time for action – creating our first Subreport

The steps for creating our first Subreport are as follows:

1. We will create our first Subreport and place it in the Report Header section. Then we will edit the internally used Parameters and import the value of the field `country_id`. Finally, we will create a JDBC data set that will be filtered by the value imported from the main Report. We add a Sub-report object (Sub) to the Group Header section. We drag-and-drop it in the area that we have left empty.
2. After doing this, PRD will ask us if we want the Subreport to be **Banded** or **Inline**. We should click on the **Inline** button. PRD will ask us about the data set to be used. We click on the option **Cancel**. We name our Subreport so it is easier for reference. We go to the **Structure** tab, choose the sub-report node, and configure the following:
    - **Attributes.name** = `SubReportBarChartAs`: This Subreport will display information related to the country that the final user chooses. We should make the Subreport receive the country that will be displayed in the main Report. To do so, we will use the Parameters for internal use between Reports and Subreports.
3. Next, we go to the **Data** tab, select the **Parameters** node, right-click on it, and choose the option **Edit Sub-report Parameters...** as shown in the following screenshot:

    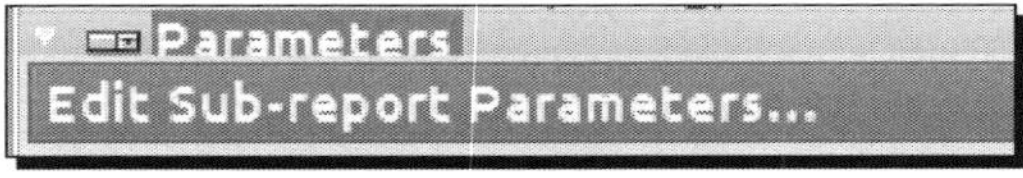

    We will see the following window:

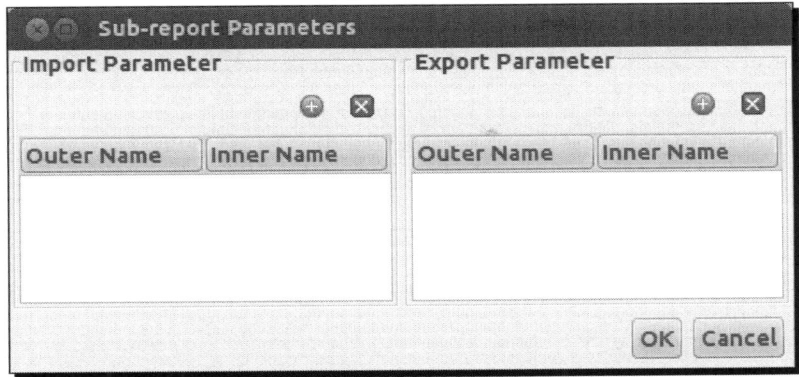

4. To the left-hand side is where we configure the values that will be imported from the main Report, and to the right-hand side is where we configure the values that will be exported to the main Report.
5. In this case, we configure a value to be imported. It is the country identification (`country_id`).
6. In the table on the left-hand side (**Import Parameter**), we click on the [+] button to create a new row and then establish the following:
   - **Outer Name** = `country_id`. The field of the main Report from which the value should be obtained is placed here.
   - **Inner Name** = `importCountryId`. This will be the Subreport's internal use variable that will take on the value that is imported.

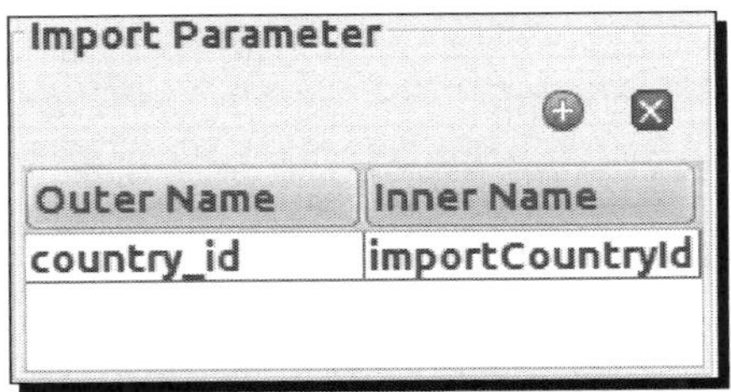

7. Now we create the data set for this Subreport. It will be a JDBC data set, and we will configure it as follows:
   - **Connections** = `sakila db`
   - **Query Name** = `RatingAmount`

- **Query** =

```
SELECT film.rating, SUM(payment.amount) sum_amount
FROM payment
INNER JOIN rental ON rental.rental_id=payment.rental_id
INNER JOIN inventory ON inventory.inventory_id=rental.
inventory_id
INNER JOIN film ON film.film_id=inventory.film_id
INNER JOIN customer ON customer.customer_id =
rental.customer_id
INNER JOIN address ON address.address_id = customer.
address_id
INNER JOIN city ON city.city_id = address.city_id
WHERE city.country_id = ${importCountryId}
GROUP BY film.rating
```

We can see that the SQL query is filtered by the value of the variable we created earlier.

What just happened?

We added an inline Sub-report object to the Group Header section. We created an internally used Parameter called `importCountryId` that will take on the value of the `country_id` field in the main report. Then we created the Subreport's data set and configured it so the SQL query is filtered by `importCountryId`.

Time for action – configuring our first Subreport

The steps for configuring our first Subreport are as follows:

1. We will configure the size of the Sub-report in our report. Then we will open the Subreport and add and configure a bar chart. We go to the main Report and enlarge the area covered by the Sub-report object so that it fills the empty space as shown in the following screenshot:

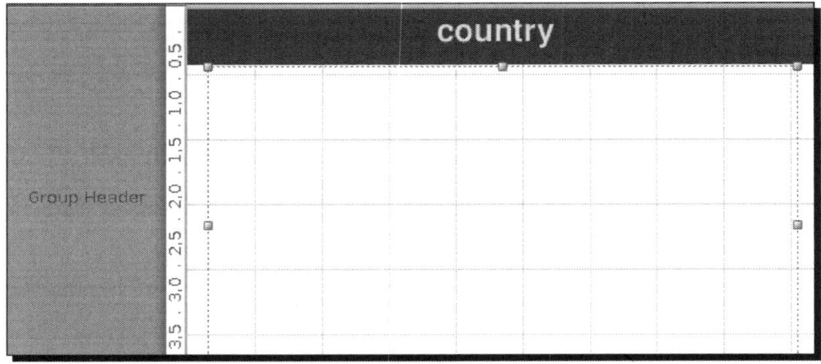

The size of the Sub-report in the main Report will be the available size that we have later in the Subreport.

2. We go the Subreport **SubReportBarChart** and begin to design it. We can double-click on the Sub-report object we placed in the report or click on the tab that refers to this object.

3. We add a chart object to the **Report Header** section and enlarge it so it looks like the following screenshot:

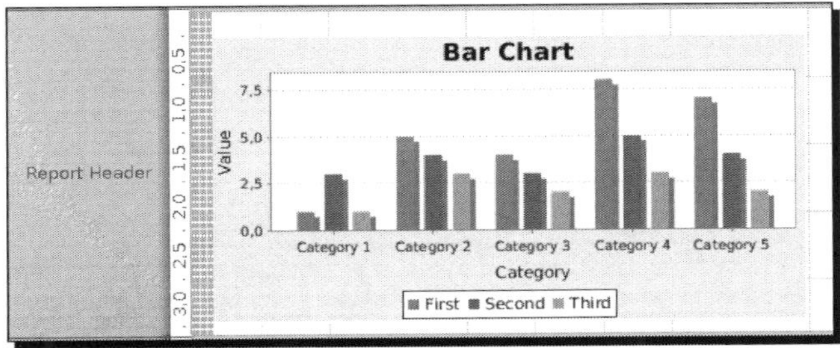

We can see that to the left-hand side there is a kind of gray grid. This grid represents the area that we cannot use in the Subreport. The size of the gray grid depends on the size we have given the Sub-report object in the main Report and will help us to design our Subreport, as it tells us what area is visible and what is not.

4. We configure the chart object, establishing the following:

   In the upper part, we choose the chart type bar chart as shown in the following screenshot:

   In the right-hand part we configure it as follows:

   - **category-column** = `rating`
   - **value-columns** = `[sum_amount]`
   - **series-by-field** = `[rating]`

And in the left-hand part as follows:

- **bar-borders** = `True`
- **x-axis-title** = `Ratings`
- **y-axis-title** = `Amount`
- **y-tick-fmt-str** = `$`
- **show-item-labels** = `Show Labels`
- **text-format** = `${2}`
- **show-legend** = `False`

Next, click on **OK** to continue.

If we preview it, we will see the following:

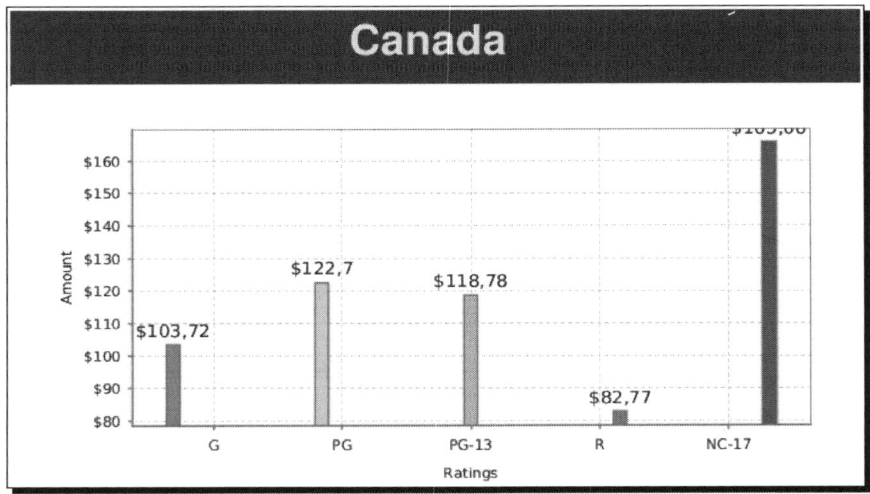

What just happened?

By clicking on the different tabs, first we went to the main Report and enlarged the size of the Sub-report object. Then we went to the Subreport **SubReportBarChart** and began its design. We added a chart object to the Report Header section and configured it as indicated in the guide.

Time for action – creating and configuring the second Subreport

We will create another Subreport, but this time we will place it in the Details section so that it is executed for each row. Then we will edit the internally used Parameters and import the value of the field `city_id`. We will create a JDBC data set that will be filtered by the value imported from the principal Report. Finally, we will configure the layout of the Subreport. The steps for creating and configuring the second Subreport are as follows:

1. We add a Sub-report object (Sub) to the Details section. We drag-and-drop it to the area that we have left empty.
2. After doing this, PRD will ask us if we want the Subreport to be **Banded** or **Inline**. We should click on the **Inline** button.
3. When PRD asks us about the data set to be used, we click on the option **Cancel**.
4. We go to the **Structure** tab, choose the **sub-report** node, and configure the following:
   - **Attributes.name** = `SubReportTable`
5. This Subreport will display information related to different cities that belong to the country chosen by the user. To make this happen, we need to make the Subreport receive the city that the main Report is currently analyzing.
6. We go the **Data** tab, select the **Parameters** node, right-click on it, and choose the option **Edit Sub-report Parameters...**.
7. In this case, the value to be imported is the city identification (`city_id`).

   In the table on the left-hand side (**Import Parameter**), we click on the button to create a new row and then establish the following:
   - **Outer Name** = `city_id`
   - **Inner Name** = `importCityId`
8. Now we create the data set for this Subreport. It will be a JDBC data set, and we will configure it as follows:
   - **Connections** = `sakila db`
   - **Query Name** = `Actors`

- **Query** =

```
SELECT actor.actor_id, CONCAT(actor.last_name,", ",actor.
first_name) AS full_name, SUM(payment.amount) sum_amount
FROM payment
INNER JOIN rental ON rental.rental_id=payment.rental_id
INNER JOIN inventory ON inventory.inventory_id=rental.
inventory_id
INNER JOIN film ON film.film_id=inventory.film_id
INNER JOIN customer ON customer.customer_id = rental.
customer_id
INNER JOIN address ON address.address_id = customer.
address_id
INNER JOIN film_actor ON film_actor.film_id = film.film_id
INNER JOIN actor ON actor.actor_id = film_actor.actor_id
WHERE address.city_id = ${importCityId}
GROUP BY actor.actor_id
ORDER BY sum_amount DESC
LIMIT 0,10
```

9. We will configure the size of the Sub-report in our report. Then we will open the Subreport and add and configure a small table. We go to the main Report and enlarge the area covered by the Sub-report object so that it fills the empty space as shown in the following screenshot:

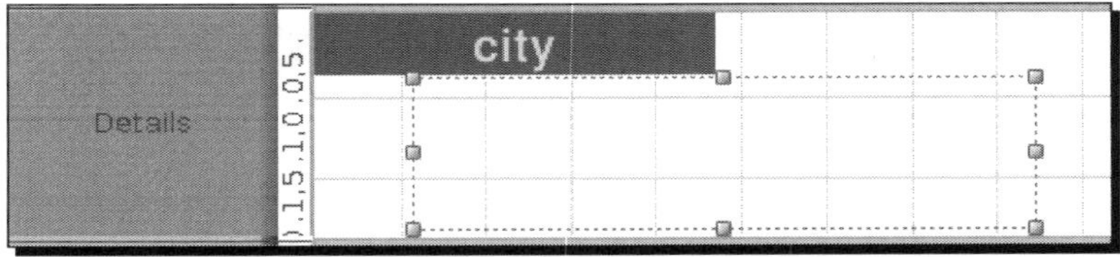

10. We go to the Subreport **SubReportTable** and begin to design it. We create the following layout:

11. In the **Details Header** section, we place two labels and a horizontal line and configure them according to the previous image.

12. In the **Details** section, we place the fields `full_name` and `sum_amount` and configure them according to the previous image.

13. In the **Details Footer** section, we place a horizontal line and configure this as well according to the previous image.

If we preview it, we will see the following screenshot:

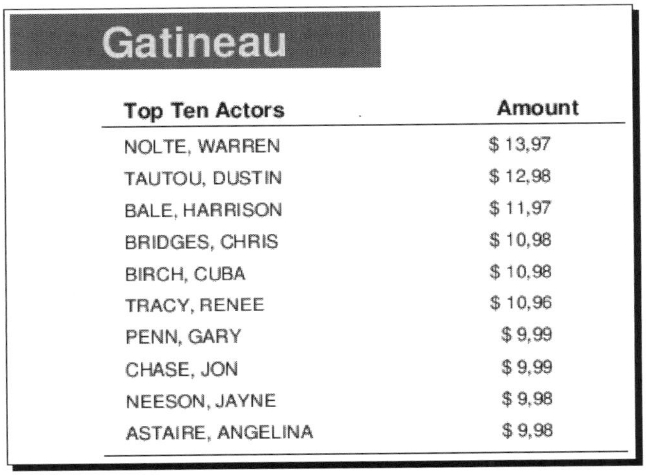

Gatineau

Top Ten Actors	Amount
NOLTE, WARREN	$ 13,97
TAUTOU, DUSTIN	$ 12,98
BALE, HARRISON	$ 11,97
BRIDGES, CHRIS	$ 10,98
BIRCH, CUBA	$ 10,98
TRACY, RENEE	$ 10,96
PENN, GARY	$ 9,99
CHASE, JON	$ 9,99
NEESON, JAYNE	$ 9,98
ASTAIRE, ANGELINA	$ 9,98

What just happened?

We added a Sub-report object to the Details section and configured it to be of the inline type. We created an internally used Parameter called `importCityId` that will take on the value of the `city_id` field in the main report. Then we created the Subreport's data Set and configured it so the SQL query is filtered by `importCityId`.

In the main Report, we enlarged the size of the Sub-report object, SubReportTable. Then in **SubReportBarChart**, we created a table as indicated in the guide. This table displays a list of actors and amounts.

Have a go hero

Now we propose that you modify the report you have already created, and that you add a Subreport to show the country information. Within this Subreport, you will create a data set that will be filtered by the values taken from the main Report, and the information will then be represented by a Scatter Plot chart. The first page of the report will display two pre-existing charts, and the second page will display the Subreport as shown in the following screenshot:

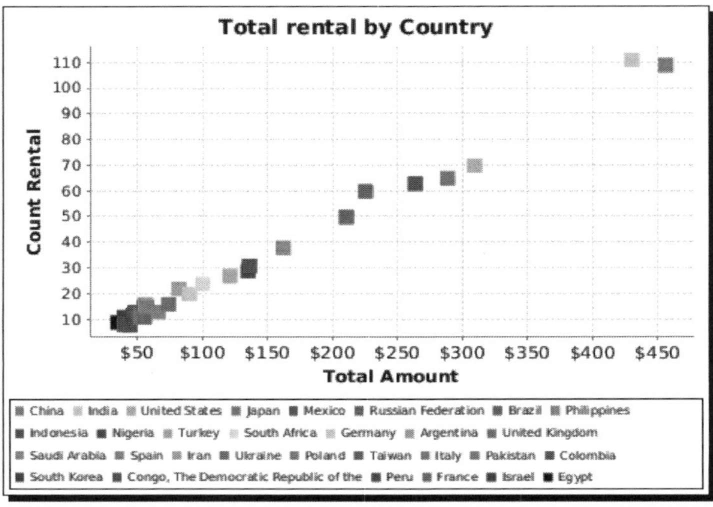

The steps you should follow, broadly speaking, are as follows:

1. Create a copy of the report `11_Adding_Charts.prpt` and save it with the name `14_Adding_Subreports_Plus.prpt`.
2. Place a Sub-report object in the Report Header section under the last chart.
3. Go to the Subreport, create a JDBC data set, and configure it as follows:
    - **Connections** = `sakila db`
    - **Query Name** = `CountryAmount`
    - **Query** =

```
SELECT country.country, SUM(payment.amount) AS sum_amount,
count(1) AS count_rental
FROM payment
INNER JOIN rental ON rental.rental_id=payment.rental_id
INNER JOIN inventory ON inventory.inventory_id=rental.
inventory_id
INNER JOIN customer ON customer.customer_id = payment.
customer_id
INNER JOIN address ON address.address_id = customer.
address_id
INNER JOIN city ON city.city_id = address.city_id
INNER JOIN country ON country.country_id = city.country_id
WHERE year(payment.payment_date)=${importSelectYear}
AND month(payment_date) = ${importSelectMonth}
GROUP BY country.country
ORDER BY sum_amount DESC
LIMIT 0,30
```

4. Go to the Subreport and add a chart object to the Report Header section.

Pop quiz – Subreports

State whether the following are true or false.

Q1. Within a Subreport, you cannot add other Subreports.

Q2. The behavior and general use of a Subreport is similar to a normal report except for a few exceptions.

Q3. Within a Subreport, Parameters can be defined so that the end user can choose a value.

Q4. When importing Parameters from a Subreport, if the name of the variable that contains the value to be imported is `country_id`, the name of the variable that will receive this value can also be named `country_id`.

Q5. If a Sub-report object is placed in the Report Header section or the Details section, its behavior will be the same regardless of the design of the main Report.

Q6. If we add a banded type Sub-report, we will not be able to modify its size or position.

Summary

We created a report from scratch and created and configured its data set. We created and established the default value for a Parameter, SelectCountry.

We talked about Subreports, defined what they are, what they let us do, and what new possibilities they bring. We also talked about their behavior and general use. We explained the relationship that exists between the main Report and the different Subreports and how they can communicate. We explained step-by-step how to create and configure our own Subreports.

We added two Subreports to our report, one at a time, and made each of them inline type Subreports. Then we defined the Parameters that the Subreport should import from the main Report.

Next, we created the data sets for the Subreports and configured them to be filtered by the values imported from the main Report.

We also designed the content of both Subreports. In the first, we added and configured a charts, and in the second we created a table.

Finally, to practice what we had seen in this chapter, we proposed that you modify an existing report and add a Subreport to it.

In the next chapter we will learn about Pentaho BA Server and how to publish, display, and work with our reports in Pentaho User Console.

11

Publishing and Running Reports in Pentaho BA Server

In this chapter we talk about Pentaho, the fastest growing, most active, most popular, and most heavily invested in **Open Source Business Intelligence** *(***OSBI***) suite in recent years. We analyze its principal characteristics and the principal projects included in the suite.*

With Pentaho **Business Analytics** *(***BA***) Server, we have full BI analytic power at our fingertips through a GNU* **General Public License** *(***GPL***).*

We will see how **Pentaho Report Designer** *(***PRD***) and Pentaho BA Server interact, and how we can use them to run our reports from* **Pentaho User Console** *(***PUC***). At the end of this chapter, we will have Pentaho BA Server running and will be able to access our reports from a web browser.*

In this chapter we will do the following:

- Download and install Pentaho BA Server
- Configure the MySQL JDBC driver in Pentaho BA Server
- Run Pentaho BA Server and log in with Pentaho User Console (PUC)
- Create a solutions folder in our Pentaho BA Server repository
- Publish a report from PRD in the BI Server
- See how to import PRD reports from PUC, how to create a URL for our reports, and how to create a schedule

Finally, we propose that you complete a series of tasks related to the topics in this chapter.

Learning Pentaho

Pentaho is an open source / free software project whose goal is to create Business Intelligence solutions. Pentaho's license is the GNU GPL and its principal functionalities are as follows:

- Business reporting and analysis
- Dashboards
- Data mining
- Data integration, alerts, subscriptions, and so on

Its logo is as shown:

Some important links for Pentaho are as follows:

- Main site: `www.pentaho.com`
- Official forum: `http://forums.pentaho.com`
- Official community: `community.pentaho.com`

Defining Pentaho

We can define Pentaho as a solutions-oriented and process-centered platform:

- It is solutions oriented because when we talk about developing or implementing a project in Pentaho, we are talking about developing or implementing a solution. Physically creating a solution in Pentaho means creating a folder with a given path (we will discuss this more in depth soon) The resources and components that will attack this particular business problem are found in a structure in this folder.
- It is process centered because each component, for example, a report, must go through a process to be run, and this process is generally the same. Pentaho has a process motor in its kernel that basically supports inputs, a series of ordered tasks (process chain), and a final output. At the same time, each Pentaho process can be run within other processes, allowing for carrying out very complex tasks, and gives great flexibility. Pentaho processes are described in XML.

Many Pentaho processes are created automatically and in a very habitual manner. One way to create a process is for the user to select the option **create a new report**. What Pentaho does in this case is create, invisibly to the user, the process that will carry out the task with its respective inputs, process chain, and outputs.

Pentaho components

The Pentaho suite is made up of multiple independent components that carry out specific functions of sending mails, visualizing graphics, and so on, and that work together to create and distribute Business Intelligence solutions.

Pentaho works through the combined use of these components.

In the following diagram, we can see the big picture of how the Pentaho components relate to each other:

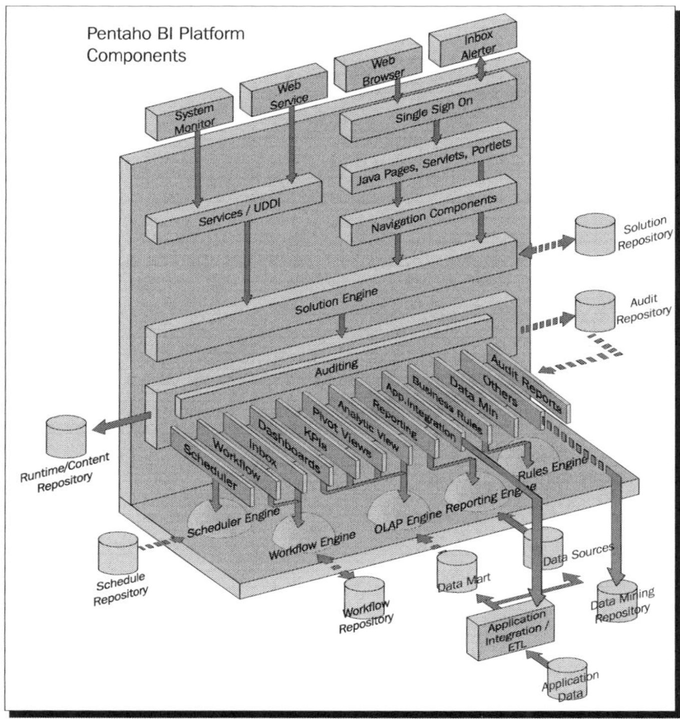

We will not go into detail about this diagram, but we want to highlight Pentaho's modular and layered design. It is this design that lets Pentaho replace or modify its components and in doing so add new functionalities by, for example, using other programs from outside the suite, such as Eclipse BIRT and Jasper Reports.

In the Pentaho Users' Community, there are many projects that develop new plugins or components or modify existing ones in order to meet the needs of this group of users faced with a business problem. What Pentaho Corporations does in these cases is evaluates these projects and, if it sees fit, adopts them. A good example of this is the CTools of Webdetails, whose company was acquired by Pentaho recently.

Principal Pentaho projects

Pentaho is made up of a series of independent projects that make it a complete Business Intelligence suite. Among the most important projects in the Pentaho suite, we find the following:

- **Pentaho BA Server**: A web application that makes up one of the fundamental pieces of the Pentaho suite. One of its principal functions is to let the user access and interact with BI content, for example, by easily visualizing PRD reports. Pentaho BA Server's graphic interface is called PUC.
- **Pentaho User Console** (**PUC**): This is the web application through which the user can navigate and interact with business components, such as reports, dashboards, analysis, and so on, and also administer and configure the BI server.
- **Pentaho Report Designer** (**PRD**): This is the reporting tool used to create advanced and highly complex reports, which is the subject of this book.
- **Pentaho Data Integration** (**PDI**): This is a powerful data integration tool.
- **Pentaho Analysis** (Mondrian OLAP server): This is a multidimensional engine that resolves Interactive analysis or OLAP analysis queries.
- **Pentaho Data Mining** (Weka): This is a versatile data mining tool.
- **Pentaho Metadata Editor** (**PME**): This is a tool that lets us create, edit, and publish Business Models. Business Models are used to create ad hoc reports.
- **Pentaho Schema Workbench** (**PSW**): This is the tool used to create, edit, and publish either multidimensional models or Mondrian schema.
- **Pentaho Aggregate Designer** (**PAD**): This is the tool that is used to improve the performance of multidimensional queries. It creates a series of precalculated data that will be used automatically by Mondrian to reduce the cost of the queries.
- **Saiku**: This is an attractive OLAP viewer with a very pleasant UI.
- **CTools**: This is a set of tools used principally for the creation of dashboards.

It is worth mentioning that all the programs in the Pentaho suite that we have mentioned have open source and/or Free Software licenses.

A brief historical review

Pentaho Corporation was founded in 2004, and since 2008, there has been an Enterprise version of the suite, that is, a paid version that is, in some ways, different from the community version.

The evolution of different versions of the Pentaho BA Server can be seen in SourceForge via the following link: `http://sourceforge.net/projects/pentaho/files/Business%20Intelligence%20Server/`. The following graph shows the evolution of the Pentaho BA Server:

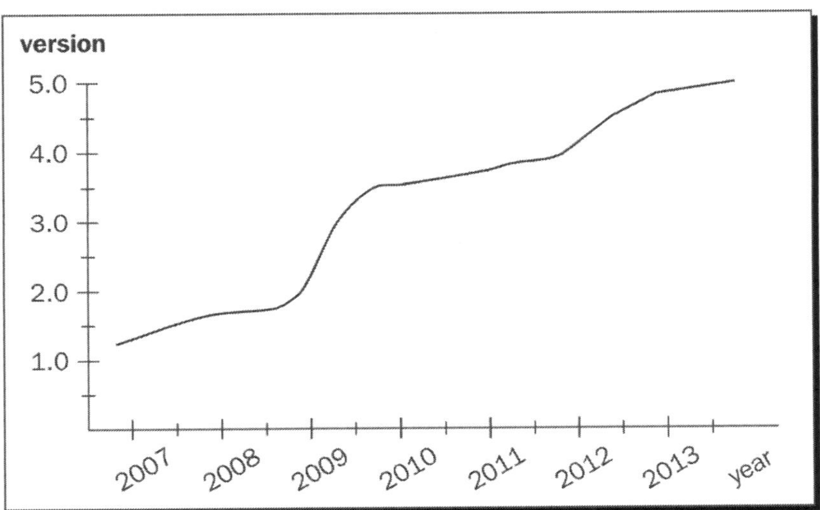

It is worth noting that over the years there has been a reduction in the time taken between the publication of each new version and between the injection of new technologies into each new version.

Principal characteristics of Pentaho

In the following section, we point out some of the characteristics of Pentaho 5 that we consider most important:

- Pentaho is completely programmed in Java, and the web component, the platform, in JEE. This characteristic makes Pentaho scalable, integrable, and portable software.
- Pentaho can run on any compatible application servers with JEE architectures, such as JBOSS AS, WebSphere, Tomcat, WebLogic, and Oracle AS.

- Pentaho accesses the database via JDBC and can use IBM DB2, MS SQL Server, MySQL, Oracle, PostgreSQL, NCR Teradata, Firebird, and Informix, among others.
- Pentaho can run in various operating systems because it is programmed in Java. As long as there is a Virtual Machine (JVM) for the platform, it should function without complications.
- The most important languages and technologies used to deploy the various Pentaho applications are Java, JavaScript, JSP, XSL, XSLT, XPath, and XSL-FO.
- Pentaho's data repository is based on the JCR specification (Content Repository API for Java).
- All the publication components are presented through web services; this facilitates integration with **Service Oriented Architecture** (**SOA**). It uses **Representational State Transfer** (**REST**) services.
- Pentaho can be accessed from a simple web browser embedded in portals (LifeRay), management systems (Alfresco), or web systems in general.

Downloading Pentaho BA Server

To download Pentaho BA Server, go to the link `http://sourceforge.net/projects/pentaho/files/Business%20Intelligence%20Server`. Then click on the folder **5.0.0-stable**. This will show you a series of files.

- In Linux, look for and download the file `biserver-ce-5.0.0-stable.tar.gz`
- In Windows, look for and download the file `biserver-ce-5.0.0-stable.zip`

> Usually, the names of the files that are downloaded contain a series of commonly used abbreviations to indicate the version type; refer to the following examples:
>
> - `GA` (general availability) or `stable` (stable version)
> - `RC-X` or `RCX` (release candidate) indicates a beta or alpha version
> - `Milestone X` or `MX` indicates that the version includes a specific set of functions that have been tested previously

System requirements

To correctly execute the Pentaho BA Server, the requirements are as follows:

- **Java Runtime Environment** (**JRE**) 1.7 or higher needs to be installed
- The `JAVA_HOME` variable needs to be configured
- The `PATH` variable entry is configured that points to `[JAVA_HOME]/bin`

If we pay attention, we can see that these are the same requirements for PRD that we configured in *Chapter 2, Installation and Configuration*. That is, in this case we do not need to make any modifications as Pentaho BA Server will use the established configuration.

Time for action – installing and running Pentaho BA Server

Next, we will install Pentaho BA Server in a folder of our choice and then copy the MySQL JDBC driver. We run Pentaho BA Server and use a web browser to access Pentaho User Console (PUC). Finally, we log in with our username and password and we can see the PUC UI.

1. We select the file that we just downloaded and we decompress it. After doing this, we get a folder called `biserver-ce-5.0.0-stable`. In this folder, we find the subfolder called `biserver-ce`.

> From here on, we will refer to the path of the folder `biserver-ce` with the name `[PUC_HOME]`.

2. We configure the MySQL JDBC driver in Pentaho BA Server.
3. We go to the path `[PUC_HOME]/tomcat/lib`.
4. We should verify that the MySQL JDBC driver is included by default and if the version included is the one we are using. If it isn't, we should delete the default driver and paste the driver that we are currently using: `[PRD_HOME]/lib/jdbc/mysql-connector-java-X.X.XX-bin.jar`.
5. Next, we run the Pentaho BA Server as follows:
   - In Linux:
   1. We open a terminal.
   2. We go to the path `[PUC_HOME]`:
      ```
      shell > cd [PUC_HOME]
      ```
   3. We execute the file `start-pentaho.sh`:
      ```
      shell > sh start-pentaho.sh
      ```
   - In Windows:
   1. We open a terminal.
   2. We go to the path `[PUC_HOME]`:
      ```
      shell > cd [PUC_HOME]
      ```
   3. We execute the file `start-pentaho.bat`:
      ```
      shell > start-pentaho.bat
      ```

Remember that each time we see `[PUC_HOME]`, we should write the complete path to the folder `biserver-ce`.

After completing these actions, we will have run Pentaho BA Server and we will be able to use Pentaho User Console (PUC) to navigate, explore our BI solutions, and manage and configure the BI Server. PUC is Pentaho's public face.

6. Now we run PUC and log in with a username and password.
7. We direct our preferred web browser to the following URL:

   `http://localhost:8080/pentaho`

   This will show us the following welcome and login page:

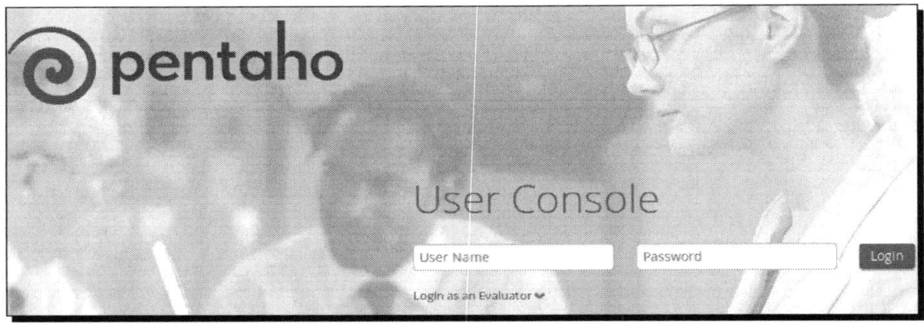

8. We click on **Evaluation Login** to see the default users and their respective profiles in Pentaho BA Server. The user console page will look like the following screenshot:

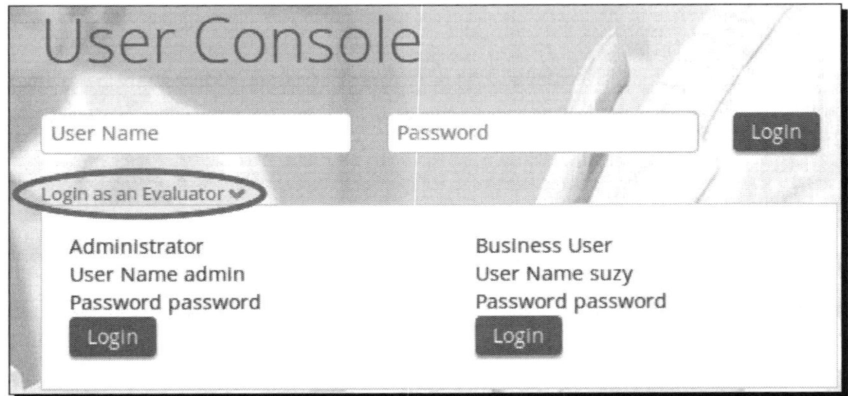

In our case, the user `admin` already has a profile and Administrator privileges.

9. We go to the right-hand panel where the login data should be entered and insert the following:

- **User Name** = admin
- **Password** = password

To continue, we click on the **Login** button.

After logging in, we can see the PUC UI as shown in the following screenshot:

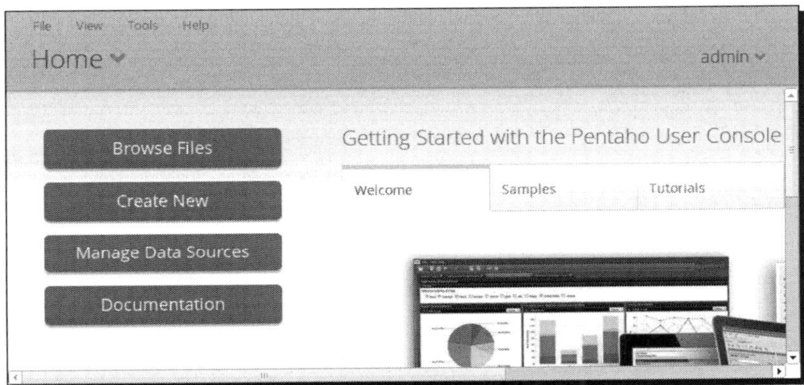

What just happened?

We decompressed the file that we downloaded from SourceForge in a folder of our choice. Then we copied the MySQL JDBC driver to the `[PUC_HOME]/tomcat/lib` folder.

We ran Pentaho BA Server according to our operating system. Then we accessed PUC using a web browser through a URL, `http://localhost:8080/pentaho`. Then we logged in with the user `admin` and entered PUC. Finally, we used a PUC option to view the BI solutions explorer.

General layout of Pentaho User Console

In the following section, we will see the general layout of PUC and familiarize ourselves with the console.

In the upper part of the page, we have the classic options menu as shown in the following screenshot:

A little farther down, on the left-hand side, we find the perspective selector as shown in the following screenshot:

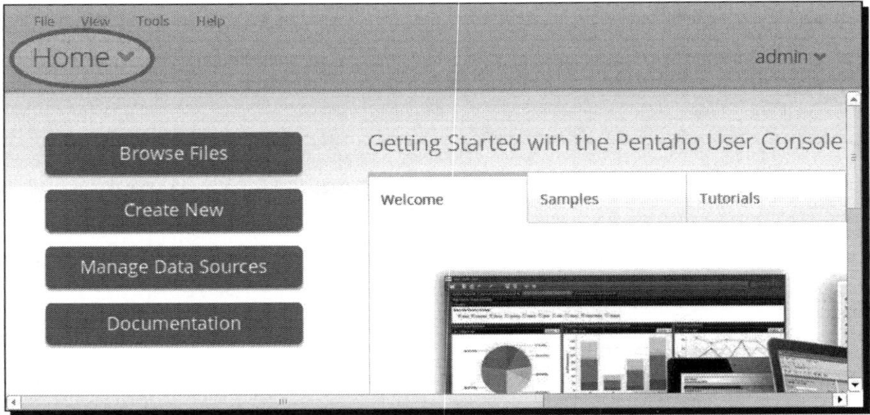

As you can see, the current perspective is **Home**; but, we can change the perspective by clicking on the selector as shown in the following screenshot:

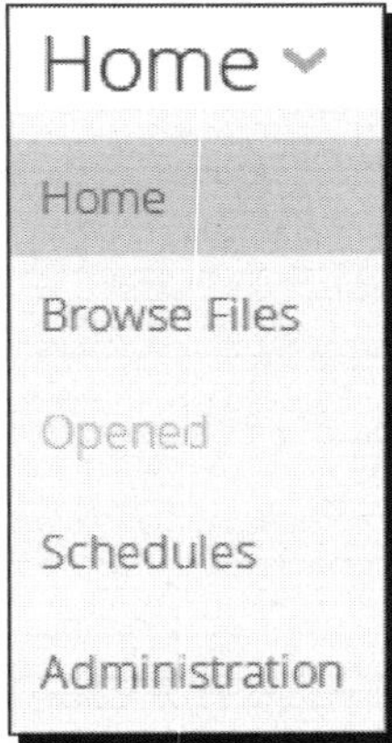

The Home perspective

In the Home perspective on the lower left, the following options are available:

- **Browse Files**: This is used to navigate through our solutions folders and subfolders.
- **Create New**: This is used to create analyses and reports.
- **Manage Data Sources**: This is used to create and edit data sources.
- **Documentation**: This is used to access Pentaho documentation.

In the lower-right corner, we have the following three panels:

- **Welcome**: This panel contains Pentaho examples and tutorials.
- **Recent**: This panel saves a list of the analyses and reports recently visited by the current user.
- **Favorites**: This panel saves the analyses and reports that the user has marked as favorites.

The Browse Files perspective

If we choose the **Browse Files** perspective in the perspective selector, we will see the following screenshot:

Here we have the following three panels:

- **Browsing home**: This is used to navigate through our BI solutions folders and subfolders.
- **home Files**: This shows the analyses, reports, and so on that are in the selected folder in the **Browsing** panel.
- **Folder Actions for home**: This shows a list of actions that we can realize on our folders, analyses, reports, and so on.

The Opened perspective

This perspective lets us visualize and interact with the analyses and reports that are running.

The Schedules perspective

If we choose the **Schedules** perspective in the perspective selector, we will see the following screenshot:

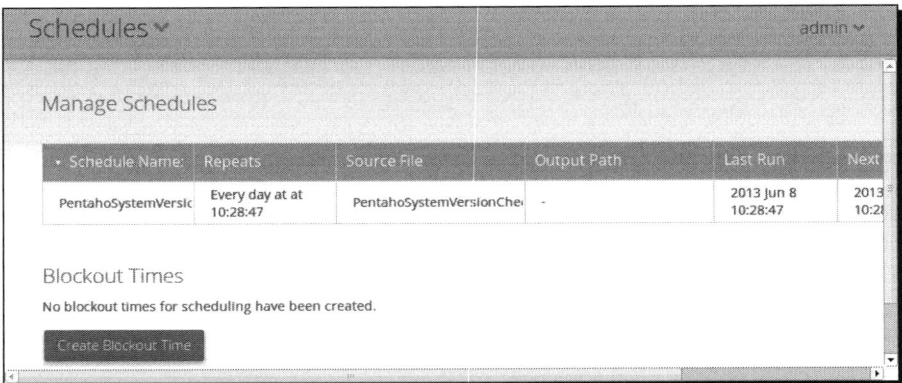

This perspective lets us manage our schedules. Later we will look at this perspective in more detail.

The Administration perspective

If we choose the **Administration** perspective in the perspective selector, we will see the following screenshot:

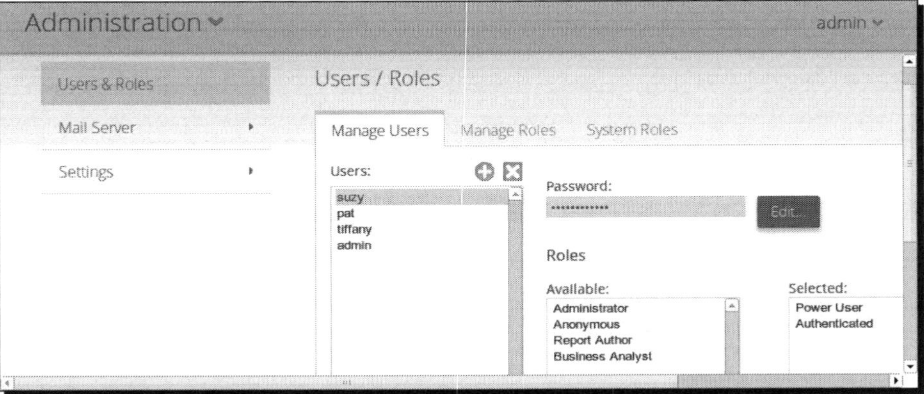

Using this perspective, we can manage **Users & Roles** and configure the **Mail Server** and other options (**Settings**).

Creating a new solutions folder

We will create a new `solutions` folder in PUC so we can use it later in the exercise. To do so, we go to the **Browse Files** perspective:

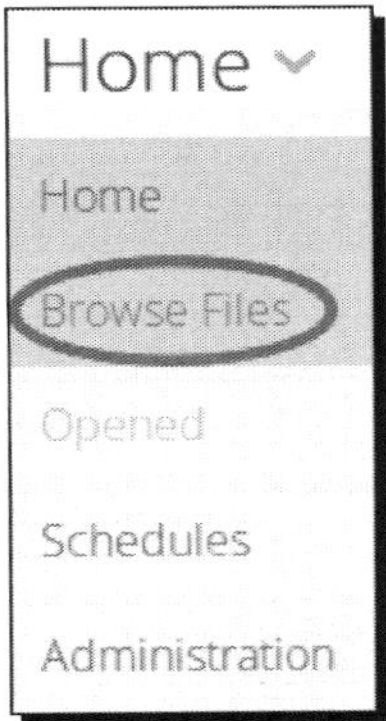

Then, we choose the **public** folder and click on the **New Folder...** button as shown in the following screenshot:

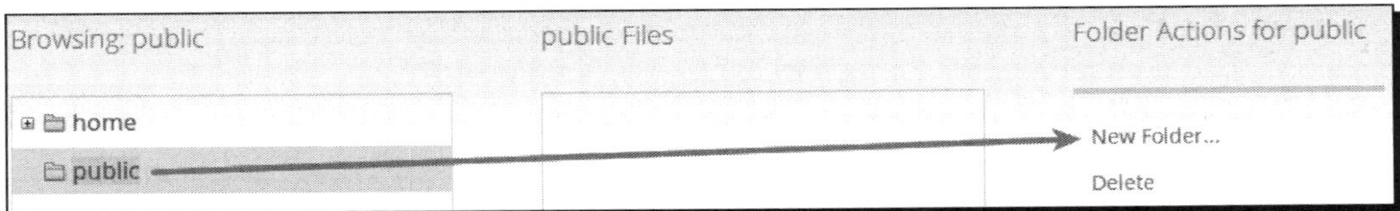

This will open a window where we can enter the name of the folder, which in this case will be `Reporting`, as shown in the following screenshot:

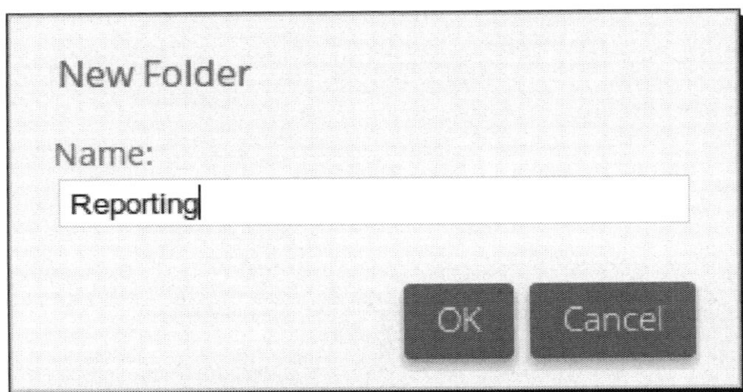

Next, we click on **OK** to continue.

Time for action – publishing reports in Pentaho BA Server

Using PRD, we will open a report we created in earlier chapters and then publish it in Pentaho BA Server. We will configure the connection data required by Pentaho BA Server and then configure the data related to the publication. Finally, we will use PUC to run the report we have published.

1. We start PRD and open a report of our choice; in this case, the report we propose is the one we created in the previous chapter: `13_Adding_Subreports.prpt`.

When publishing a report, Pentaho BA Server must be running.

2. We publish this report in our Pentaho BA solutions folder (the `Reporting` folder).
3. We select the following option in the shortcuts bar:

We can also do the preceding task by navigating to **File** | **Publish...**.

4. The previous action will open a window for us to log in to Pentaho BA Server as shown in the following screenshot:

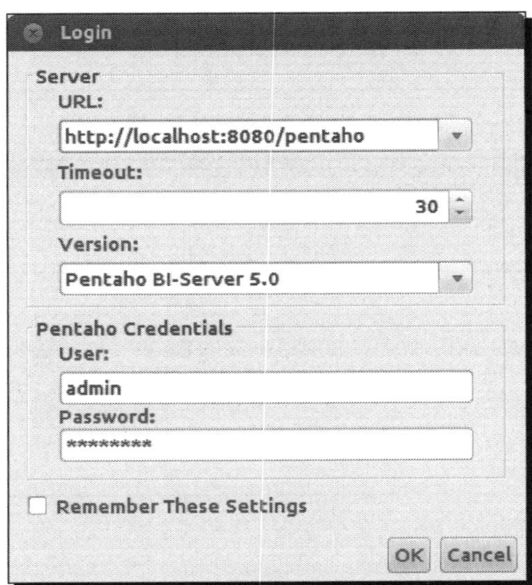

Here we should complete the required information as follows:

- **URL:** = `http://localhost:8080/pentaho`. This is the base URL where Pentaho BA Server is listening.
- **Timeout:** = `30`.
- **Version:** = `Pentaho BA-Server 5.0`.
- **User:** = `admin`. This is the Pentaho BA Server user that has permissions to publish content.
- **Password:** = `password`. This is the `admin` user's password.

Next, click on **OK** to continue.

5. If we entered the data correctly, PRD will connect to Pentaho BA Server and we will see the following window:

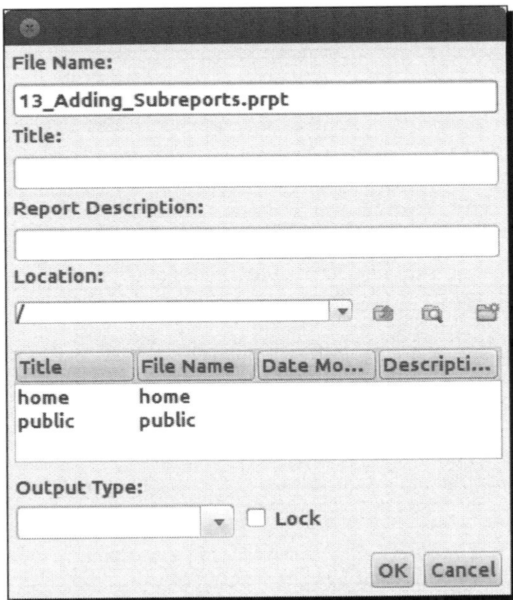

Here we should complete the options as follows:

- **File Name:** Is the name that the file will be saved with in the Pentaho BA Server solutions repository. Here we leave the default value.
- **Title:** Is the report identifier that we will later see in PUC. Here we leave the default value.

- **Report Description:** Is the value that PUC will display as a tool tip. For this to work, the option **Use Descriptions For Tooltips** in **View** must be enabled in PUC. Here we leave the default value.
- In **Location:** We must select the solutions folder where we want to save the file. We double-click on the **public** folder and then on the **Reporting** folder.
- **Output Type:** Is used to establish the default output format when running the report. We choose the option **HTML (Stream)**. The **Lock** option lets us block the output type selection so only the default value is used. The page will look as shown in the following screenshot:

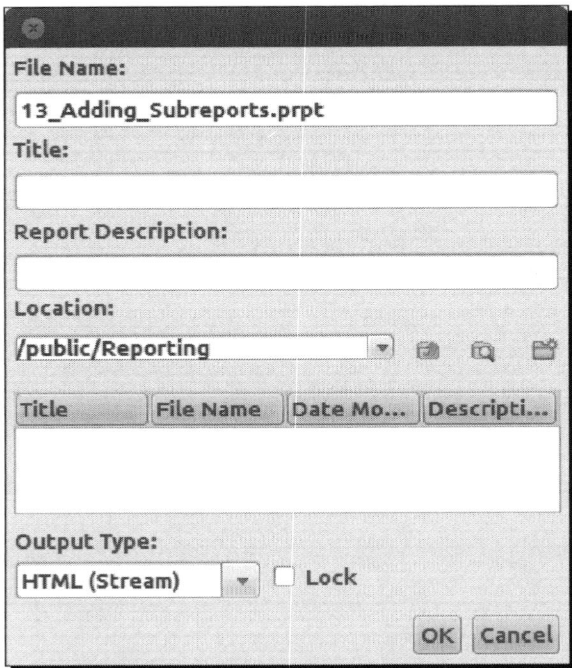

To publish the report, we click on **OK**.

If the publication was successful, we will see the following message:

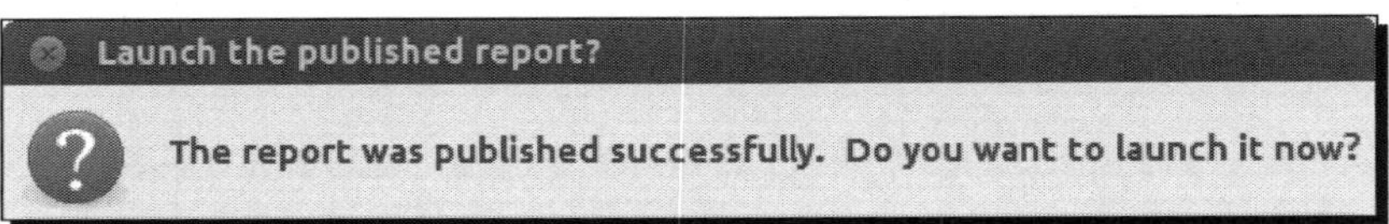

If we want to run the published report now, we choose the option **Yes**; but what we want to do now is see this report from PUC, so we will choose the option **No**.

6. Next we use PUC to run the report we just published.

7. We open PUC in our preferred web browser by typing the following URL:

   `http://localhost:8080/pentaho`

8. We log in with the user `admin` (whose password is `password`).

9. We go to the **Browse Files** perspective.

10. In the **Browsing** panel, we choose the folder **public** and then **Reporting**. Now in the **Files** panel, we will see the report we just published as shown in the following screenshot:

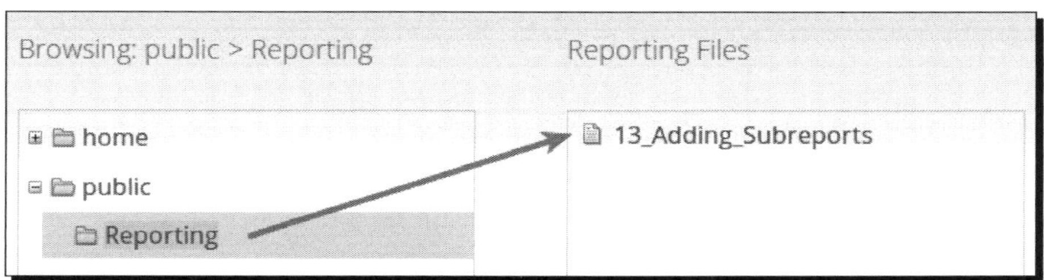

11. In the **Files** panel, we double-click on the report **13_Adding_Subreports**.

12. Finally, we can see what our report looks like when we run it in PUC:

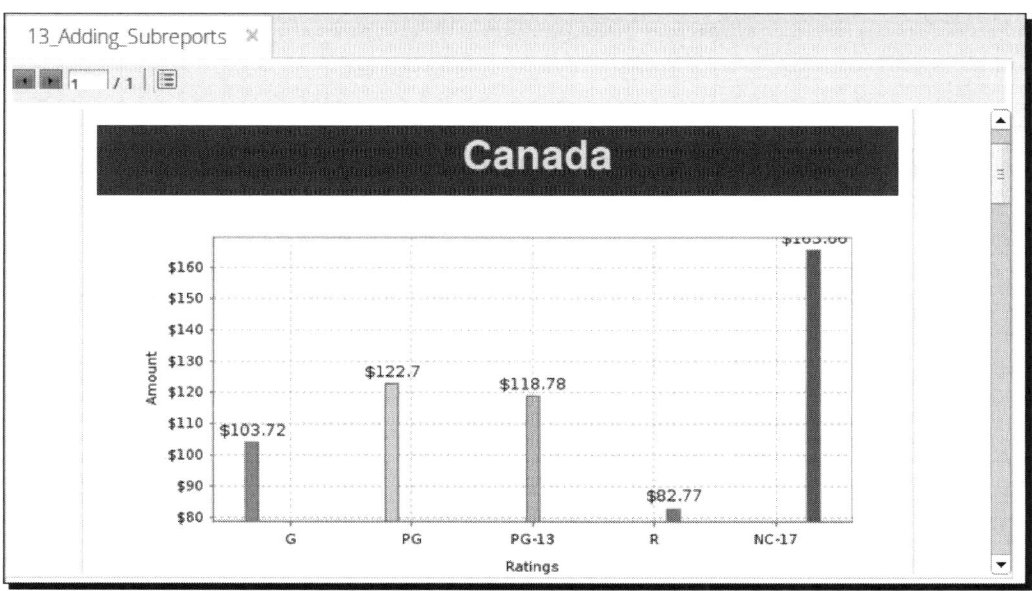

What just happened?

We used PRD to open the report `13_Adding_Subreports.prpt` and publish it. We configured the connection data for Pentaho BA Server; among them, we configured the URL and the authentication credentials. Then we specified the solutions folder where the report was saved and established a default value for the output type. Finally, we accessed PUC using our preferred web browser and executed the published report.

Executing reports in Pentaho BA Server

As you can see, the report looks better when executed in PUC than when it is executed in PRD. The selector area is more stylized and can even be hidden.

Also, the solutions structure that Pentaho BA Server offers, that is, the folders and files, gives users great familiarity with the environment and drastically reduces their resistance to change.

To run the report, first we had to find it (`/public/Reporting`), which means we needed to know its exact location. Suppose a user with little technological experience needs to run a given report. What information should we give him or her? The login URL, the steps to follow to see the **Browse Files** perspective, a brief explanation on how to use the **Browsing** and **Files** panels, and finally, where the report in question is located. It seems like a lot, doesn't it?

But there is a solution to this problem. We can send the user a URL through which he/she only has to log in to see the report.

Doing this is very easy:

1. We find the desired report and select the option **Open in a new window**.
2. A new web browser window will open as shown in the preceding screenshot, showing only the report, without the PUC UI. What we should do is copy the URL and send it to the corresponding user. Refer to the following example:
    - `http://localhost:8080/pentaho/api/repos/:public:Reporting:13_Adding_Subreports.prpt/viewer?`

    Now suppose that the user needs the report to show the information for the country `Egypt` by default. The URL we should send is as follows:

    - `http://localhost:8080/pentaho/api/repos/:public:Reporting:13_Adding_Subreports.prpt/viewer?SelectCountry=29`

The option of sending just the URL to reference and access a report is an enormous facilitation to distribution. It avoids unnecessary delays in looking for a particular report and facilitates access to information.

Creating a schedule

One of the options that Pentaho 5.0 offers is the possibility of scheduling PRD reports. When scheduling a report, Pentaho BA Server precalculates the report data and saves a copy in the chosen format (HTML, PDF, and so on) so we do not have to wait for the data to load to see the report.

To create a schedule for a report, follow these basic steps:

1. Find the desired report and select the option **Schedule...** as shown in the following screenshot:

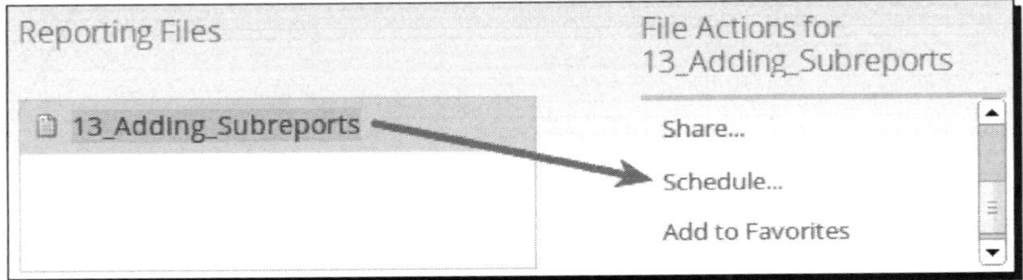

   Now the following wizard will open:

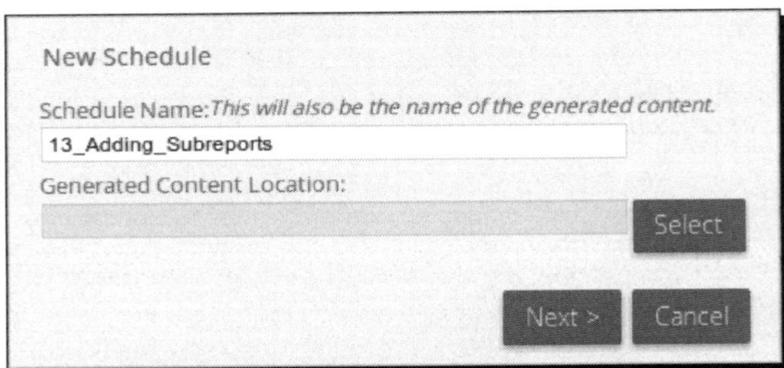

2. We need to complete the following information:
   - **Schedule Name:** Is the name the report will have once it is generated. For example, `13_Adding_Subreportes_Egypt`.
   - **Generated Content Location:** Is where the report will be saved once it is generated. For example, `/public/`Reporting.

The page will look like the following screenshot:

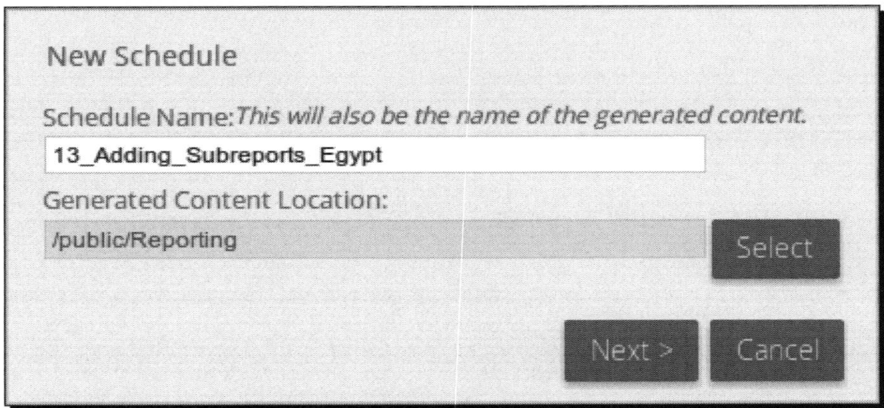

Now click on **Next >** to go to the next step in the wizard. The page will look like the following screenshot:

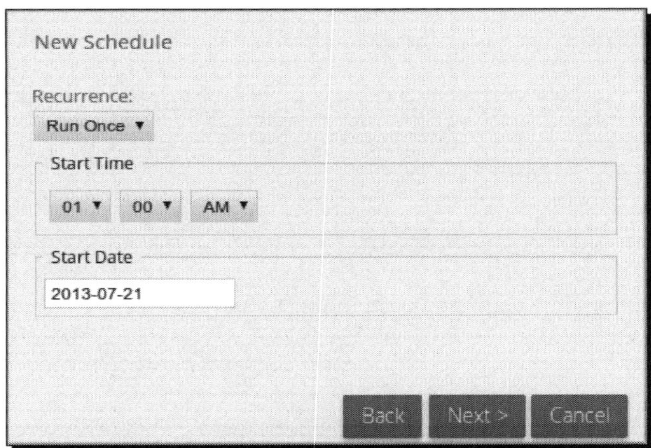

3. \We should enter the schedule's **Recurrence** (**Run Once**, **Daily**, **Yearly**, and so on), its **Start Time**, and the details of the selected **Recurrence** option.

   To continue, click on **Next >**. The following page will open:

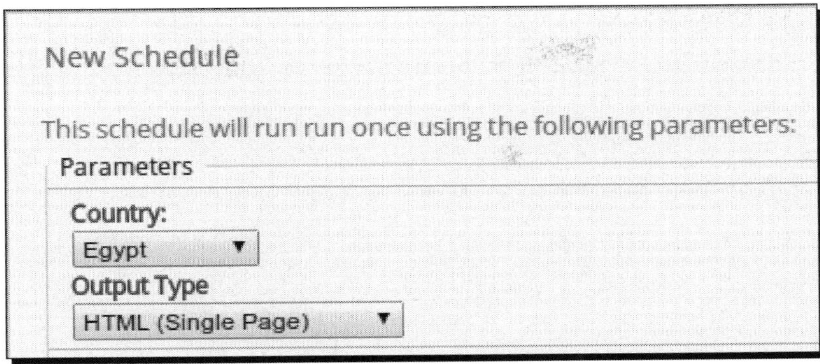

4. The next step is to choose the report's **Parameters** and **Output Type** option. To save the schedule, click on **OK**.

   To see the schedules, choose the **Schedules** perspective. The page will look like the following screenshot:

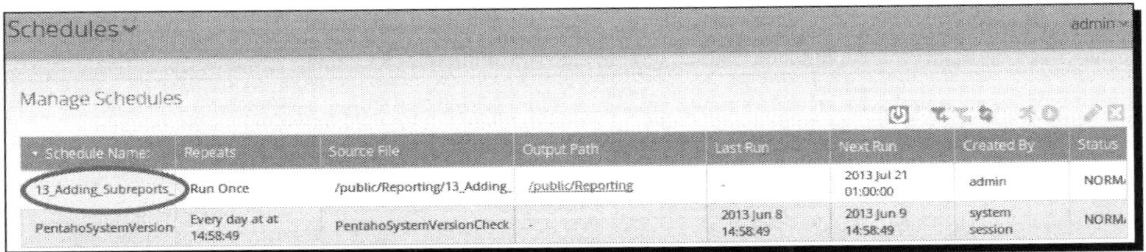

Once the schedule has been executed, we can see the precalculated reports. We can also choose a schedule and click on [icon] to run it now.

The precalculated reports are generated in the specified folder. In this case, if we go to the **Browse Files** perspective, we will see the following screenshot:

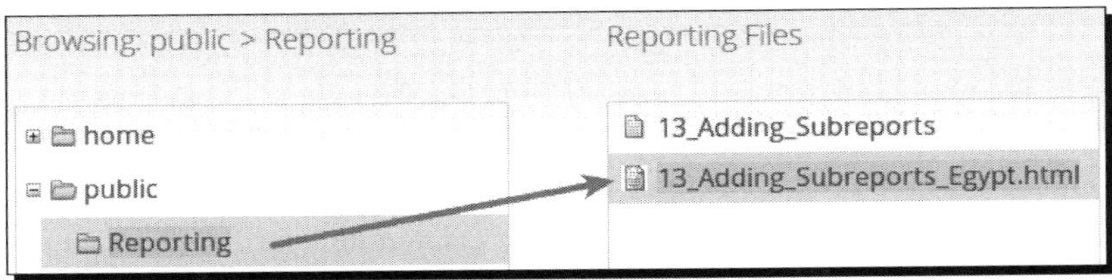

Uploading reports

We have seen how to publish reports in Pentaho BA Server using the PRD UI. Now we will see how to import reports from PUC. This is a new characteristic in Pentaho 5.0.

The first thing to do is select the solutions folder where the report will be imported. Then, click on the option **Upload...** as shown in the following screenshot:

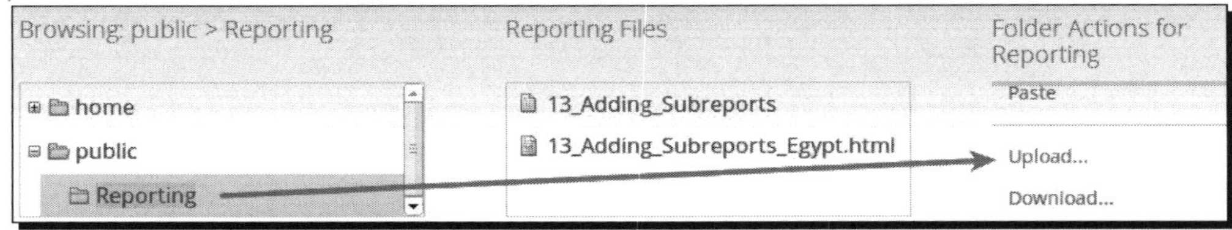

Finally, find and select the desired report using the **Browse...** button, verify the **Advanced Options** option, and click on **OK** as shown in the following screenshot:

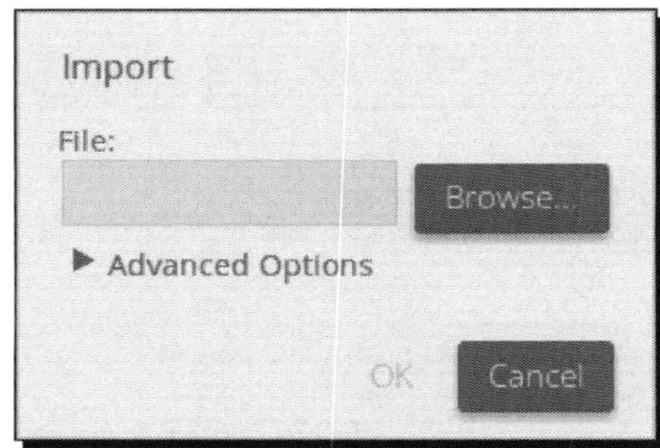

Have a go hero

We propose a series of tasks for you to carry out as follows:

- Use PRD to publish the reports `01_Hello_World.prpt`, `03_Adding_Relational_DS.prpt`, and `05_Adding_Groups.prpt`
- Use PUC to import the reports `07_Adding_Parameters.prpt`, `09_Using_Formulas.prpt`, and `11_Adding_Graphics.prpt`
- Compare the time and number of steps you had to take to publish and import the reports
- Generate a URL for the report `07_Adding_Parameters.prpt` in which the rating `PG`, the year `2005`, and the month `May` are selected by default
- Add a schedule to the report `09_Using_Formulas.prpt` so that it is executed every day at 7:00 in the morning

Pop quiz – Pentaho

Q1. State whether the following statements are true or false:

1. Pentaho's license is the GNU LGPL.
2. The Pentaho suite is made up of multiple components that interact with each other.
3. Pentaho is written in Java.
4. Pentaho BA Server, as well as PRD, requires JDK or JRE.
5. The path where the JDBC drivers should be copied in order for the Pentaho BA Server to use them is `[PUC_HOME]/tomcat/jdbc`.
6. If we want to publish a report with PRD, Pentaho BA Server needs to be running.
7. When we are importing a report from PUC, it is possible to indicate the default parameters that the report should have.
8. In PUC, when we create a schedule for a report, we should always indicate the value of its parameters.

Summary

In this chapter, we talked about Pentaho's functionalities, indicated what license it uses, and defined it. We also talked about Pentaho's modular design and the interaction of its components. We also reviewed the principal projects that integrate the Pentaho suite. We saw a brief historical summary of the different versions of Pentaho BA Server and detailed their principal characteristics. We downloaded Pentaho BA Server and specified its system requirements. We installed Pentaho BA Server, configured the MySQL JDBC driver, and ran it. Using a web browser, we logged in to Pentaho User Console (PUC), saw the general layout of this console, and created the solutions folder `Reporting`. Using PRD, we published a report in Pentaho BA Server and then ran it from PUC. We saw how to obtain a URL for Pentaho BA Server reports. At the end of the chapter, we talked about Scheduling and how to import reports from PUC. We suggested a series of tasks for you to carry out, to practice what we saw in this chapter.

In the next chapter, we will see how to create, configure, and use hyperlinks and sparklines in our reports.

12

Making a Difference – Reports with Hyperlinks and Sparklines

In this chapter we will see how to create and configure Hyperlinks. Hyperlinks give us great flexibility in designing our reports, as they let us drill down (see Detail section). Using Hyperlinks, we can create a network of reports and also re-use reports.

Here we will also see a very interesting object that we can add to our reports, which will present specific information graphically: the sparkline.

In this chapter we will do the following:

- Create and configure a Hyperlink on a text-field object
- Create and configure a Hyperlink on each portion of a pie chart
- Create and configure a bar-type sparkline
- Create and configure a line-type sparkline

Finally, we propose that you modify the report we create in this chapter and add a pie-type sparkline.

Starting practice

In this chapter we will copy a report we created earlier and modify it step-by-step so that it ends up looking like the following screenshot:

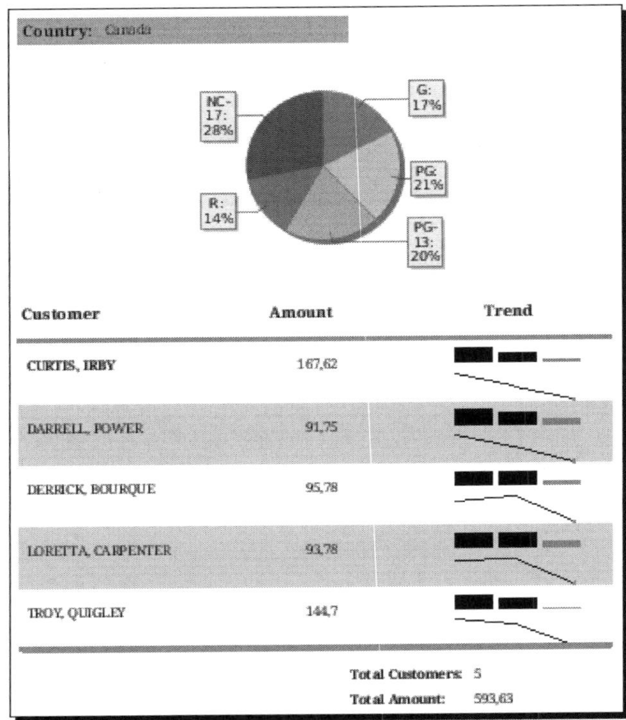

This report will have the feature that, when we click on the name of a country, a new report will open with more detailed information about that country. We will also configure the pie chart so that when we click on one of its areas, a report will open with more information about the selected item.

In the report detail, we will add two sparklines that will analyze the payment history tendency of each client.

First we will talk about hyperlinks, then about sparklines.

Time for action – configuring the layout

In the following section, we will make a copy of a report created in the previous chapter and configure its layout according to the needs of this chapter.

1. We create a copy of the report we created earlier. Open the report `05_Adding_Groups.prpt` and save it with the name `15_Adding_Hyperlinks_Sparklines.prpt`.
2. We modify the report so that it looks like the following screenshot:

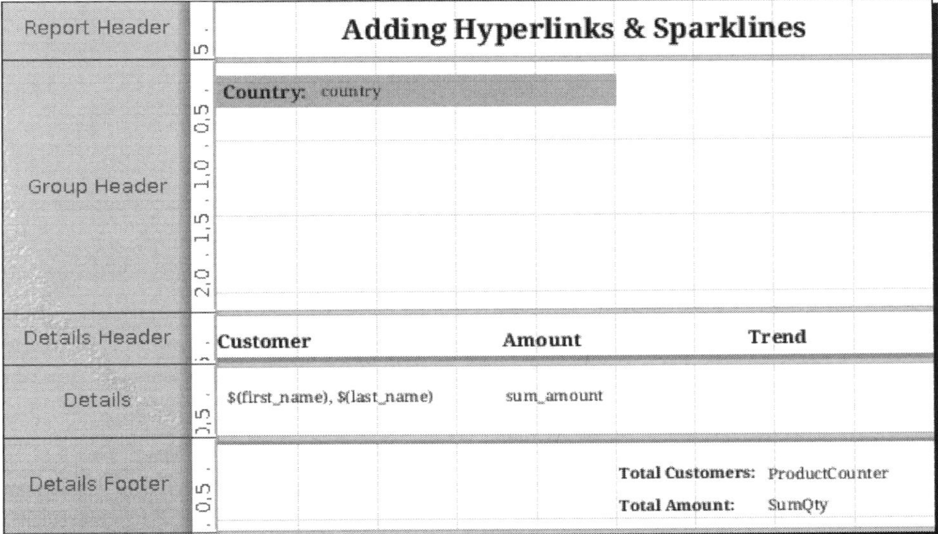

- In the **Report Header** section, we assign the following value to the **Attributes.value** property of the label: `Adding Hyperlinks & Sparklines`.

In the **Group Header** section, we leave a blank space where we can add a Sub-report later.

- In the **Details Header** section, we move the labels **Customer** and **Amount** to the left-hand side and add a label to show the value **Trend**.

In the **Details** section, we eliminate the horizontal line and move the two objects found here to the left so that they stay below their respective headers. We increase the width of this section, as we will later place a Sub-report here.

- To give this report a different style, we configure its colors to be green tones.

What just happened?

We made a copy of the report `05_Adding_Groups.prpt` and saved it with the name `15_Adding_Hyperlinks_Sparklines.prpt`. Then, using an image as a guide, we adapted the layout of the report. We changed the value of the title, moved some objects to the left-hand side, deleted a horizontal line, left blank spaces, and added a label to show the value **Trend**.

Learning about hyperlinks

A **Hyperlink** lets us access an external resource, which could mean opening a website or a report, downloading a file from the Internet, and so on. It also lets us navigate internally; that is, go to specific positions within a web page, report, and so on.

A Hyperlink has two well-differentiated parts:

- The **link**, which is the element that will contain the Hyperlink. Usually, when we hover over the link, the pointer changes to a hand, and if the link is a text, it will be blue and underlined.
- The **target**, which is the element the Hyperlink will point to.

In PRD, Hyperlinks work similarly. For example, we can select an object (link) and use it to create a Hyperlink whose target is another report. But it doesn't stop there. PRD lets us send values to that report's Parameters, that is, we can obtain detailed information from the link we click on, and by doing so, simulate the drill down typical of an OLAP analysis.

Up to here, this is all pretty common, but PRD goes a bit further. PRD lets us create Hyperlinks in parts of our graphics, that is, we can take a pie chart and configure a Hyperlink so that when we click on a portion of the pie, a report opens with more information about the selected item.

Types of hyperlinks in PRD

PRD includes the following options for creating Hyperlinks:

- **Self**: Lets us give values to the Parameters of the current report.
- **URL**: Lets us access an external resource, such as a website, image, or file.
- **Pentaho Repository**: Lets us link reports, xactions, and so on from the Pentaho repository. The Pentaho BA Server must be running, as it will render the reports, xactions, and so on.
- **Manual Linking**: Lets us configure a Hyperlink manually and navigate within the report using HTML anchors.

For more information about HTML anchors, you can visit the following link: `http://en.wikipedia.org/wiki/HTML_anchor#Anchor`.

Interaction between PRD and Pentaho BA Server

The use of Pentaho Repository Hyperlinks is another clear demonstration of how the different tools in the Pentaho suite interact. While it does not have to be the Pentaho BA Server that centralizes and renders our reports, it is a very good option. In fact, in the following chapters we will see how to render a report without using the Pentaho BA Server.

Hyperlinks let us re-use reports, as one report can be linked to many times. For example, a report with sales details for a certain film could be linked to from many other reports that need to make a more detailed analysis about that film.

Also, this lets us create a network of interconnected reports, making possible a really spectacular and extraordinary interactive analysis. We can really navigate the information from one extreme to another and analyze specific or general data, with just a click of the mouse.

Restarting practice

Now that we have explained the basic theoretical concepts related to Hyperlinks, we will put these concepts into practice. First, we will create a Hyperlink on a text-field object, and then we will create another Hyperlink, this time on a pie chart.

Time for action – creating our first hyperlink

Now we will create a Hyperlink that lets us open a PRD report. We will create the Hyperlink on a text-field that contains the name of the country currently under analysis. Clicking on the Hyperlink will open a report that gives us information about that country.

1. We create a Hyperlink on the text-field object that has the value `country` in the field **Attributes.field**. We select the object, right-click on it, and in the **context** menu choose **Hyperlink...** as shown in the following screenshot:

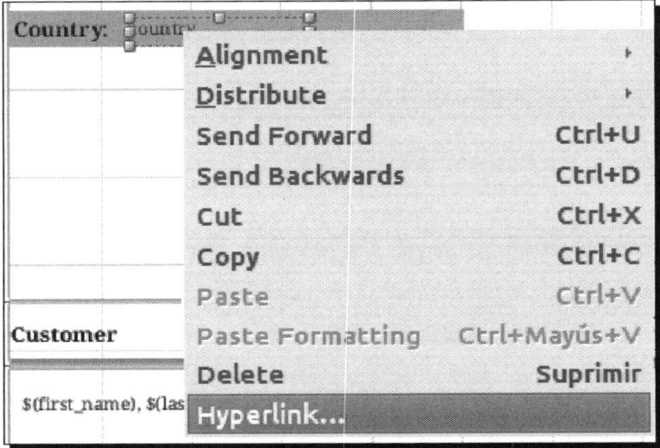

This will open the Hyperlink's Editor as shown in the following screenshot:

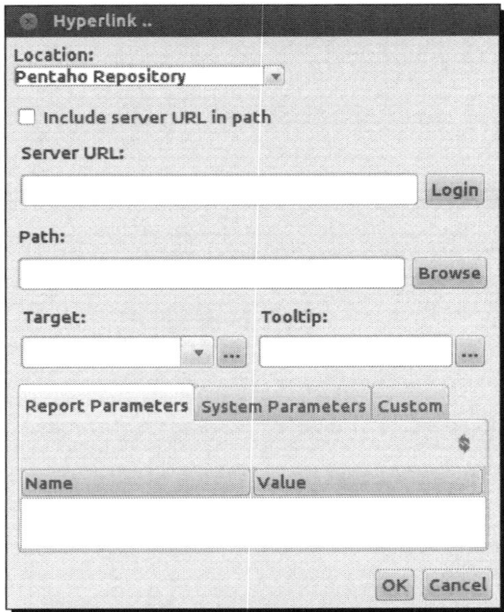

2. The purpose of this Hyperlink is to link to a Pentaho BA Server solutions report and assign a value to its Parameter, according to the country the user clicks on.

   To accomplish this, we complete the Editor's formula as follows:

   - **Location:** = `Pentaho Repository`.
   - **Include server URL in path** = `True`. With this option, the Hyperlink includes in its definition the value of **Server URL:**.
   - To complete the value of **Server URL:**, we click on the **Login** button. This will open a window, as shown in the following screenshot, for us to log in to the Pentaho BA Server (which must be running):

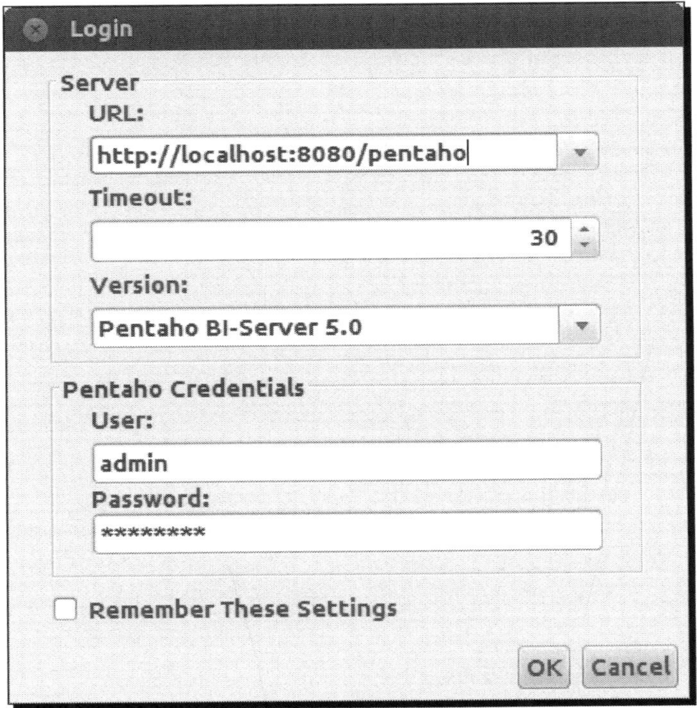

   We complete the login information as follows:

   - **User:** = `admin`
   - **Password:** = `password`

   Then we click on **OK**. Once we are logged into the Pentaho BA Server, the following options will be much easier to complete, as we will be able to navigate through the solutions folders and see the Parameters of the report we choose. The user we use to log in should be an admin.

- In the field **Path** we should enter the location of the report to link to. We click on the **Browse** button, navigate to the path `/public/Reporting`, and choose the report `13_Adding_Subreports.prpt` as shown in the following screenshot:

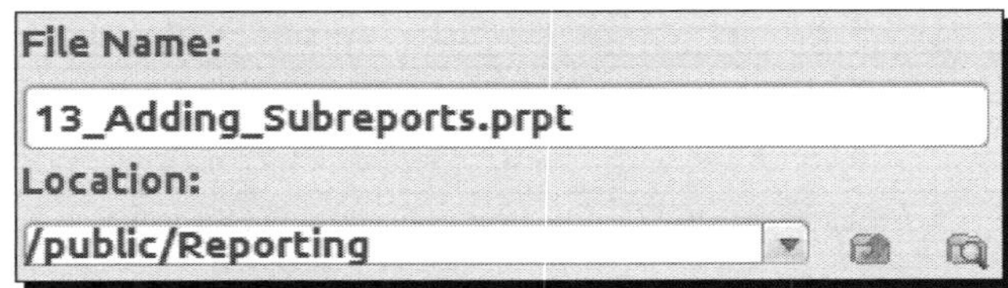

Next, we click on **OK** to continue.

- **Target** = `_BLANK`. This will open the report in a new window.

> The values this attribute can take are the same as the HTML specifications for the tag `<a>`. For more information, visit the following page: `http://www.w3schools.com/tags/att_a_target.asp`

- **Tooltip** = `Press click for more details...`; this is the text that will appear if we hover over the text for a few seconds.
- In **Report Parameters**, we find a table with the Parameters that the report we are creating a Hyperlink to receives. We should assign the value `[country_id]` to the Parameter **SelectCountry** as shown in the following screenshot:

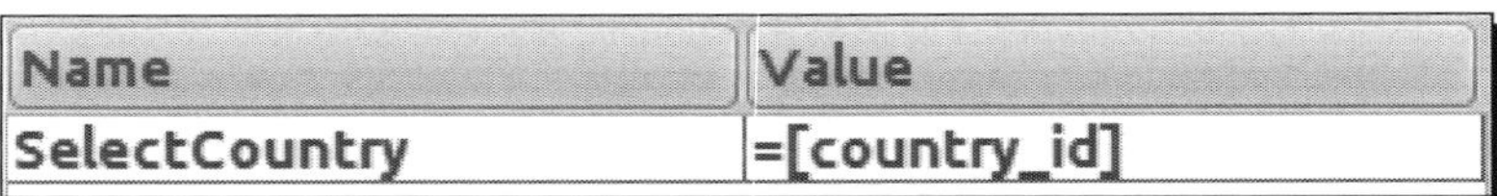

Name	Value
SelectCountry	=[country_id]

Next, we click on **OK** to continue.

3. Now we run our report as HTML to test the Hyperlink we just created. We click on **Canada** as shown in the following screenshot:

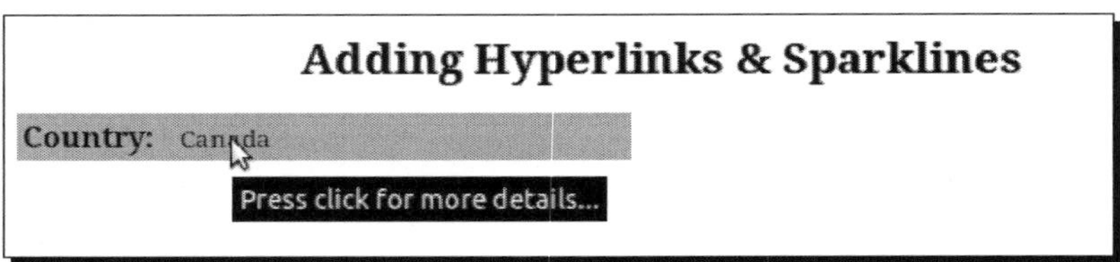

As we can see, this will open a new tab in the web browser, where the selected country will be passed to the report `13_Adding_Subreports.prpt` as shown in the following screenshot:

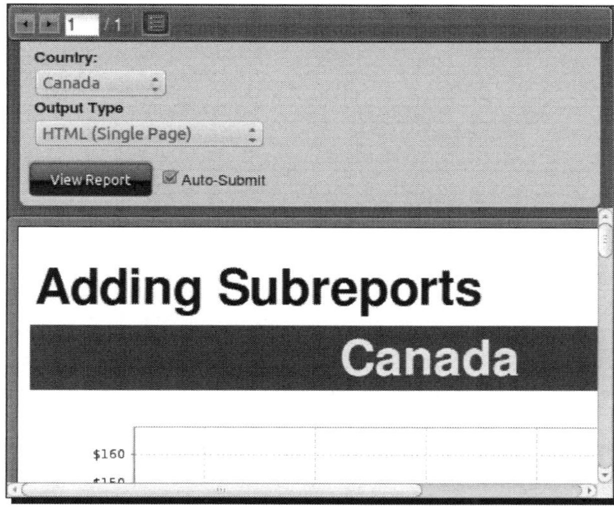

4. Next, we will see where the configuration of the Hyperlink we created is saved.
   - We select the text-field in question
   - We click on the **Structure** tab, and in the **Style** panel we look for the category **links** as shown in the following screenshot:

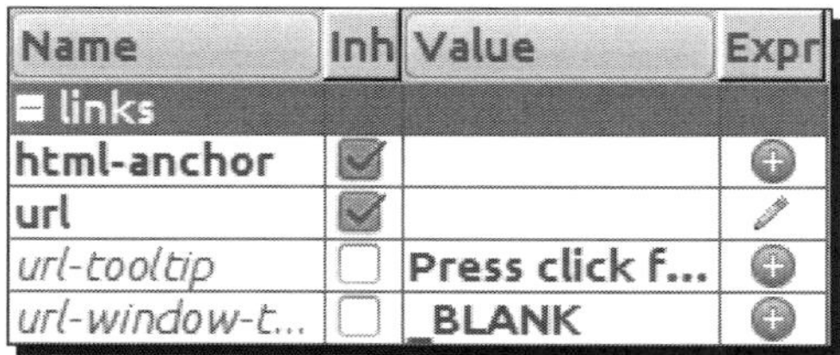

Name	Inh	Value	Expr
links			
html-anchor	☑		⊕
url	☑		✎
url-tooltip	☐	Press click f...	⊕
url-window-t...	☐	_BLANK	⊕

If we look closely, we will see that the configuration of our Hyperlink has been saved in **Style.url**, **Style.url-tooltip**, and **Style.url-window-target**.

If we click on the ✎ icon located to the right-hand side of **Style.url**, we will see that the Hyperlink's logic is created through the **Open Formula** `DRILLDOWN` function:

```
=DRILLDOWN("remote-sugar"; "http://localhost:8080/pentaho";
{"SelectCountry"; [country_id] | "::pentaho-path"; "/public/
Reporting/13_Adding_Subreports.prpt"})
```

For more information about `DRILLDOWN`, visit the following page: `http://wiki.pentaho.com/display/Reporting/DrillLinking`.

What just happened?

We chose the text-field that has the value `country` and we created a Hyperlink on it. We configured the Hyperlink to run the report `13_Adding_Subreports.prpt` and send the value of `[country_id]` to its Parameter, `SelectCountry`. We saw where and how the information related to the Hyperlink is saved. Finally, we analyzed the Open Formula `DRILLDOWN` function.

Time for action – hyperlinks in charts

We will add and configure a Sub-report in our report. Then we will add a pie chart to the Sub-report and configure it so that each of its portions has a Hyperlink to a PRD report.

1. In the space that we left blank in the **Group Header** section, we add a Sub-report.
2. We enlarge the Sub-report to occupy the empty space and then double-click on it to begin configuring its contents.

   We configure its **Import Parameter**. In the **Data** tab, we right-click on **Parameters** and choose the option **Edit Sub-report Parameters...**.

   In the table on the left-hand side (**Import Parameter**), we click on the button to create a new row and then establish the following:

   - **Outer Name** = `country_id`
   - **Inner Name** = `importCountryId`.

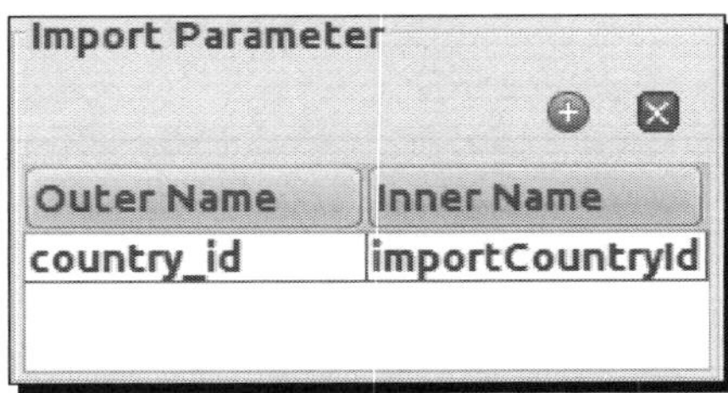

Import Parameter

Outer Name	Inner Name
country_id	importCountryId

   We add a JDBC type **Data Set** with the following configuration to the Subreport:

   - **Connections** = `sakila db`
   - **Query Name** = `RatingAmount`

- **Query** =

```
SELECT
  film.rating,
  SUM(payment.amount) AS sum_amount
FROM film
INNER JOIN inventory ON film.film_id = inventory.
film_id
INNER JOIN rental ON inventory.inventory_id = rental.
inventory_id
INNER JOIN payment ON rental.rental_id = payment.
rental_id
INNER JOIN customer ON payment.customer_id = customer.
customer_id
INNER JOIN address ON customer.address_id = address.
address_id
INNER JOIN city ON address.city_id = city.city_id
WHERE
  city.country_id = ${importCountryId}
GROUP BY film.rating
```

We add a chart to the Report Header section of our Subreport and configure it as follows:

3. In the upper part, we choose the chart type pie chart:

In the right-hand part, we configure the data source as follows:

- **value-column** = `sum_amount`
- **series-by-field** = `[rating]`

In the left-hand part, we configure the following:

- **label-font** = `SansSerif-PLAIN-10`
- **label-format** = `{0}: {2}`
- **url-formula** =

```
=DRILLDOWN("remote-sugar"; "http://localhost:8080/
pentaho"; {"SelectRating"; ["chart::key"] |
"::pentaho-path"; "/public/Reporting/09_Using_
Formulas.prpt"})
```

This formula will be applied to each portion of the pie chart. `["chart::key"]` returns the value of the field under analysis in each portion of the pie chart. To create this formula, we can use the assistant that will guide us or we can write it manually.

For more information about the fields `["chart::key"]`, `["chart::item"]`, and so on, visit the following page: `http://www.on-reporting.com/blog/drill-down-update-charting-and-images/`.

- **tooltip-formula** = **="Press click for more details..."**
- **show-legend** = `False`

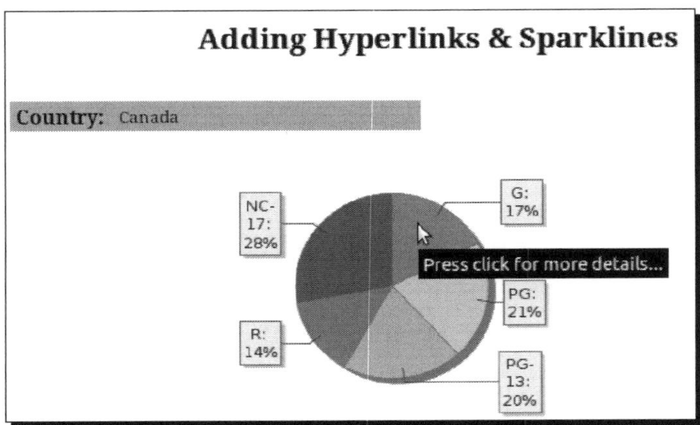

4. If we preview in HTML, we see that clicking on a portion of the pie chart opens a new tab in our web browser with the report linked to, which will receive the **Ratings** selected as a Parameter.

   For example, if we click on **G**, a new tab will open in our web browser with the report as shown in the following screenshot:

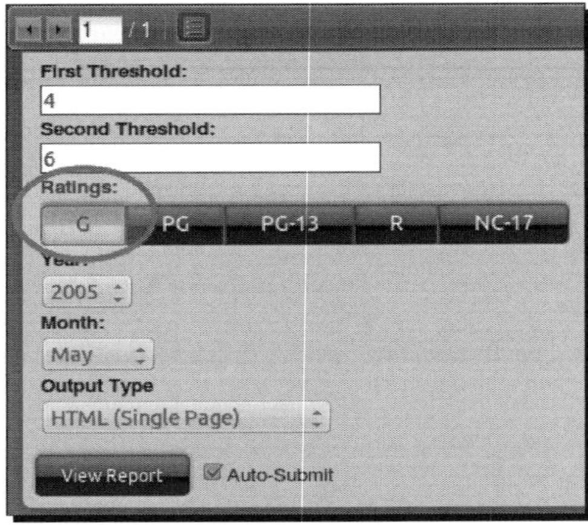

What just happened?

We added a Sub-report to the **Group Header** section and configured its **Import Parameter** and **Data Sets**. We added a pie chart to the Subreport and completed its basic configuration. In the pie chart's characteristic **url-formula**, we created a Hyperlink so that clicking on a portion of the graphic opens the report `09_Using_Formulas.prpt`, which receives the selected rating as a Parameter.

Learning about sparklines

Sparklines are very small graphics that contain very specific information. Sparklines have few characteristics to configure and are very minimalist. They cannot include axes, labels, descriptions, effects, or numbers. To get a better idea of what sparklines are, here are some examples:

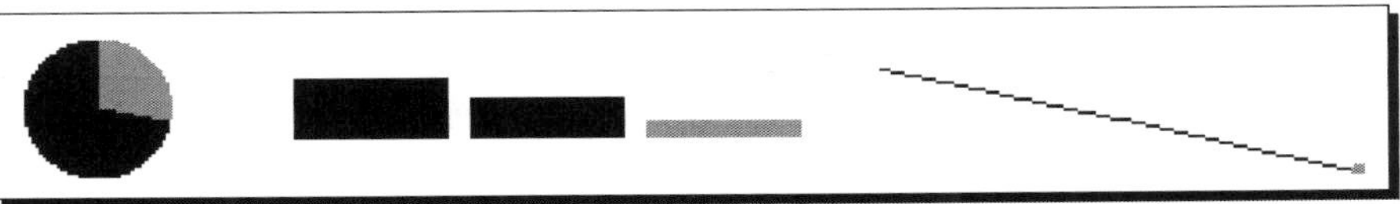

As you can see, they do not contribute any information out of context. That is why their principal role is to accompany the data present in the report, and because of their small size, we can include them in the detail level of our reports!

PRD lets us include sparklines in our reports, granting us the possibility of analyzing the variation of an item's value over time, making specific comparisons, showing what percentage of a total an item's value represents, and so on.

If we compare sparklines with the kinds of charts that we have already seen in PRD, we could erroneously conclude that sparklines display very little information to the end user. But as we saw before, this characteristic is what makes these little charts shine.

In PRD there are three types of sparklines:

- **Bar sparkline** ( ) : Lets us add a small bar chart. The characteristics we can modify for this graphic are:
    - **Style.high-color**: The color the tallest bar will have.
    - **Style.lastcolor**: The color the last bar with have.
    - **Attributes.spacing**: The spacing between bars. The default value is `2`.

- **Line sparkline** ( ) : Lets us add a small line chart. The characteristics we can modify for this graphic are:
    - **Style.lastcolor**: The color of the point on the line that represents the last value.
    - **Attributes.spacing**: The spacing between values. The default value is `2`.
- **Pie sparkline** ( ) : Lets us add a small pie chart. The characteristics we can modify for this graphic are:
    - **Style.low-color**: The color of each portion of the pie whose value falls in the low range. The default color is green.
    - **Style.medium-color**: The color of each portion of the pie whose value falls in the medium range. The default color is yellow.
    - **Style.high-color**: The color of each portion of the pie whose value falls in the high range. The default color is red.
    - **Attributes.low-slice**: The values between zero and this value will be considered in the low range. The default value is `0.3`.
    - **Attributes.medium-slice**: The values between the low-slice value and this value will be considered in the medium range. The default value is `0.7`.
    - **Attributes.high-slice**: The values between the medium-slice value and this value will be considered in the high range. It is usually left blank. The default value is `1`.
    - **Attributes.start-angle**: The pie's starting angle.
    - **Attributes.counter-clockwise**: The direction in which the pie will turn.

> After adding a sparkline to our report, the characteristics for configuring the graphic are found in **Styles** and **Attributes** in the category **sparkline**.

An array with the values to be displayed must be assigned to the object's bar sparkline and line sparkline. We will see how to do this soon.

All the values for the pie sparkline object must be between 0 and 1, with 0.2 representing 20 percent and 1 representing 100 percent.

Restarting practice

Now we will create a bar sparkline and a line sparkline step-by-step. Both objects will be in the **Details** section of our report in order to show two small graphics in each row.

Time for action – creating our first sparkline

We will modify our principal data set to practice each of the following points. We will create a subreport, and within it we will create and configure two sparklines.

1. We modify the SQL query of our data set to conform to the needs of this guide. We add the field `customer_id` at the end of the list of fields in the `SELECT` statement. Our query should look like the following:

   ```
   SELECT country.country_id, country.country, customer.first_name,
   customer.last_name, SUM(payment.amount) sum_amount, payment.
   customer_id
   FROM payment
   INNER JOIN customer ON customer.customer_id=payment.customer_id
   INNER JOIN address ON address.address_id=customer.address_id
   INNER JOIN city ON city.city_id=address.city_id
   INNER JOIN country ON country.country_id=city.country_id
   WHERE country.country_id IN (20,24,29,34,48,67,74)
   GROUP BY payment.customer_id
   ORDER BY country.country, customer.first_name
   ```

   In the **Details** section, beside the label **Trend**, we place a subreport object. Now we begin to work on the subreport.

2. In the **Data** tab, we go to the node's Parameters, right-click on it, and select the option **Edit Sub-report Parameters....**

   Here we add an **Import Parameter** and configure it as follows:

   - **Outer Name** = `customer_id`
   - **Inner Name** = `importCustomerId`

3. We create a JDBC type data set with the following characteristics:

   - **Connections** = `sakila db`
   - **Query Name** = `LastDateAmount`
   - **Query** =

     ```
     SELECT
     YEAR(payment.payment_date) AS payment_year,
     MONTH(payment.payment_date) AS payment_month,
     SUM(payment.amount) AS sum_amount
     FROM payment
     WHERE payment.customer_id = ${importCustomerId}
     GROUP BY 1, 2
     ORDER BY 1, 2 DESC
     LIMIT 0,3
     ```

   Next, we click on **OK** to continue.

4. In the **Report Header** section, we add a bar sparkline and a line sparkline, and establish their sizes and positions so they look like the following:

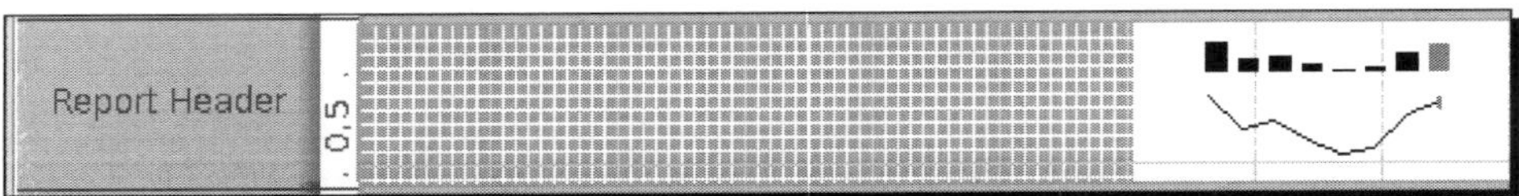

5. First we configure the bar sparkline and then the line sparkline. We click on the **Bar-sparkline** and establish the values it needs in order to draw the bars:

   - **Attributes.value** = `=MULTIVALUEQUERY("LastDateAmount"; "sum_amount")`

   What the `MULTIVALUEQUERY` function does in this case is it receives as its first parameter the name of the data set that we are going to work with, and as its second parameter, the name of the field in the data set that we will use. What the `MULTIVALUEQUERY` function will do is create a string with the values of `sum_amount` separated by commas. For example, the field `sum-amount` in the Subreport's data set, for the customer `CURTIS, IRBY` from the country `Canada` will return three rows as shown in the following screenshot:

86,83
54,86
22,94

   So, in this case, after applying the `MULTIVALUEQUERY` function, we get the following:

86.83, 54.86, 22.94

   Attributes.value receives numerical data separated by commas. The technique suggested in the preceding section can be used for this purpose or some other, for example, using the `group_concat` function in SQL, or by a PDI transformation, and so on.

> There is another very interesting function: `SINGLEVALUEQUERY`. This receives the same parameters as `MULTIVALUEQUERY`, but returns only the first row.

6. We configure the rest of the bar sparkline's details:
   - **Attributes.spacing** = `4`
   - **Style.lastcolor** = `#cc9329`
7. Now we edit the line sparkline as follows:
   - **Attributes.value** = `=MULTIVALUEQUERY("LastDateAmount"; "sum_amount")`
   - **Attributes.spacing** = `4`
   - **Style.lastcolor** = `#cc9329`

   The two sparklines we added to our report have the same data, but this way we can see more clearly the way each one represents information.

   If we preview, we will see the following screenshot:

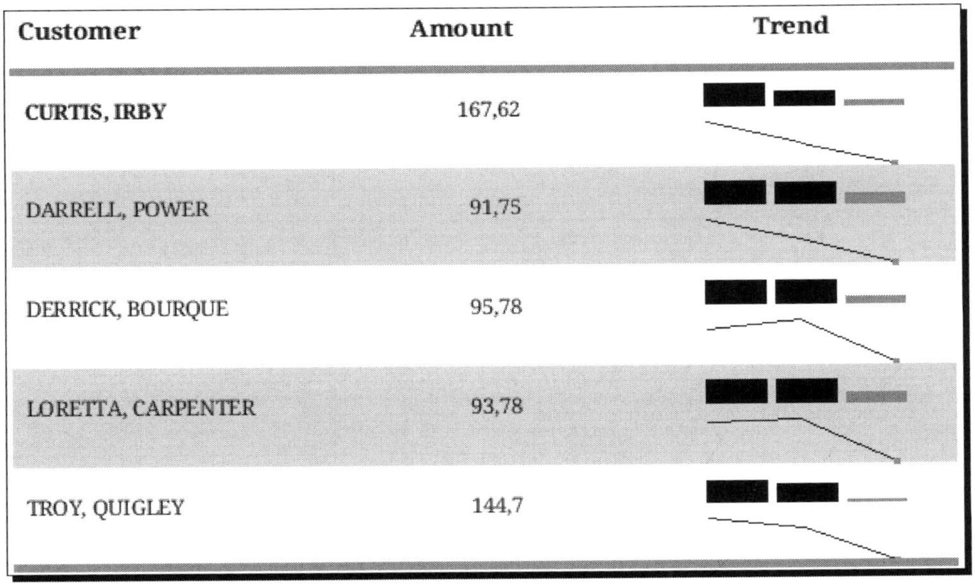

Customer	Amount	Trend
CURTIS, IRBY	167,62	
DARRELL, POWER	91,75	
DERRICK, BOURQUE	95,78	
LORETTA, CARPENTER	93,78	
TROY, QUIGLEY	144,7	

What just happened?

We added the field `customer_id` to our report's principal data set in order to work with this field later. In the Details section, we added a subreport and configured it to import the value of the field `customer_id`. We also created a data set for the subreport and added two sparklines to the **Report Header** section. First we configured the bar sparkline and then the line sparkline. Finally, we explained the `MULTIVALUEQUERY` function.

Have a go hero

We propose that you make a copy of the report we just created and modify it so it looks like the following:

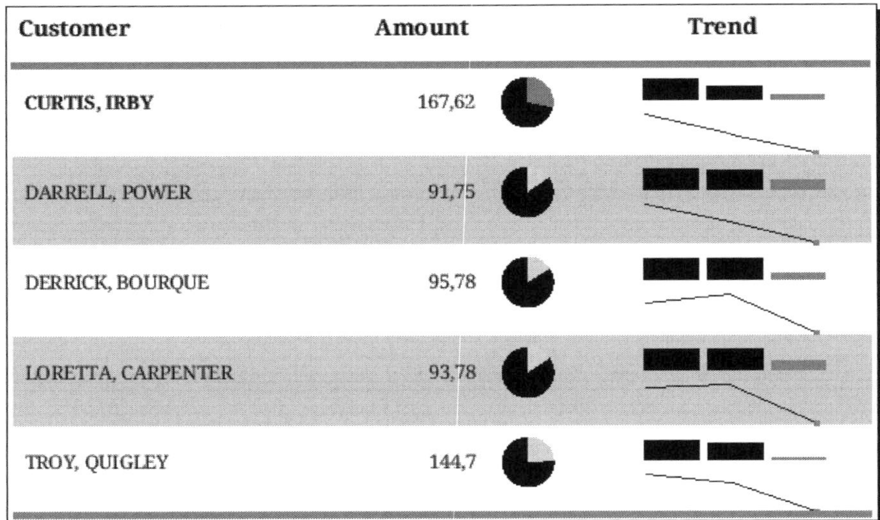

What you should do is create a pie sparkline, place it in the **Details** Section, and configure it so it shows the portion of the pie corresponding to the current **Amount**.

The steps you should follow, broadly speaking, are as follows:

1. Create a copy of the report `15_Adding_Hyperlinks_Sparklines.prpt` and save it with the name `16_Adding_Hyperlinks_Sparklines_Plus.prpt`.

2. Place a pie sparkline in the **Details** Section to the right-hand side of the number-field that has the value `sum_amount`, and configure it as follows.

   - **Attributes.value** = `=[sum_amount]/[TotalAmount]`
   - **Attributes.low-slice** = `0.15`
   - **Attributes.medium-slice** = `0.25`
   - **Style.low-color** = `#cf4646`
   - **Style.high-color** = `#2ead03`

Pop quiz: Hyperlinks and Sparklines

Q1. State whether the following statements are true or false.

1. Hyperlinks in PRD only let us reference and pass values to the parameters of other PRD reports.
2. Hyperlinks in PRD let us navigate within our reports in the same way we would in a traditional web page.
3. To create a hyperlink in PRD, we must use the Pentaho BA Server.
4. A sparkline in PRD has a very minimalist format, but we can still assign values to the X and Y axes.
5. In PRD, sparklines let the end user make a rapid analysis of data at the detail level.
6. The three types of sparklines in PRD receive an array of comma-separated data as their input.

Summary

We created a copy of the report `05_Adding_Groups.prpt` and modified its layout.

We explained what a hyperlink is, how to use it, and what it is used for. We talked about the different types of hyperlinks that can be created in PRD. We detailed the interaction between PRD and the Pentaho BA Server when using hyperlinks.

We created a hyperlink on a text-field that returns the value of the field country. We configured this hyperlink to open the report `13_Adding_Subreports.prpt` and passed it the desired country as a parameter.

We explained how and where the information related to Hyperlinks is saved and analyzed the `DRILLDOWN` function.

We added a subreport to the Report Header Section and configured it and added a pie chart to it. We configured a hyperlink on this pie chart, so that clicking on each portion of the pie chart shows the report `09_Using_Formulas.prpt` filtered by the value of the selected portion.

We explained what sparklines are and what they are used for. We explained the characteristics of each of the three types of sparklines.

We added a subreport to the Details Section and configured it. We added a bar sparkline and a line sparkline to the subreport and configured them.

We talked about the `MULTIVALUEQUERY` and `SINGLEVALUEQUERY` functions.

Finally, we proposed that you modify the current report and add a pie sparkline to it.

In the next chapter we will talk about environment variables, stylesheets, and crosstabs.

13
Environment Variables, Stylesheets, and Crosstabs

This chapter is dedicated to environment variables, stylesheets, and crosstabs. We will treat each of them in detail, defining what they are about and how to implement them in **Pentaho Report Designer** *(***PRD***).*

Using **Environment Variables** *allows us to interact with the BA Server that is executing our reports. That is, we can obtain the username of the user who is currently logged in and his or her roles, among other information.*

With **Style Sheets***, we can configure our report so that its look and feel varies according to certain* **CSS Rules***. These CSS Rules are easy to configure, save, and import.*

Finally, we will take a look at one of PRD's new jewels, **Crosstabs***. Using Crosstabs, we can show OLAP-style analytic information in our reports.*

In this chapter we will do the following:

- See examples of environment variables and use them to configure our objects in order to create CSS Rules for them
- Create a new stylesheet and add our own rules to format objects' look and feel according to the user currently logged in
- Save the stylesheet and assign it to our report
- Create our own crosstab and configure it to show a crosstab analysis of year-month and ratings
- Finally, we propose that you modify a previous report and configure the visibility of a graphic according to the user who is currently logged in

Learning about environment variables

Environment variables are basically variables whose values depend on the environment in which they are being used. For example, an environment variable can return to the application using it as a description of the current operating system or the complete path where the application is being executed.

In Pentaho Report Designer (PRD) there exists a series of predefined environment variables that will help us interact with the BA Server that is executing them. Making use of these variables, we can modify the behavior and content of our reports.

Environment variables in PRD

The environment variables that we can use in PRD are found in the **Data** tab, under the **Environment** node as shown in the following screenshot:

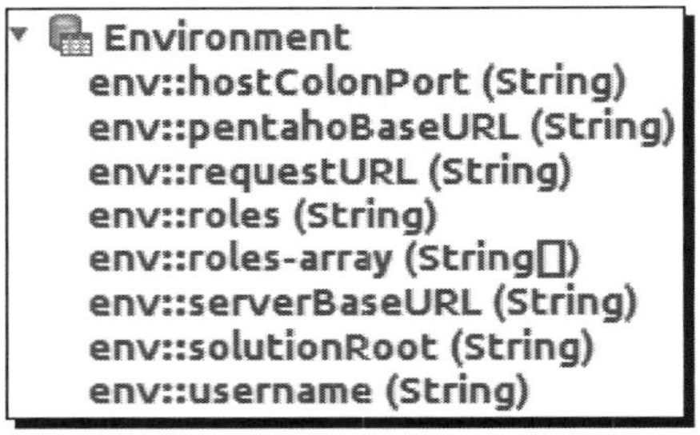

Environment
env::hostColonPort (String)
env::pentahoBaseURL (String)
env::requestURL (String)
env::roles (String)
env::roles-array (String[])
env::serverBaseURL (String)
env::solutionRoot (String)
env::username (String)

In the following list, we describe each of these:

- **env::hostColonPort**: This environment variable specifies the IP address and port where Pentaho BA Server is being executed, separated by a colon. For example: `localhost:8080`.
- **env:serverBaseURL**: This environment variable specifies the protocol, IP address, and port where Pentaho BA Server is being executed. For example: `http://localhost:8080`.
- **env::pentahoBaseURL**: This environment variable specifies the protocol, IP address, port, and base URL where Pentaho User Console (PUC) is being executed. For example: `http://localhost:8080/pentaho/`.
- **env::username**: This environment variable specifies the username of the user who is currently logged in. For example: `Admin`.
- **env::roles**: This environment variable specifies the roles of the user who is currently logged in, separated by commas. For example: `Administrator, Authenticated`.

- **env::roles-array**: This environment variable is the same as the previous variable, but with the difference that here we obtain an array. For example: `{"Administrator"}, {"Authenticated"}`.
- **env::solutionRoot**: This environment variable specifies the complete path where the pentaho-solutions folder is physically located. For example: `[BISERVER_HOME]/pentaho-solutions/`.

Using the environment variables

Using the environment variables is simple and similar to what we have already seen. We can drag-and-drop environment variables in our reports and/or use them as part of a formula or expression, as a filter condition in a SQL query, and so on.

That is, we now have the capacity to vary the content of our report accordingly; for example, according to the user who runs it. We can, for example, show or hide charts, establish dynamic filters in our data sets, configure the look and feel (colors, images, and so on), hide the selector section, and so on.

We can take a wide variety of actions depending on the specific need of each case.

On practice

As we mentioned earlier, there are many examples that can be given for environment variables, from something as simple as displaying them to really complex actions such as varying the look and feel of our report. What we will do in this chapter with environment variables is configure the look and feel of our report in a simple and pleasant exercise that, although it is simple, still shows the capacities we want to analyze.

Before we formally begin the exercise, we need to talk about one of the new and impressive characteristics of PRD, stylesheets!

Learning CSS

Cascading Stylesheets (**CSS**) is a language used to describe the visual presentation of a tag-structured document; for example, HTML, XHTML, XML, SVG, and XUL.

CSS is based on a group of **Rules** through which we can configure the color, position, visibility, size, borders, and so on of the content of any tag in our document. CSS lets us reference these tags in different ways; for example, through their name, class, ID, and so on.

Basically, a CSS Rule consists of two parts: the tag selector and the style to be applied.

For more information on CSS, visit:

- http://www.w3.org/Style/CSS/
- https://en.wikipedia.org/wiki/Cascading_Style_Sheets

Stylesheets in PRD

PRD uses CSS3 to implement stylesheets, which allows, among other things, correct integration with the most popular web browsers.

The stylesheets' code in PRD is stored in an XML file with the extension `.prptstyle`. This file can be created, exported, and modified from the PRD UI using the **Style Definition Editor**. Also, this file can be embedded in our report or simply linked to it.

Using stylesheets in PRD will make the design of the final presentation of our reports easier and will save us a lot of manual configuration time, in addition to separating the presentation logic from the report logic. That is, we can create our stylesheets just once and then apply them to all of our reports. If, for example, our company changes its logo, colors, font face, and so on, we don't have to modify each and every report. We just modify the CSS assigned to the reports.

The Style Definition Editor

To open the **Style Definition Editor**, navigate to the main menu and then to the option **Extras** | **Style Definition Editor**.

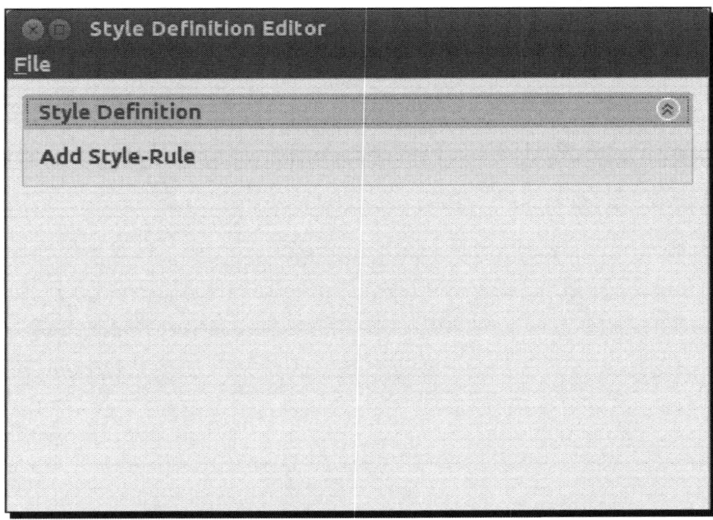

To open a `.prptstyle` file, navigate to the option **File** | **Open...**.

To add a new CSS Rule, click on the **Add Style-Rule** option as shown in the following screenshot:

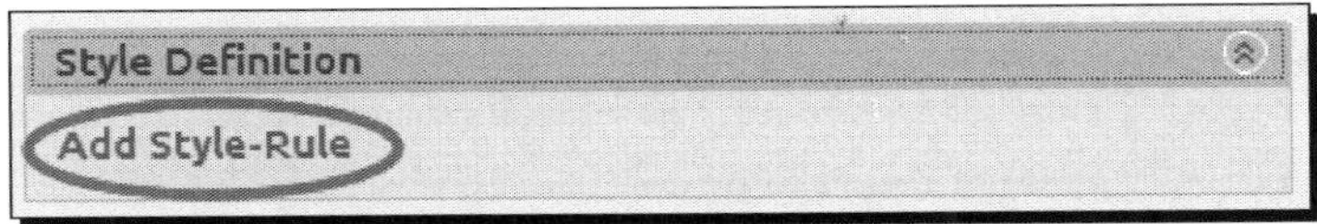

This will create an empty CSS Rule as shown in the following screenshot:

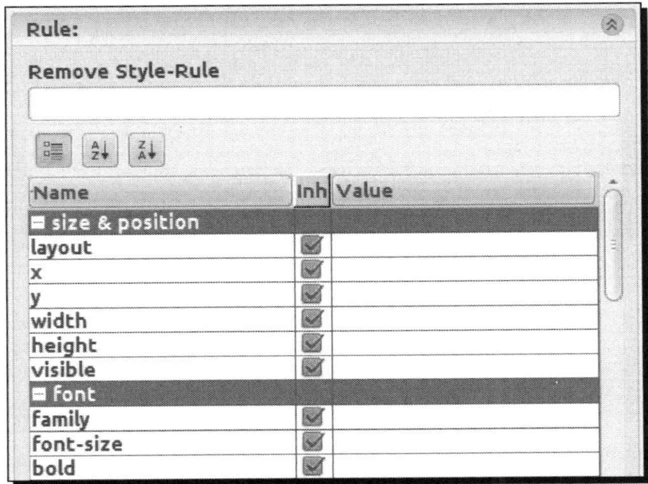

Type the tag selector in the upper field and use the options below it to describe the style.

To save the changes, navigate to **File** | **Save** or **File** | **Save As...**, whichever is appropriate.

To delete a CSS Rule, click on the **Remove Style-Rule** option.

Applying CSS

In order for our report to use a `.prptstyle` file's CSS Rules, we select the **Master Report** node in the **Structure** tab and configure the value of **Attributes.style-sheet-reference**.

When creating tag selectors in our CSS Rules, we can reference any node in our report's structure; that is, a complete section or an object. Also, by using the options **Attributes.style-class** and **Attributes.id**, we can reference any node by its class or ID, respectively.

Starting practice

In this section, we will apply all that we have seen up to now in practice. Using environment variables and stylesheets, we will make our report present content and styles depending on the user who is currently logged in.

Time for action – configuring the layout

We will create a new report and configure its layout in order to be able to carry out this chapter's exercises. The most important configuration is establishing the values of **Attributes.style-class** and **Attributes.xml-id**, as later these will be used for creating CSS Rules.

1. Create a new report and save it with the name `17_Adding_Style_Sheets.prpt`.
2. Configure the layout of our report so that it looks like the following screenshot:

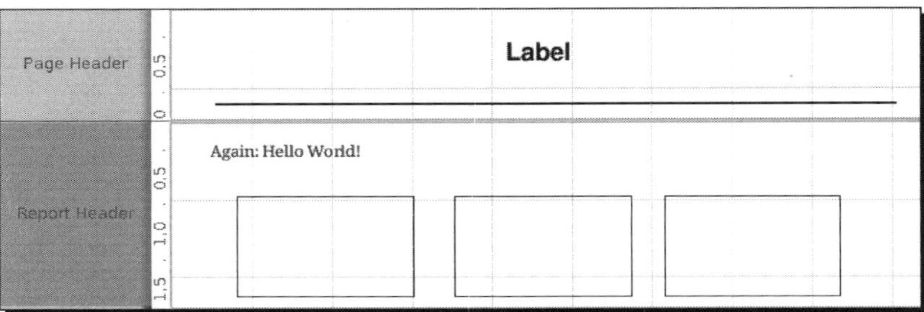

3. In the **Page Header** section, add a **Label** and configure it as follows:
   - **Attributes.value=** `=CONCATENATE("Welcome ";["env::username"])`
   - **Attributes.style-class=** `=["env::username"]`
   - **Style.family=** `FreeSans`
   - **Style.font-size=** `16`
   - **Style.bold=** `true`
4. In the **Page Header** section, add a **Horizontal-line** and configure it as follows:
   - **Attributes.style-class=** `=["env::username"]`
   - **Style.stroke=** `solid, 2.0`
5. In the **Report Header** section, add a **Label** and configure it as follows:
   - **Attributes.value=** `Again: Hello World!`
   - **Attributes.style-class=** `=["env::username"]`

6. In the **Report Header** section, add three **Rectangles** that, respectively, will have the values `=CONCATENATE("r1_";["env::username"])`, `=CONCATENATE("r2_";["env::username"])`, and `=CONCATENATE("r3_";["env::username"])` in **Attributes.xml-id**.

What just happened?

We created a new report and named it `17_Adding_Style_Sheets.prpt`. We added a label and a horizontal line to the **Page Header** section, and a label and three rectangles to the **Report Header** section. We configured these objects so we can later apply style sheets to them.

Time for action – creating and applying our stylesheet

We will create our own stylesheet using the **Style Definition Editor** UI, then save it, and look at the XML code that has been created. Then we will assign the stylesheet to our report.

1. To create our stylesheet, navigate to the option **Extras | Style Definition Editor** in the upper menu.
2. Click on the **Add Style-Rule** option to create a new CSS rule and configure it as follows:
   - **Rule**= `horizontal-line[style-class="Designer"]`
   - **Style.text-color**= `#339900`

   The CSS rule says that it will apply the style (green color) to all the horizontal lines that have the value `Designer` in their **Attributes.style-class**.

`Designer` is the default user used when previewing reports in PRD.

3. Click on the **Add Style-Rule** option to create a new CSS rule and configure it as follows:
   - **Rule**= `horizontal-line[style-class="Admin"]`
   - **Style.text-color**= `#f02929`

   The CSS rule says that it will apply the style (red color) to all the horizontal lines that have the value `Admin` in their **Attributes.style-class**.

Remember that `Admin` is the name of a Pentaho BA Server User.

4. Click on the **Add Style-Rule** option to create a new CSS Rule and configure it as follows:
    - **Rule=** `report-header label[style-class="Designer"]`
    - **Style.font-size=** `18`
    - **Style.bold=** `true`

    The CSS Rule says that it will apply the style (large and bold font) to all the labels in the **Report Header** section that have the value `Designer` in their **Attributes. style-class**.

5. Click on the option **Add Style-Rule** to create a new CSS rule and configure it as follows:
    - **Rule=** `report-header label[style-class="Admin"]`
    - **Style.italics=** `true`

    The CSS Rule says that it will apply the style (italic) to all the labels in the **Report Header** section that have the value `Admin` in their **Attributes.style-class**.

6. Click on the **Add Style-Rule** option to create a new CSS rule and configure it as follows:
    - **Rule=** `[xml-id="r3_Designer"]`
    - **Style.visible=** `false`

    This CSS Rule says that it will apply the style (invisible) to the node (section or object) that has the value `r3_Designer` configured in its **Attributes.xml-id**.

7. Save the file. To do so, navigate to the option **File | Save As...**. Name it `styles.prptstyle`.
8. Open the file `styles.prptstyle` in your favorite text editor. In the part designated for CSS rules we should find something like this:

```
<rule>
  <selector>horizontal-line[style-class="Designer"]</selector>
  <styles>
    <content-styles color="#339900"/>
  </styles>
</rule>
<rule>
  <selector>horizontal-line[style-class="Admin"]</selector>
  <styles>
    <content-styles color="#f02929"/>
  </styles>
</rule>
```

```
<rule>
  <selector>report-header label[style-class="Designer"]</selector>
  <styles>
    <content-styles color="#00cc99"/>
    <text-styles bold="true"/>
    <text-styles font-size="18"/>
  </styles>
</rule>
<rule>
  <selector>report-header label[style-class="Admin"]</selector>
  <styles>
    <content-styles color="#ff6600"/>
    <text-styles italic="true"/>
  </styles>
</rule>
<rule>
  <selector>[xml-id="r3_Designer"]</selector>
  <styles>
    <common-styles visible="false"/>
  </styles>
</rule>
```

To better understand the code for the `<selector>` tags, we have replaced the string `"` with the character `"`.

If we pay attention to the XML code, we will see that it is very simple, and with a little practice we can even create our Stylesheets without having to use the PRD UI.

9. Now we will make a report on our stylesheet. Go to the **Structure** tab, click on the **Master Report** node, and in the option **Attributes.style-sheet-reference** click on the ... button. In the window that opens, for **Source**, search for and choose the stylesheet you just created and select the option **Embed in Report** as shown in the following screenshot:

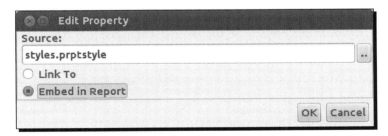

What just happened?

We opened the **Style Definition Editor** UI and using the option **Add Style-Rule** we added one by one of the CSS rules proposed in the exercise. We created CSS rules that take into account the name of the user who is currently logged in. We created CSS rules for `Designer`, the PRD default user, and for `Admin`, a Pentaho BA Server user. Finally, by using **Attributes.style-sheet-reference**, we assigned the stylesheet we just created to the **Master Report** node.

Trying out stylesheets

To try out the stylesheets we just created, run them through PRD, whose default user is Designer, and from the Pentaho BA Server, logging in with the user `Admin`.

Then, on one hand, preview the report in PRD.

On the other hand, publish the report in Pentaho BA Server, in the same folder where we published previous reports. When asked if you want to execute the report now, click on the **Yes** option.

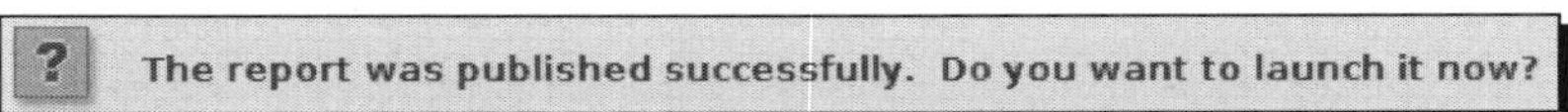

In the following screenshot we have placed the results of the two executions of the report side by side for comparison. On the left is the report executed in Pentaho BA Server, and on the right is the report executed in PRD:

Welcome Admin

Again: Hello World!

Welcome Designer

Again: Hello World!

If we review the CSS rules that we have defined, we can see that we have done an important job using environment variables and stylesheets.

Next, we will talk about another new feature in Pentaho Report Designer: Crosstabs!

Learning about crosstabs

A crosstab is a table where we can analyze and compare the relationship of the results of two or more study variables. Its name comes from the fact that a cross is carried out between the values of the study variables in order to analyze something. That is, in a crosstab we can have years and months on one side and film ratings on the other, and analyze their intersection, the quantity of films of each rating rented in each month and year. Crosstab is similar to Excel pivot tables.

Crosstabs are used in OLAP analysis, where the user can place study variables at the head of a row or column.

For more information on crosstabs, you can visit Wikipedia: `http://en.wikipedia.org/wiki/Crosstab`

The crosstabs in PRD

Before we begin, we would like to quote a nice introduction by Thomas Morgner (the software architect for Pentaho Report Designer) regarding crosstabs:

> *Crosstabs have been on the horizon for several years now. They lived a happy, undisturbed life along with the unicorns and gnomes guarding the pot of gold at the end of the rainbow.*
>
> *With an endless recession and central banks selling off their gold reserves, the unicorn has been sold to a meat factory and the gnomes now assemble luxury cell-phones in a Chinese factory.*
>
> *So the day had to come that crosstabs have to work for a living. That day is now.*

Crosstabs themselves are nothing new. They have been in development for many years. They could even be included in PRD 3.5, although in an experimental and complex manner.

With crosstabs, we can include in our reports the analytic capacity that OLAP analysis offers, although in a predefined and totally static way.

Using crosstabs

To create a crosstab in PRD, drag-and-drop the object in the desired section.

We will see that the way crosstabs are implemented is very similar to Subreports.

After doing this, the UI will ask us if we want our crosstab to be **Banded** or **Inline**. Next we choose or create the data set we want to use. Finally, the **Crosstabs Editor** window will open, as shown in the following screenshot, which we will use to configure the data to be displayed.

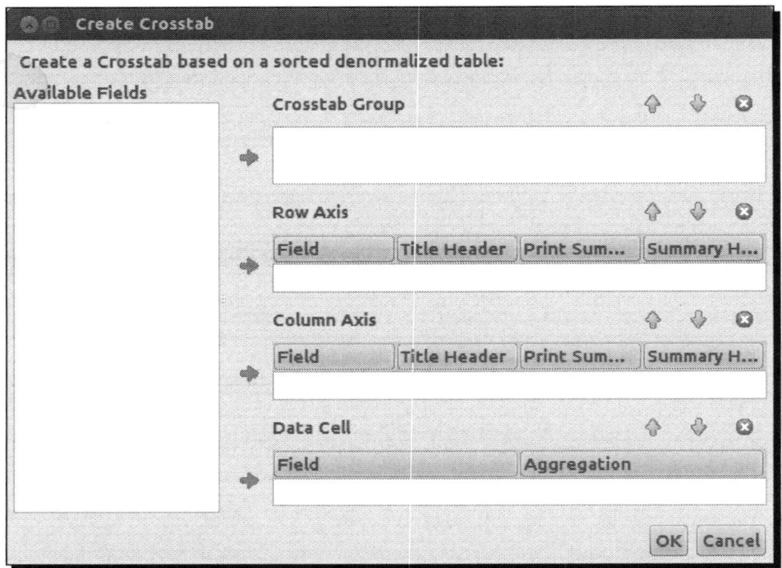

Crosstabs editor

In the preceding screenshot we saw the crosstabs editor UI. Now we will describe each of its sections.

- Available Fields: In this section we find all the fields we can add to our Crosstab.
- Crosstab Group: Here we place the fields by which the crosstab will be grouped. For example, if we place the films' ratings here, we will obtain a Crosstab for each rating.
- Row Axis: Here we place the fields to be analyzed horizontally.
- Column Axis: Here we place the fields to be analyzed vertically.
- Data Cell: Here we place the fields that we want to measure (facts). These are the fields that will fill our table, and their value will depend on the intersection of the fields of the rows and columns. For this reason, we also must choose the aggregation criteria for these fields.

When adding fields to the crosstab's sections, the order they appear in is important, as a parent-child hierarchy will be formed for each one that we place in a given section. The order of the hierarchy is descendent; that is, the first field will be the parent and the second will be the child. If there is a third field, it will be the child of the second, and so on.

Starting practice

Now we will create our own crosstab and configure it to obtain a final result as shown in the following screenshot:

		Ratings	Ratings	Ratings
Year	Month	G	PG	R
2005	5	$ 928	$ 859	$ 933
	6	$ 1647	$ 1901	$ 2010
	7	$ 5013	$ 5696	$ 5436
	8	$ 3972	$ 4787	$ 4809
2006	2	$ 105	$ 95	$ 83

Time for action – configuring the layout

Next, we will create a new report, create its data set, and add a crosstab. Then we will configure the crosstab to show us the values of `amount` analyzed after crossing `years-months` with `ratings`.

1. Create a new report and save it with the name **18_Adding_Crosstabs.prpt**.
2. Create a JDBC data set and configure it as follows:
   - **Connections**= `sakila db`
   - **Query Name**= `DateRatingAmount`
   - **Query**=

```
SELECT YEAR(payment.payment_date) AS payment_year,
MONTH(payment.payment_date) AS payment_month, film.rating,
SUM(payment.amount) AS sum_amount
FROM payment
INNER JOIN rental ON rental.rental_id=payment.rental_id
INNER JOIN inventory ON inventory.inventory_id=rental.
inventory_id
INNER JOIN film ON film.film_id=inventory.film_id
WHERE film.rating IN ("G","PG","R")
payment_year, payment_month, film_rating
```

3. In the **Report Header** section, add a crosstab object:
4. Make the crosstab **Inline**, and when asked about the data set to use, choose **DataRatingAmount** and click **OK**. After doing this we will see the **Crosstabs Editor**.
5. Next, configure the crosstab.
6. In the **Row Axis** section, add the fields **payment_year** and **payment_month**, in that order. Then modify their **Titles Header** section to be `Year` and `Month`, respectively.
7. In the **Column Axis** section, add the field **rating**, and in **Title Header** type `Ratings`.
8. In the **Data Cell** section, add the field `sum_amount`, and choose the **Aggregation** criteria as `sum`.

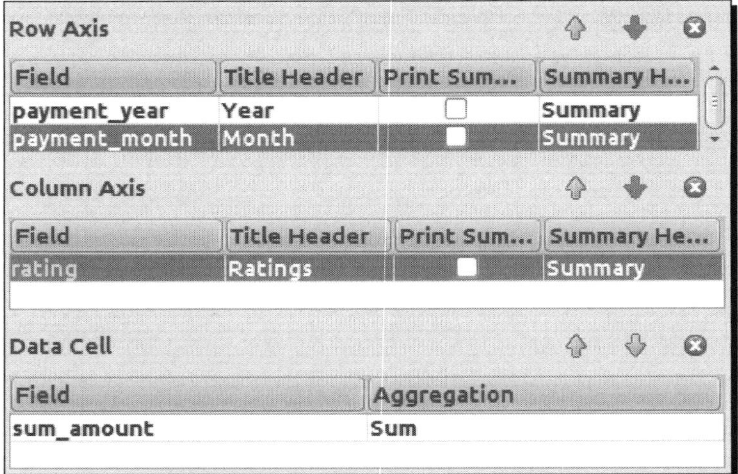

9. Next, click **OK** to continue.
10. Return to the main report and enlarge the crosstab so it fills the page width.
11. Go back to the crosstab and modify its final presentation as we please: bold, fonts, formats, and so on.

What just happened?

We created a new report and named it `18_Adding_Crosstabs.prpt`. Then we created its JDBC data set and established its SQL query. We added a crosstab to the **Report Header** section, made it be **Inline**, and established its data set. Then we configured the sections **Row Axis**, **Column Axis**, and **Data Cell** for the crosstab.

Have a go hero

In this chapter we propose that you hide a graphic if the user executing the report is not `Admin`.

The steps you should follow, broadly speaking, are:

1. Create a copy of the report `11_Adding_Graphics.prpt` and save it with the name `19_Adding_Style_Sheets_Plus.prpt`.
2. Select the second graphic and configure its **Style.visible** with a formula that will return `True` if the user currently logged in is `Admin`, and return `False` otherwise.

Pop Quiz – environment variables, stylesheets, and crosstabs

Which of the following statements are true?:

Q1. PRD's environment variables let us know some information about the BA Server where the report is being executed.

Q2. In order for PRD to include the values of the environment variables, they must be previously enabled.

Q3. PRD uses CSS3 to implement stylesheets.

Q4. We can manually create our .prptstyle file and then include it using PRD.

Q5. In stylesheets, we can create CSS Rules only if we know the class or ID of the object in question.

Q6. Crosstabs in PRD function dynamically when executed in Pentaho BA Server.

Summary

We talked about environment variables, what they are, how they are used in PRD, and what information each of them provides us.

We also talked about stylesheets, what they are, what they let us do, and what CSS rules are. Then we saw how PRD implements stylesheets, how they are saved, configured, and applied to our reports.

We created a simple report and applied a stylesheet to it that we created step-by-step. The CSS rules were based on the user executing the report.

Later we talked about crosstabs, what they are, what their purpose is, and how they are used and configured in PRD.

We created another report, added a crosstab to it, and configured the crosstab.

Finally, to put into practice what we saw in this chapter, we proposed that you modify an existing report and modify the visibility of a chart according to the user currently logged in.

In the next chapter we will see how to embed and run PRD reports in our web applications.

14
PRD Reports Embedded in Web Applications

At this stage, with the amount of knowledge we have of Pentaho Report Designer (PRD), we can confidently say we are fairly good PRD developers.

This chapter attempts at taking not only one step forward with PRD, but many.

Once this chapter is finished and the concepts presented here are understood, we will be able to create a web portal that allows users to access PRD reports, send parameters to them, and select the final presentation format.

We will also be able to perform every configuration needed to have the portal working as well as have it packaged so that we can transport it and deploy it in a different environment with little modification.

In this chapter we will do the following:

- We will explain what **Java Platform Enterprise Edition** (**JEE**) is and its main components.
- We will explain what **Apache Tomcat** is. We will download it, install it, configure it, and start it.
- We will explain what **Eclipse** and **Eclipse Web Tools Platform** (**WTP**) are. We will download Eclipse, install it, set it up, and configure its perspectives.
- By means of Eclipse, we will create a **Dynamic Web** type project and configure it.
- We will create and configure an Apache Tomcat instance in our project.
- We will create a JDBC/JNDI connection pool.

- We will add to our project MySQL's JDBC driver as well as the required libraries and report we will be working on.
- We will create and configure a **Listener** and a **Servlet**.
- We will also create and configure a **Web Client**.
- We will package our project and deploy it on Apache Tomcat.

Finally, we will invite you to perform every step needed to execute a report through Apache Tomcat.

Tools and technologies we will be using

Before starting with the practical part, we will present and discuss (summary-wise) the tools and technologies required to perform our practice.

Learning JEE

Java Platform Enterprise Edition (JEE) is the part of the Java platform that allows the execution of components based on application servers. JEE promotes the construction of modular software distributed over N layers and is defined by various specifications. Software providers must comply with a series of standards defined within the specifications so that their products obtain JEE compliance.

JEE covers an important amount of components and specifies how each of them is supposed to work. Some of the most popular components of this platform are as follows:

- **Servlets**: These are software components that are executed on the server side, are oriented mostly to workflows and calculations, and are commonly used on web applications.
- **Java Server Pages** (**JSP**): These are web components oriented to presenting information and generating content with which the final user will interact.
- **Enterprise Java Beans** (**EJB**): These are components that specify how application servers should provide objects. EJB objects possess a series of features, such as security, the handling of transactions, concurrency control, remote communications, and so on.
- **Web Services** (**WS**): These are components that allow the exposure of functionality via the web. They are commonly used on current applications.

One of JEE's most attractive features is the low cost with which one can begin to create applications. Many of the available implementations are **free and open source software** (**FOSS**) and have an excellent quality. There also exist a fair amount of FOSS developer tools with a quality that, in many cases, is superior to that of commercial versions.

JEE is also a technology stack with a maturity and robustness highly proved and thoroughly tested. A very important number of current applications are written in Java.

Learning Apache Tomcat

Apache Tomcat, also known as **Jakarta Tomcat** or simply Tomcat, is a multiplatform server that works as a servlets container. Tomcat implements Oracle's servlet and Java Server Pages specifications. It includes a compiler named **Jasper** that transforms JSP into servlets.

Tomcat is currently being used in environments of high concurrency and where high availability is required.

Tomcat can work as a standalone web server, is written in Java, and is distributed under an Apache 2.0 license.

Tomcat is currently on Version 7, with support for Servlet 3.0, JSP 2.2, and **Expression Language** (**EL**) 2.2. For more information, please refer to the project's main page at `http://tomcat.apache.org/`.

Time for action – installing and starting Apache Tomcat

We will now download and install Tomcat. Later on, we will initiate it and test it with a web browser.

1. We will download Tomcat Version 7. To do so, we will direct our web browser to the following URL:

   `http://tomcat.apache.org/download-70.cgi`

   Once there, we will find a page similar to the following screenshot:

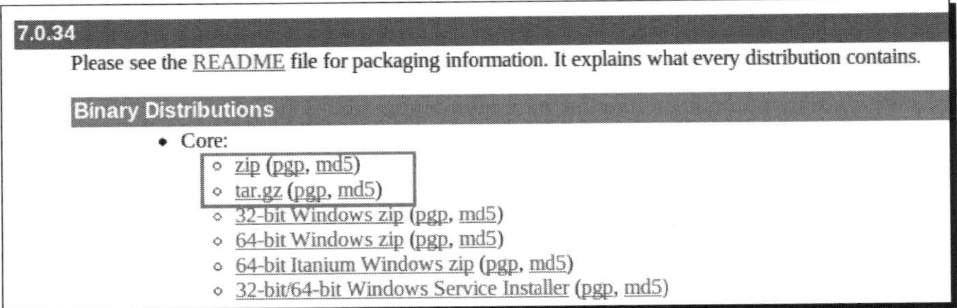

It is possible that a newer version of Tomcat will be available by the time you read this book. If that is the case, please use the **Quick Navigation** section of the web page and select the correct version. We recommend downloading Version 7.x to avoid possible inconveniences and incompatibilities with the rest of the exercises of this chapter.

2. Next, we will download the file corresponding to our operating system:
   - If on a Linux environment, we will choose `.tar.gz`
   - If on a Windows environment, we will choose `.zip`
3. We will now install Tomcat. We will choose a folder and uncompress the file we just downloaded. As a result, we will now have a folder named `apache-tomcat-7.0.34`.

   From now on, the complete filesystem path to this folder will be referred to as `[TOMCAT_HOME]`.
4. We are now ready to start Tomcat. In order to do so, we need to do the following (remember to replace `[TOMCAT_HOME]` with the full path to our uncompressed directory):
   - On a Linux environment:
   1. Open a terminal and type the following command:

      ```
      shell> cd [TOMCAT_HOME]/bin
      ```
   2. Start the service:

      ```
      shell> sh startup.sh
      ```

   In order to stop the service, we need to execute the following command:

   ```
   shell> sh shutdown.sh
   ```
   - On a Windows environment:
   1. Open a terminal and type the following command:

      ```
      shell> cd [TOMCAT_HOME]\bin
      ```
   2. Start the service:

      ```
      shell> startup.bat
      ```

In order to stop the service, we need to press *Ctrl* + *C* on the shell instance on which we started it, or execute the `shutdown.bat` file in the other terminal into the `[TOMCAT_HOME]\bin` path.

5. To test it, we will open our preferred web browser and direct it to the following URL: `http://localhost:8080`

We should be presented with a page similar to the following screenshot:

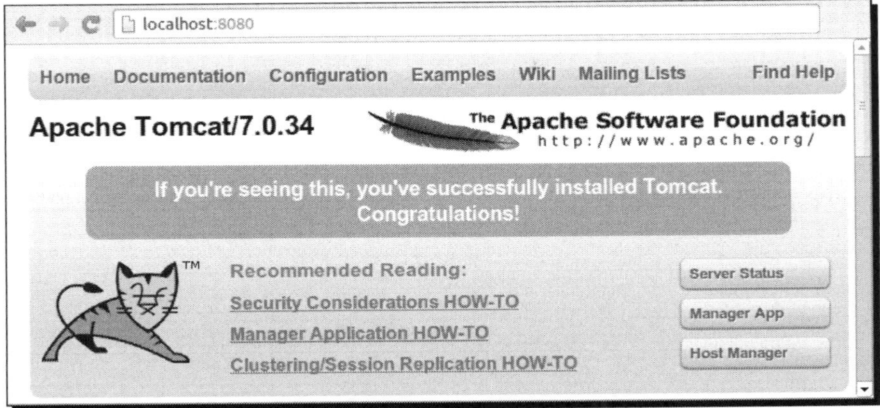

6. We can now stop the previously explained service.

> By default, Tomcat listens on port 8080; if we want to change this, we should edit the [TOMCAT_HOME]/conf/server.xml file and make the necessary changes in the <Connector port="8080" protocol="HTTP/1.1"...> tag.

What just happened?

According to our operating system, we downloaded Tomcat 7 and then uncompressed it on a folder of our choice. By means of a terminal, we started the service and then used a web browser directed to http://localhost:8080 to test it. Finally, we used the terminal again to stop the service.

Learning Eclipse and WTP

Eclipse is a FOSS, multiplatform **Integrated Development Environment** (**IDE**) that is used to develop software and is used as a base for **Rich Client Application** (**RCA**). One of the most popular examples of an RCA is the **Java Development Toolkit** (**JDT**); it extends Eclipse by adding tools that allow for the creation and management of Java projects.

There exists a pretty big number of projects based on Eclipse; among them we can find administrators and graphic managers for databases, application servers' administrators, business intelligence visualization tools, and so on.

Eclipse Web Tools Platform (**WTP**) is a project that extends Eclipse by adding tools for web development and the creation of JEE applications. It includes graphical and source code editors for many languages, wizards to aid and simplify common tasks such as the creation of a new project, and tools and libraries that provide support to deploy, execute, and test our applications.

Both Java Development Toolkit and Eclipse Web Tools Platforms can coexist on a single Eclipse paltform, as well as on many other tools, since they are added as **plugins**.

> There exists a series of Eclipse distributions providing a preinstalled set of plugins that facilitate the development of various kinds of projects. The last known version is called **Juno,** the previous one was called **Indigo**, and so on. These distributions are published once a year in the month of June.

Time for action – installing and initiating Eclipse WTP

Next, we will download and install Eclipse WTP. We will then initiate it and establish a path for the required Eclipse workspace.

1. We will direct our browser to the following URL, on which we will be able to download the Juno version of Eclipse WTP:

   `http://www.eclipse.org/downloads/`

2. Once there, we will select our operating system on the corresponding selector.
3. Finally, depending on our architecture, we will download either the 32-bit or 64-bit version as shown in the following screenshot:

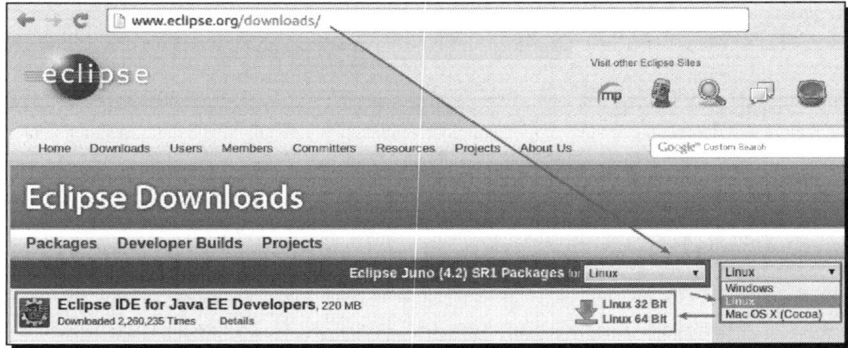

4. We will now install Eclipse, and in order to do so we will need to uncompress the file we just downloaded on a folder of our choice.

   As a result, we will obtain a new folder named `eclipse`. From now on, the full filesystem path to this folder will be referred to as `[ECLIPSE_HOME]`.

5. We are now ready to start Eclipse. To do so, we will need to follow the instructions corresponding to our operating system:

   - On a Linux environment:

   1. Open a terminal and type the following command:

      ```
      shell> cd [ECLIPSE_HOME]
      ```

   2. Start Eclipse:

      ```
      shell> ./eclipse
      ```

   - On a Windows environment:

   1. Open a terminal and type the following command:

      ```
      shell> cd [ECLIPSE_HOME]
      ```

   2. Start Eclipse:

      ```
      shell> eclipse.exe
      ```

6. Once Eclipse has started, it will present us with a dialog box where we will be asked for the path to our workspace. We will use the path proposed by default and add `-prd5_book` to the end of the string, as can be seen in the following screenshot. We will call this folder `[WORKSPACE_HOME]`:

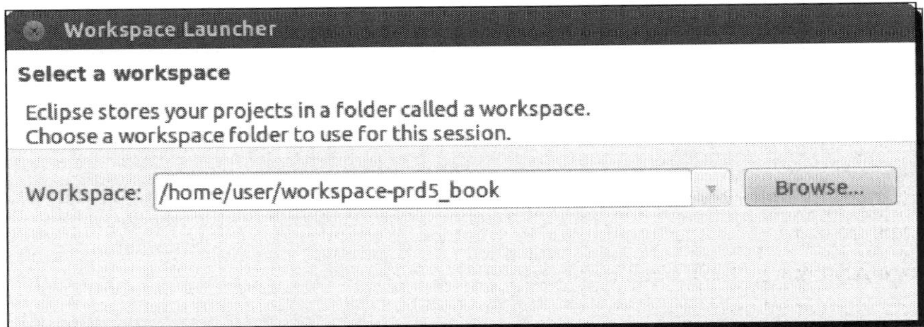

> The workspace is a directory that will contain the projects we create on Eclipse as well as the metadata that defines them. It is also possible to create links to projects on other locations.

7. We will click on the **OK** button to continue.

What just happened?

We went to Eclipse's download area and, according to our operating system and architecture, proceeded to download the Eclipse WTP Juno version. We then uncompressed this file and used a console to initiate Eclipse. Finally, we configured the path to our workspace.

Time for action – creating a new Dynamic Web project

We will create a project of the Dynamic Web type for which we will define a new runtime. We will specify the version and location of our recently installed Apache Tomcat. We will also specify the version and location of our JRE. Finally, we will configure the section dedicated to Java and the Web module.

1. We will create and configure a new project of the Dynamic Web type. To do so, once we have initiated Eclipse, we will head to the main menu and go to **File | New | Other...**.
2. A new assistant will be opened that will help us create and configure our project. On this new window, we will select the **Dynamic Web Project** item, which is found inside the **Web** category as shown in the following screenshot:

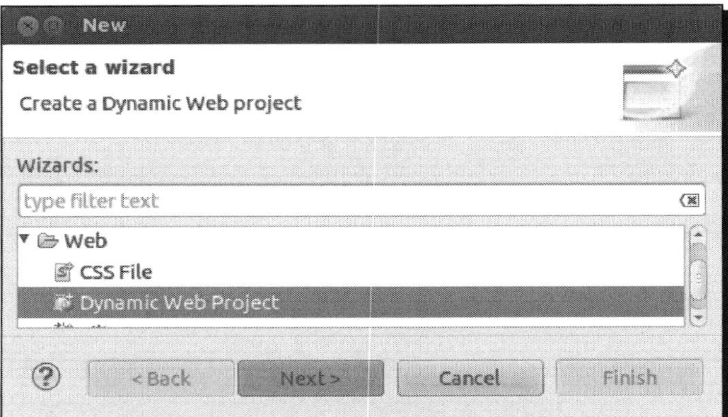

3. We will click on the **Next >** button to continue.
4. We will place the value `prd5Ch14` in the **Project Name** textbox and click on the **New Runtime** (New Runtime...) button.

5. On this new window, we will select the **Apache Tomcat v7.0** item inside the **Apache** category as shown in the following screenshot:

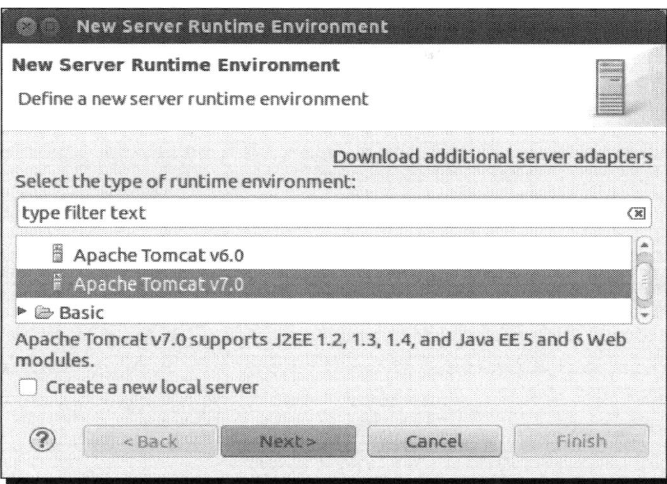

6. We will click on the **Next >** button to continue.
7. We need to inform the wizard where Apache Tomcat is installed. To do so, we will complete **Tomcat installation directory** with the full path to `[TOMCAT_HOME]`.
8. On the **JRE** selector, we need to select the JRE to be used; in our case, the right value will be `java-7-oracle`.

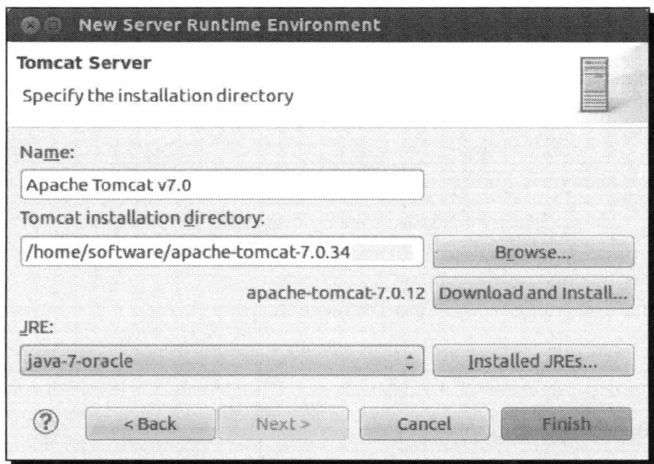

9. If when pressing the **JRE** selector we find out that `java-7-oracle` is not available, we will need to do the following:
   1. Click on the **Installed JREs...** button.
   2. Click on **Add...** to add a new JRE.
   3. Select **Standard VM** from the list of JRE types and click on the **Next >** button.
   4. On **JRE home**, place the full path to our JRE. On Linux it is usually found at `/usr/lib/jvm/java-7-oracle/jre` while on Windows the usual location is `C:\Program Files\Java\jdk1.7.0_04`. For **JRE name**, we will put `java-7-oracle`.
   5. Finally, we will click on the **Finish** button.
   6. In the main window, we must make sure that **java-7-oracle** is checked and then click on **OK**:

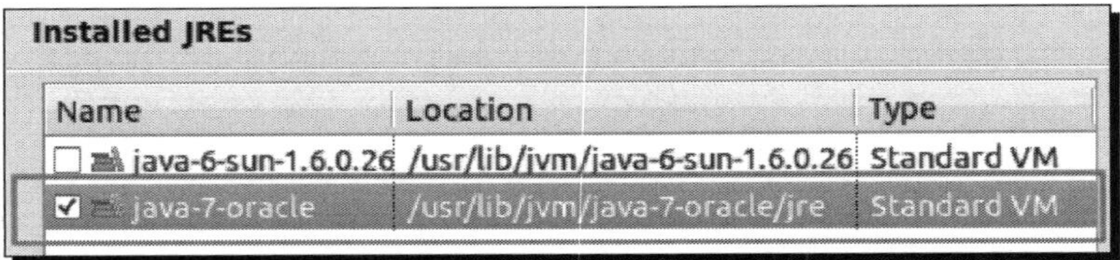

   7. To continue, we will click on the **Finish** button.

With the previous steps, we complete the configuration of our server:

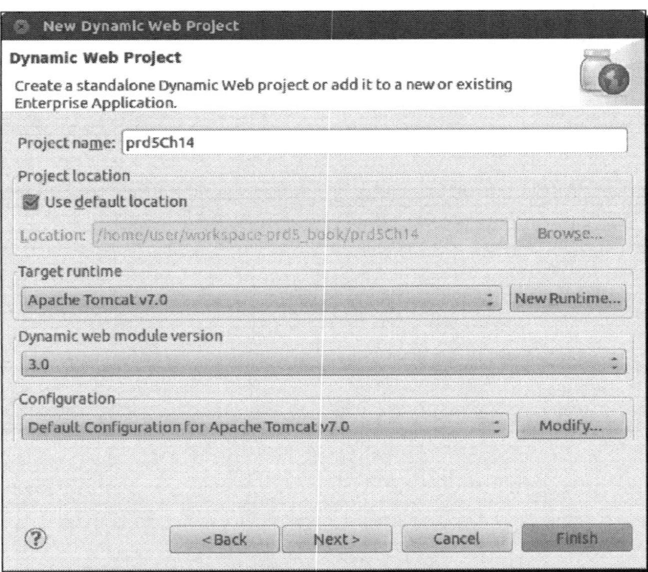

10. We will click on the **Next >** button to continue. We will now proceed with the Java configuration:

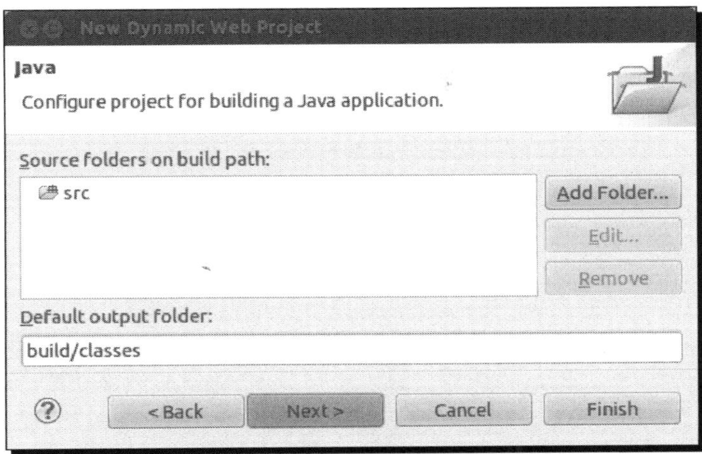

We will leave the default configuration as it is and click on the **Next >** button.

11. Next we will need to configure the web module. In **Context root**, we will place the value `prdweb` and check the **Generate web.xml deployment descriptor** option as shown in the following screenshot:

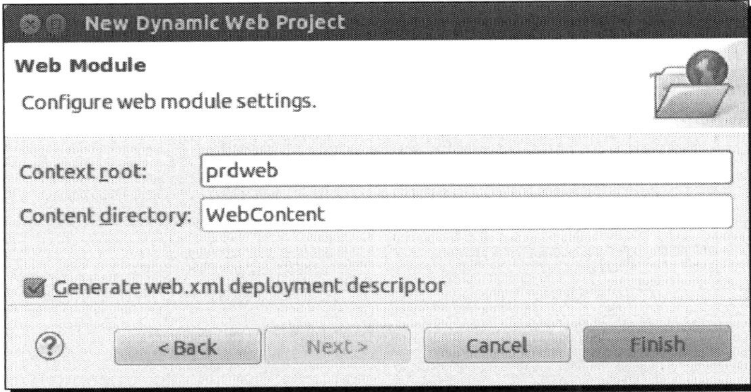

Context root will be the name of the web application. Later on we will see that to access it, we will need to use this name in addition to the URL previously used to test Tomcat, that is, `http://localhost:8080/`**`prdweb`**.

12. We will finally click on the **Finish** button to conclude the configuration of our Dynamic Web type project.

What just happened?

We created a Dynamic Web type project, specified its name, and created a new runtime. We chose `Apache Tomcat v7.0` and indicated its location. As the JRE version to be used, we selected `java-7-oracle`. For the Java configuration, we used the default values, and when it was time to configure the web module, we modified its context root with the value `prdweb`.

Configuring Eclipse Perspectives

Once we have completed the wizard, we will obtain a base environment for a Java website that is configured and working. The environment is configured by default on the **Java EE** Perspective:

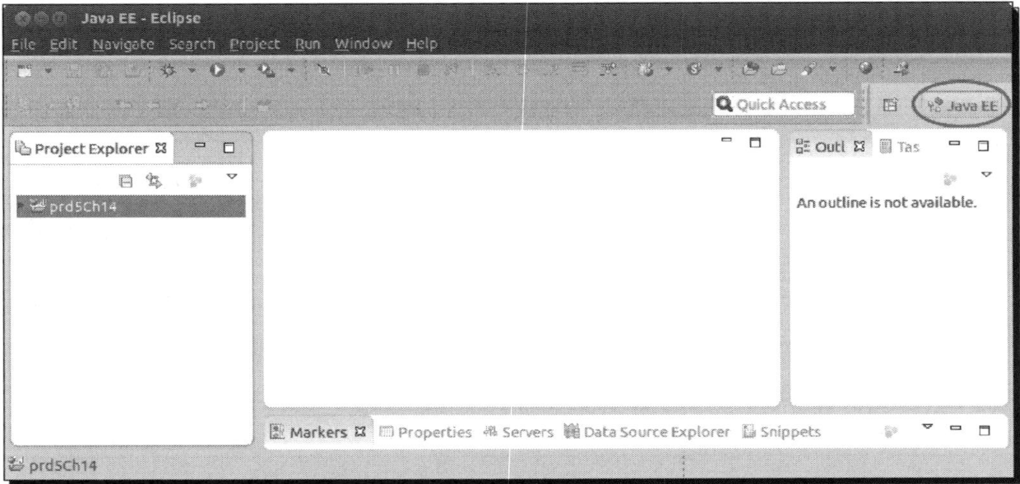

One of the basic concepts in Eclipse usage is that of **Perspectives**. A Perspective is a combination of **Views** and **Editors** thought out to perform a concrete task in an easy and intuitive way.

- **Editor**: This area allows for the creation and modification of programs or other components of the project. Editors are not only meant for source code; there are graphical editors available as well.
- **View**: This area allows us to easily visualize various items, such as the console output, navigable class outline, and outline of a project for easy schema administration. To enable a View, we should use **Window | Show View**.

In order to perform the following practice, we will be using the **Web Perspective**. We should head to the top menu and go to **Window** | **Open Perspective** | **Other...**, then search the list for the **Web** option and finally click on **OK**.

We should now be able to see that the **Web** Perspective is currently available and enabled on the Eclipse UI as shown in the following screenshot:

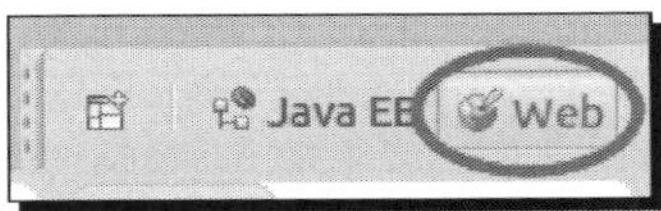

It can be observed that as we go along adding Perspectives, these will be placed in the top-right area of the Eclipse UI so that we can easily switch between them using a single click.

Infrastructure configurations

Now we will need to configure all the necessary settings to operate the application.

Time for action – creating a Tomcat instance

Next, we will create and configure an instance of Apache Tomcat within our project. We will modify the initial timeout for our server and initiate it. We will finally test our website on a web browser.

1. Our website is currently configured and functional, but in order to test it we will need to create an instance of Apache Tomcat and publish the site on the said instance. We will select the **Servers** View, which is placed in the bottom part of the **Web** Perspective, and select the **new server wizard...** option as shown in the following screenshot:

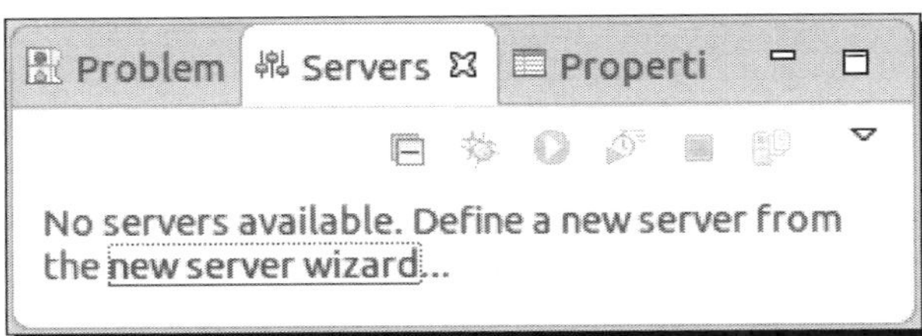

2. On the first screen of the wizard, we will make sure that **Tomcat v7.0 Server** is selected from the **Select the server type** list and leave the rest of the values unchanged:

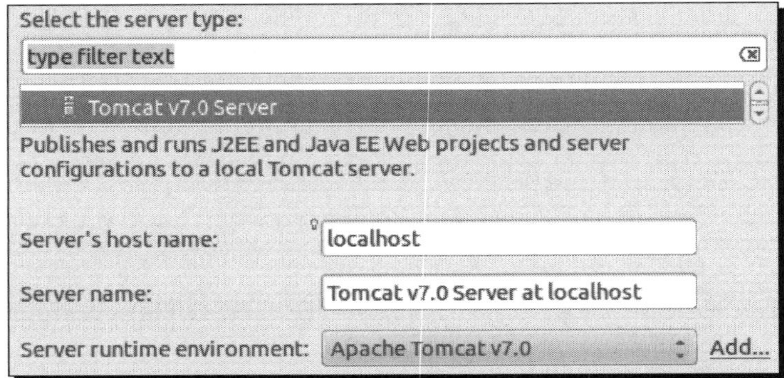

Click on the **Next >** button to continue.

3. On the next window, we will select our project from the the **Available** list (left-hand side) and add it to the **Configured** list (right-hand side) by clicking on the **Add >** button:

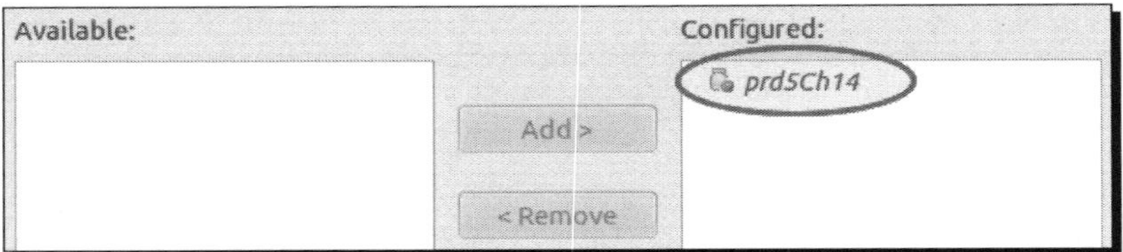

Click on the **Finish** button to continue.

4. If we look at the **Servers** View, we will notice that an item has been added reflecting the configuration we just performed:

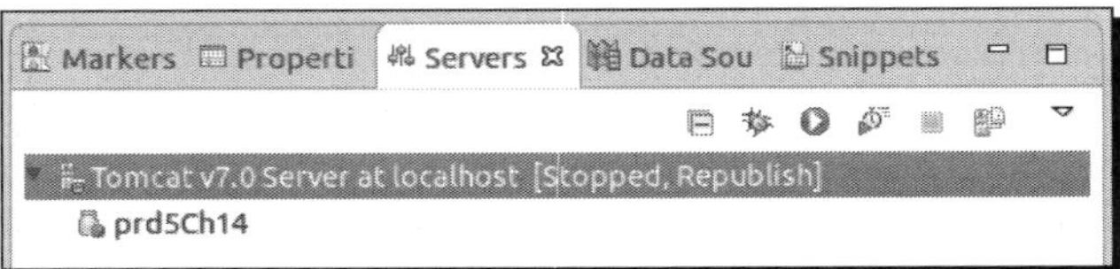

5. We will now double-click on the server (**Tomcat v7.0 Server at localhost**) to edit its initial timeout value.
6. The editor will now show us the available configuration options for this server. We will click on the **Timeouts** section and configure a higher **Start** value, for example, `300`:

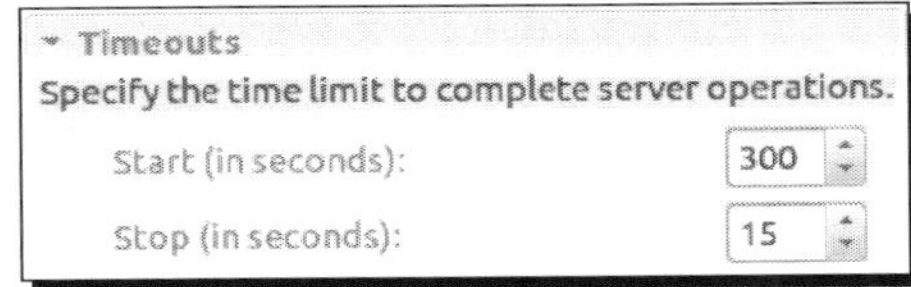

We need to enlarge the start time of our server because our application will perform the initialization of the PRD API; given that this takes a little time, the default values will probably not be enough.

7. We will save our changes to continue.
8. We should now select our server one more time and initiate it by clicking on the button.

If we wish to stop the server, we should simply select it and then click on the button.

9. We are now ready to test our site. To do so, we need to open our favorite web browser and direct it to the following URL:

```
http://localhost:8080/prdweb
```

We will receive an **HTTP 404** error message since, momentarily, there is no resource to be served.

What just happened?

We created a new Apache Tomcat instance, selected **Apache Tomcat v7.0**, and added our site to the list of resources for this server. We then modified the initial timeout value for the server and initiated the instance. Finally, we tested our website on a web browser using the `http://localhost:8080/prdweb` URL.

Time for action – setting a JNDI/JDBC connection pool

We will now create a JDBC connection pool, which will be available via JNDI. Within our project, we will create an XML file and edit it to contain information about the previously mentioned pool. Finally, we will copy MySQL's JDBC driver into our project.

1. We will head to the **Project Explorer** panel, which is located on the left of the UI, and navigate through **prd5ch14** | **WebContent** | **META-INF**; once there, we will go to **New** | **Other...** and lastly select **XML** | **XML File**. We will then click on **Next >**, save the file with the name `context.xml`, and click on **Finish** to continue.
2. Once the XML file is created, we will automatically be presented with an XML editor in the central part of the UI. We will click on the **Source** tab to edit our code as shown in the following screenshot:

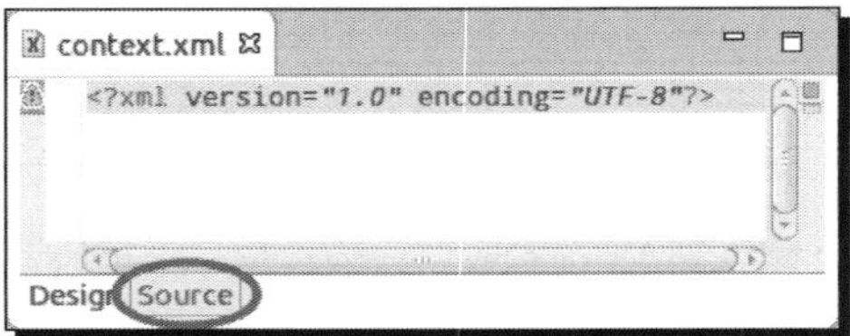

3. We will now enter the following XML code into our file:

```
<?xml version="1.0" encoding="UTF-8"?>
<Context>
  <Resource auth="Container" description="Sakila DB Connection"
    name="jdbc/sakila" type="javax.sql.DataSource"
    password="root" driverClassName="com.mysql.jdbc.Driver"
    maxIdle="2" maxWait="5000" validationQuery="select 1"
    username="root"
    url="jdbc:mysql://localhost:3306/sakila" maxActive="4" />
  <WatchedResource>WEB-INF/web.xml</WatchedResource>
  <WatchedResource>META-INF/context.xml</WatchedResource>
</Context>
```

4. Then, we will save our changes by either clicking on the save (💾) button or pressing *Ctrl* + *S*.

   The contents of this file define a resource of the type `javax.sql.DataSource`, which is a Java object implementing the JDBC connection pool. This resource can be accessed by its name `jdbc/sakila` by means of **Java Naming and Directory Interface** (**JNDI**) that provides an abstraction level; this allows us to modify connection parameters without having to modify the source code and recompile it. It is mandatory to complete the username and password fields with values that are appropriate for the MySQL instance being used.

To obtain further information on JNDI, you can visit the Wikipedia page at `http://en.wikipedia.org/wiki/Java_Naming_and_Directory_Interface`.

5. We should now copy MySQL's JDBC driver into our project. We will search for the file named `mysql-connector-java-x.x.xx-bin.jar`, which should be placed at `[PRD_HOME]/lib/jdbc`, and copy it (*Ctrl* + *C*). Then in Eclipse, we will select the node named **prd5ch14** by going to **WebContent** | **WEB-INF** | **lib** and press *Ctrl* + *V* to paste it there.

   At this stage, the contents of the nodes **META-INF** and **WEB-INF/lib** should look similar to the following screenshot:

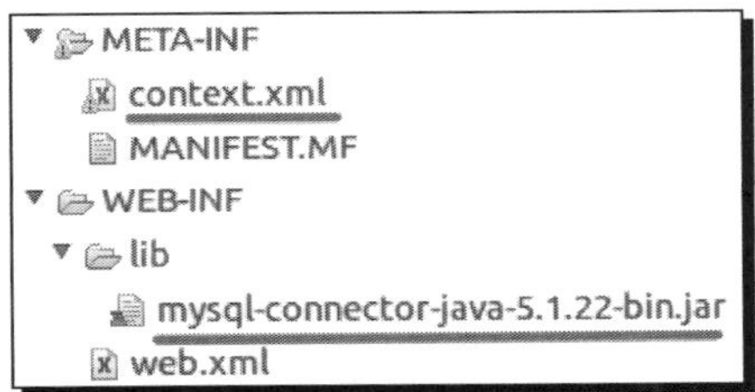

It is recommended to use connection pools on environments in which a medium or high concurrency is expected. Since they implement the efficient management of database connections, they are highly configurable and reduce the overhead produced every time a new connection is required.

What just happened?

We created the `context.xml` file within the **META-INF** node and edited it to contain the configuration for our MySQL connection pool, which is accessible via JNDI. We then copied MySQL's JDBC driver (`mysql-connector-java-x.x.xx-bin.jar`) into the **WEB-INF/lib** node.

Time for action – configuration of libraries and the PRD report

We are going to copy PRD libraries into our project. We will then create a new folder within our project and copy a PRD report inside it. Finally, we will modify the connection type of this report so that it utilizes JNDI.

1. We will copy the libraries that compose PRD's **Application Programming Interface** (**API**) into our project.
2. Head to the `lib` folder in `PRD_HOME]`, select every file in there, and copy it with *Ctrl* + *C*; then in Eclipse, select the node named **prd5ch14** by going to **WebContent** | **WEB-INF** | **lib** and paste the copied files in there by pressing *Ctrl* + *V*.

Many of the libraries we just copied are not really necessary for the execution of this chapter's PRD report, but we decided not to add complexity to this stage by choosing them one by one; that is why we are instructing you to copy all of them indiscriminately.

3. From the bulk of libraries we just copied into our project, select the one named `jsp-api-2.0.jar` and delete it.
4. We need to include into our project the report necessary to perform this chapter's practice example. To do so, we will select the node named **WEB-INF**, right-click on it, and choose **New** | **Folder**. We will call this new folder `report`.
5. We will now head to the physical location on which we have saved all our PRD reports, select the report named `11_Adding_Charts.prpt`, and copy it (*Ctrl* + *C*). In Eclipse, we will select the node named **report** by going to **WEB-INF** and paste the copied report in there (*Ctrl* + *V*):

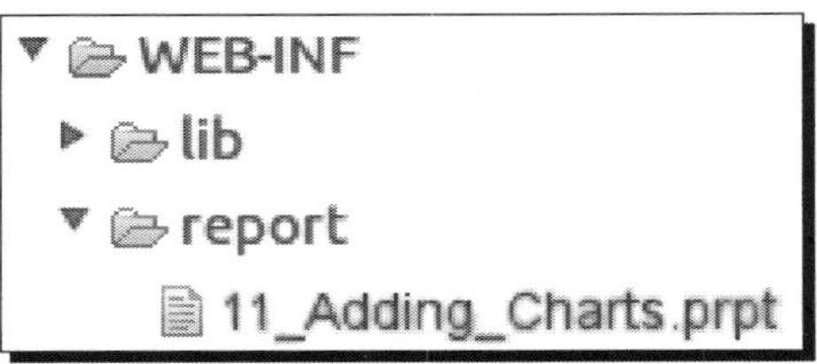

6. The report requires a modification before we can make use of it. We need to change the connection type of its data set, that is, the data set is currently of the type Native (JDBC) and we need it to be of the type JNDI so that we can use the connection pool we previously defined. To do so, we will execute PRD and open the report we just copied in the previous step; it should be located in `[WORKSPACE_HOME]/prd5Ch14/WebContent/WEB-INF/report/11_Adding_Charts.prpt`.

7. At this stage, we need to take the **Ratings** data set and change its connection type to JNDI. We can do it as follows:

    1. Once the report is opened in PRD, we will head to the **Data** tab, right-click on the **Ratings** parent node that is on **JDBC: sakila db**, and select the option **Edit Datasource...** as shown in the following screenshot:

    2. On the **Connections** panel, we will click on the button and configure the new connection as follows:

    - **Connection Name:** = `sakila jndi`
    - **Access:** = `JNDI`
    - **JNDI Name:** = `sakila`

The dialog will look like the following screenshot:

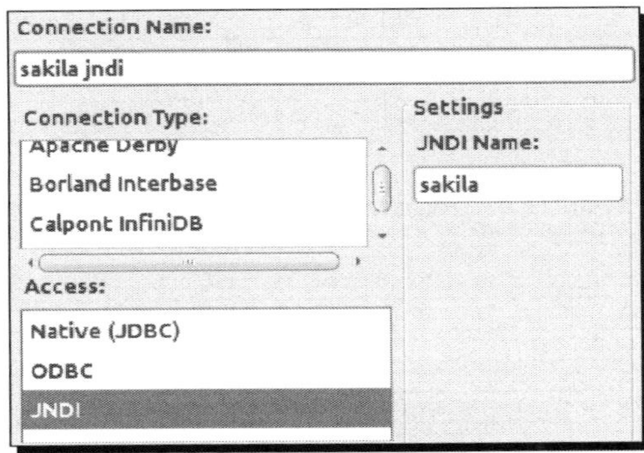

In **JNDI Name** we will set the value **sakila**, but you may have noticed that in the file `context.xml` we used the value name `jdbc/sakila`. This is because the API will take care of completing the name for us by following the standard.

We will click on **OK** to save the new connection.

1. We will now assign this new connection to the ratings query. We will head to the **Connections** panel and select the item named **sakila jndi**, then we will select the **Ratings** item within the **Available Queries** panel and click on **OK**.

8. At this stage, we should repeat steps 1 and 3 of step 5 for the **ListYears** and **ListMonths** data sets.

9. Once the **Ratings**, **ListYears**, and **ListMonths** data sets are correctly configured, we can save the report.

> If we want to use this report from the publisher through JNDI, we need to edit the file `default.properties` present in the location `[User_home]/.pentaho/single-jndi` and add the following configuration at the end:
>
> ```
> sakila/type=javax.sql.DataSource
> sakila/driver=com.mysql.jdbc.Drivers
> sakila/user=root
> sakila/password=root
> sakila/url=jdbc:mysql://localhost:3306/sakila
> ```
>
> For more information visit `http://infocenter.pentaho.com/help/index.jsp?topic=%2Freport_designer_user_guide%2Ftask_jndi_data_source.html`.

What just happened?

We copied the PRD libraries placed in `[PRD_HOME]/lib` and pasted them into our project within the **lib** node located in **WEB-INF**. We also created a folder within the **WEB-INF** node, called it `report`, and pasted inside it the report named `11_Adding_Charts.prpt`. By means of PRD, we opened the previously mentioned report and edited its data sets so that they are of the type JNDI.

Code components

Now we will create the code components that make up our application.

Time for action – creating a context Listener

We will now create and configure a Listener and a Servlet respectively inside our project. Finally, we will initiate our server and test the service by executing our report inside a web browser.

1. To be able to function efficiently, PRD's API requires a process of initialization. This process will load libraries and perform tasks related to the setup of the execution environment needed to process reports rapidly. We can perform this initialization using a certain type of web components, called Listeners.

Listeners are used to process events that are divided into categories and are generated by the server at various levels. In our case, we are interested in listening to events at a container level, particularly at the time at which the container is initiated. This is done so that the users do not have to pay the price of initializing components, thus improving the users' experience in a noticeable way.

2. Next, we will create a Listener inside our project.

   We will head to the **Project Explorer** panel, select the node named **prd5Ch14**, right-click on it, and then go to **New | Other...**. In the following window, inside the **Web** category we will select the **Listener** item and then click on **Next >** so that we are presented with the corresponding wizard.

3. On the first screen of the wizard, we will complete the fields with the following data:
   - **Java package** = `com.prd.web.listeners`
   - **Class name** = `InitListener`
4. We will click on the **Next >** button to continue.
5. On the following screen, we need to define the events that our component will be listening to. Inside the Servlet context event section, we will check the option **Lifecycle**.
6. We will now click on the **Finish** button to continue.
7. Once the component is created, we will automatically be presented with the Java editor. If we take a look at the **Project Explorer** panel, within the **prd5Ch14** node present in the location **Java Resources | src** we will now find our newly created Listener as shown in the following screenshot:

8. We should now delete all the code within `InitListener.java` and replace it with the following code:

```
package com.prd.web.listeners;
import javax.servlet.ServletContextEvent;
import javax.servlet.ServletContextListener;
import javax.servlet.annotation.WebListener;
import org.pentaho.reporting.engine.classic.core.
ClassicEngineBoot;

@WebListener
```

```
public class InitListener implements ServletContextListener {

    public void contextInitialized(ServletContextEvent event) {
      ClassicEngineBoot.getInstance().start();
    }

    public void contextDestroyed(ServletContextEvent event) {
    }
}
```

> To indicate that this is a Listener, we are making use of the @ `WebListener` annotation, which is found right before the definition of the class. The interfaces implemented by `ServletContextListener` define what types of events are being listened to. In our case, we are interested in executing the PRD engine initialization code every time the container is started; that is why we included the line `ClassicEngineBoot.getInstance().start();` within the `contextInitialized()` method. We should now save the changes made to this file.

9. Next we will be creating a Servlet. Servlets are the most appropriate components to handle petitions, perform processing, and execute routings, but are not well suited to execute presentation logic. As we will discuss later in this chapter, presentation logic will be left to PRD's API and a JSP.

10. We will head to the **Project Explorer** panel, select the **prd5Ch14** node, right-click on it, and then go to **New** | **Other...**. In the following window, inside the **Web** category we will select the Servlet item and click on **Next >** to be presented with the corresponding wizard.

11. On the first screen in the wizard, we will complete the fields with the following data:

    - **Java package** = `com.prd.web.actions`
    - **Class name** = `RunReport`

    We will click on the **Next >** button to continue.

12. In the following part of the wizard, we will define **URL Mapping**; this feature allows us to define which URL the client should request to have the Servlet execute its code.

    In the **URL Mapping** section, we will select the **/RunReport** item, click on the **Edit...** button, place the name `/runReport`, and then click on **OK**.

As can be seen, all we had to do was change the first letter from upper to lowercase; this is done to honor good programming practices.

We will now click on the **Finish** button to continue.

13. Once the Servlet is created, we will automatically be presented with the Java editor. If we take a look at the **Project Explorer** panel, within the node named **prd5Ch14** located in **Java Resources | src** we can now find our newly created Servlet as shown in the following screenshot:

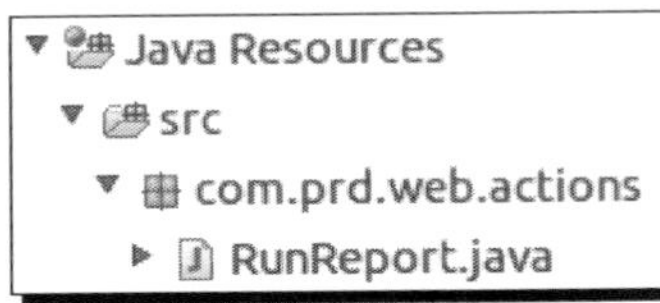

14. We will now delete all the code within `RunReport.java` and copy the following code. We should pay special attention to the comments (pieces of text within `/*` and `*/`) placed throughout the code since they will help us understand it:

```
/* Header: contains the package and necessary imports. */
package com.prd.web.actions;

import java.io.File;
import java.io.IOException;
import java.net.URL;
import javax.servlet.RequestDispatcher;
import javax.servlet.ServletException;
import javax.servlet.annotation.WebServlet;
import javax.servlet.http.HttpServlet;
import javax.servlet.http.HttpServletRequest;
import javax.servlet.http.HttpServletResponse;
import org.pentaho.reporting.engine.classic.core.MasterReport;
import org.pentaho.reporting.engine.classic.core.
ReportProcessingException;
import org.pentaho.reporting.engine.classic.core.modules.output.
pageable.pdf.PdfReportUtil;
import org.pentaho.reporting.engine.classic.core.modules.output.
table.base.StreamReportProcessor;
import org.pentaho.reporting.engine.classic.core.modules.output.
table.html.AllItemsHtmlPrinter;
import org.pentaho.reporting.engine.classic.core.modules.output.
table.html.FileSystemURLRewriter;
import org.pentaho.reporting.engine.classic.core.modules.output.
table.html.HtmlPrinter;
```

```
import org.pentaho.reporting.engine.classic.core.modules.output.
table.html.StreamHtmlOutputProcessor;
import org.pentaho.reporting.libraries.repository.
ContentIOException;
import org.pentaho.reporting.libraries.repository.ContentLocation;
import org.pentaho.reporting.libraries.repository.
DefaultNameGenerator;
import org.pentaho.reporting.libraries.repository.file.
FileRepository;
import org.pentaho.reporting.libraries.resourceloader.Resource;
import org.pentaho.reporting.libraries.resourceloader.
ResourceException;
import org.pentaho.reporting.libraries.resourceloader.
ResourceManager;

/* The next line defines that this class is a Servlet, as well as
the URL Mapping.  */
@WebServlet("/runReport")
public class RunReport extends HttpServlet {

  private static final long serialVersionUID = 1L;

  /* Method doGet(): this determines that this class will only
  respond to requests of the type HTTP GET. */
  protected void doGet(HttpServletRequest request,
                  HttpServletResponse response) throws
                  ServletException, IOException {

   /* The following three lines take the parameters sent by the
   client and assign them to variables. In our case, we need
   "year" and "month" so that we can pass them to the PRD engine,
   since in our report we have defined the parameters "SelectYear"
   and "SelectMonth" respectively. The parameter "outputType" will
   help us to determine which type of output was required by
   the user.*/
    Integer year =
    Integer.parseInt(request.getParameter("year"));
    Integer month =
    Integer.parseInt(request.getParameter("month"));
    String outputType = request.getParameter("outputType");

    String errorMsg = "";
    try {
/* The call to doReport() is the one that will finally process
the report.*/
```

```
        doReport(year, month, outputType, response);
      } catch (Exception e) {
        e.printStackTrace();
        errorMsg = "ERROR: " + e.getMessage();
      }
/* The following if checks if an error has occurred, in which
case creates a string with the error message and stores it in an
attribute of the "request" object, and then performs a redirect to
the index. */
      if (errorMsg.length() > 0) {
        request.setAttribute("errorMsg", errorMsg);
        RequestDispatcher dispatcher = getServletContext()
          .getRequestDispatcher("/index.jsp");
        dispatcher.forward(request, response);
      }
  }

  /* Method doReport(): */
  private void doReport(Integer year, Integer month, String
  type,
      HttpServletResponse response) throws
      ReportProcessingException,
      IOException, ResourceException, ContentIOException {

    /* -> Global Setup */
    ResourceManager manager = new ResourceManager();
    manager.registerDefaults();
    URL urlToReport = new URL("file:"
        + getServletContext().getRealPath(
            "WEB-INF/report/11_Adding_Charts.prpt"));
    Resource res = manager.createDirectly(urlToReport,
    MasterReport.class);
    MasterReport report = (MasterReport) res.getResource();

    report.getParameterValues().put("SelectYear", year);
    report.getParameterValues().put("SelectMonth", month);
    response.setHeader("Content-disposition", "filename=out." +
    type);

     /* -> Output Type: pdf & html */
    if (type.equalsIgnoreCase("pdf")) {
      response.setContentType("application/pdf");
      PdfReportUtil.createPDF(report,
      response.getOutputStream());
  }
```

```
        if (type.equalsIgnoreCase("html")) {
          response.setContentType("text/html");
          String fileName = "_out" + System.currentTimeMillis() +
          "." + type;
          File folderOut = new
          File(getServletContext().getRealPath(
              "/out/" + System.currentTimeMillis()));

          if (!folderOut.exists()) {
            folderOut.mkdirs();
            final FileRepository targetRepository = new
            FileRepository(
                folderOut);
            final ContentLocation targetRoot =
            targetRepository.getRoot();
            final HtmlPrinter printer = new AllItemsHtmlPrinter(
                report.getResourceManager());
            printer.setContentWriter(targetRoot, new
            DefaultNameGenerator(
                targetRoot, fileName));
            printer.setDataWriter(targetRoot, new
            DefaultNameGenerator(
                targetRoot, "content"));
            printer.setUrlRewriter(new FileSystemURLRewriter());
            final StreamHtmlOutputProcessor outputProcessor = new
            StreamHtmlOutputProcessor(
                report.getConfiguration());
            outputProcessor.setPrinter(printer);
            final StreamReportProcessor reportProcessor = new
            StreamReportProcessor(
                report, outputProcessor);
            reportProcessor.processReport();
            reportProcessor.close();

            String route = "out/" + folderOut.getName() + "/" +
            fileName;
            response.sendRedirect(route);
          }
        }
      }
    }
```

We will now save the changes to this file.

15. So far we have created the components that are to be executed at the server side and that comprise the service itself. Next, we will test the service by executing our report in a web browser:

    1. We will head to the **Server** tab (bottom part of the UI), select our **Tomcat v7.0 Server at localhost** server, and start (or restart) it using the button.
    2. Once the Server is started, we will open a web browser and direct it to the following URL:
    3. `http://localhost:8080/prdweb/runReport?year=2005&month=6&outputType=html`

    The parameters we have sent are as follows:

    - `year=2005`
    - `month=6`
    - `outputType=html`

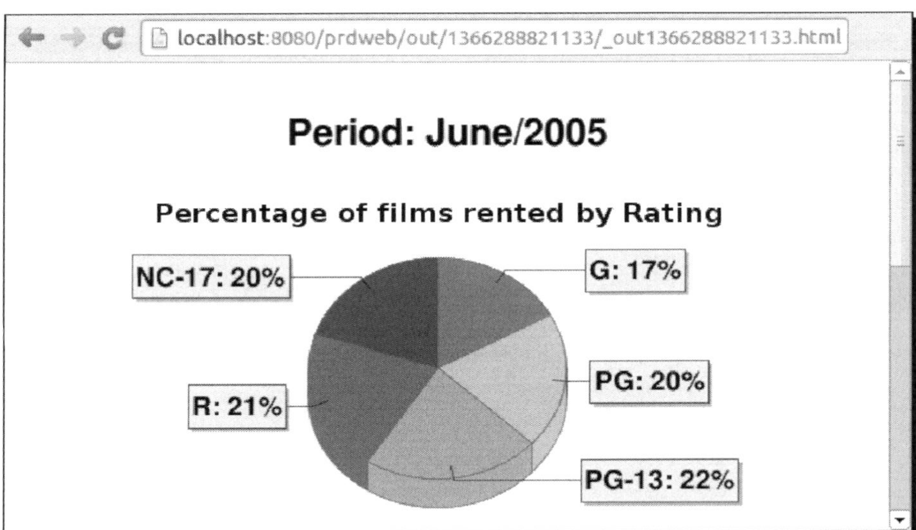

We can keep testing by changing the values of the Parameters in the URL; for example, it would be interesting to see what the output of the report is if we placed `outputType=pdf` in the URL.

What just happened?

We created a Listener inside our project so that it performs the PRD's API initialization; we configured it and modified the code within the file named `InitListener.java`. We also created a Servlet inside our project so that it manages requests, processing, and routings; we configured it and modified the code within the file named `RunReport.java`. Finally, we started our server (**Apache v7.0 Server at localhost**) and tested the service by opening the following URL inside a web browser: `http://localhost:8080/prdweb/runReport?year=2005&month=6&outputType=html`.

Time for action – creating a web client

We will create a web client using a JSP in order to give the user a friendly interface that allows for the selection of Parameters in our report. We will configure this JSP so that it contains the necessary code to achieve our goal. We will then open a web browser to see what the final presentation of our application looks like.

1. To finish the application, we will create a web client that will allow the final user to interact with the service we created in a friendly and visual way. Our client will be implemented using a JSP, given that this is the component that is better suited to create user views.
2. We will now create a JSP. We will then head to the **Project Explorer** panel and select the node named **prd5Ch14**; then we will go to **WebContent**, right-click on it, and then go to **New | Other...**.
3. In the following window, we will select the item labeled **JSP File**, which is found in the **Web** category, and click on **Next >**.
4. We will configure its **File Name** with the value `index.jsp` and click on **Finish**.
5. Once the JSP is created, we will automatically be presented with the JSP editor. We will delete the current code and replace it with the one we will present shortly. We should pay special attention to the comments (pieces of text between `<!--` and `-->`) since they will help us understand the code within our JSP.

   The logic, that is, the thing that will provide our web page with dynamism, is written using JavaScript (JS), the ultimate programming language for the manipulation of web interfaces. JavaScript allows us to access and modify the **Document Object Model** (**DOM**), which is an object representation of the page being shown in the browser.

We can visit Wikipedia to obtain further information about JS and DOM:

- JavaScript: `http://en.wikipedia.org/wiki/JavaScript`
- DOM: `http://en.wikipedia.org/wiki/Document_Object_Model`

We will paste the following code inside the JSP editor:

```
<!DOCTYPE html>
<html>
<head>
<meta charset="UTF-8">
<title>PRD 5 Book - Chapter 14</title>
<!-- The config() function is the one which will contain all of
the logic. It is executed when the "body" element is done loading,
"<body onload="config()">", in this way we will have access to
every element in the DOM. -->
<script type="text/javascript">
  function config() {
    var errMsg = document.getElementById("errorMsg");
    if ("${errorMsg}".length == 0)
      errMsg.setAttribute('class', 'hide');

    var button = document.getElementById("btnRunReport");
    button.addEventListener("click", function(event) {

      var year = document.getElementById("year").value;
      var cboMonth = document.getElementById("month");
      var month = cboMonth.options[cboMonth.selectedIndex].id;

      var cboOType = document.getElementById("outputType");
      var outputType = cboOType.options[cboOType.selectedIndex].id;

      window.location = "runReport?year=" + year +
      "&month=" + month
          + "&outputType=" + outputType;

      event.preventDefault();
    }, true);
      }
</script>
<!-- Next on is the code referring to the style section. -->
<style type="text/css">
.common {
  border-radius: 3px;
  -moz-border-radius: 3px; /* Firefox */
  -webkit-border-radius: 3px; /* Safari y Chrome */
  border: 1px solid #333;
  width: 250px;
  padding: 10px;
```

```
    text-align: center;
  }

  .form {
    background: #eee;
    height: 160px;
  }

  .errorMsg {
    background: red;
    color: white;;
  }

  .hide {
    display: none;
  }
  </style>
  </head>
  <body onload="config()">
    <h2>PRD 5 Book - Chapter 14</h2>
    <h3>Run report using API</h3>
    <div class="common form">
      <b>Report Filter Parameter</b>
      <hr />
      <!-- The "id" of every Selector and that of the button, will
      be used to obtain the values of said elements as well as to
      assign event listeners using Javascript. -->
      <!-- year Selector -->
      <label for="year">Year: </label> <input type="number"
min="2005"
        max="2006" step="1" value="2005" autofocus
placeholder="year"
        id="year" maxlength="4" size="6"> <br />
      <!-- month Selector -->
      <label for="month">Month: </label> <select id="month">
        <option id="1">January</option>
        <option id="2">February</option>
        <option id="3">March</option>
        <option id="4">April</option>
        <option id="5">May</option>
        <option id="6" selected>June</option>
        <option id="7">July</option>
        <option id="8">August</option>
        <option id="9">September</option>
        <option id="10">October</option>
```

```
        <option id="11">November</option>
        <option id="12">December</option>
      </select> <br /> <br />
      <!-- outputType Selector -->
      <label for="outputType">Output Type: </label> <select
      id="outputType">
         <option id="html" selected>HTML</option>
         <option id="pdf">PDF</option>
      </select> <br />
      <!-- report execution Button -->
      <button id="btnRunReport">Run Report</button>
    </div>
    <br />
    <div id="errorMsg" class="common errorMsg">${errorMsg}</div>
</body>
</html>
```

Then we will save the changes.

6. We will now open a web browser and direct it to the URL `http://localhost:8080/prdweb` to see what our little UI, created via a JSP, looks like.

   The page will look like the following screenshot:

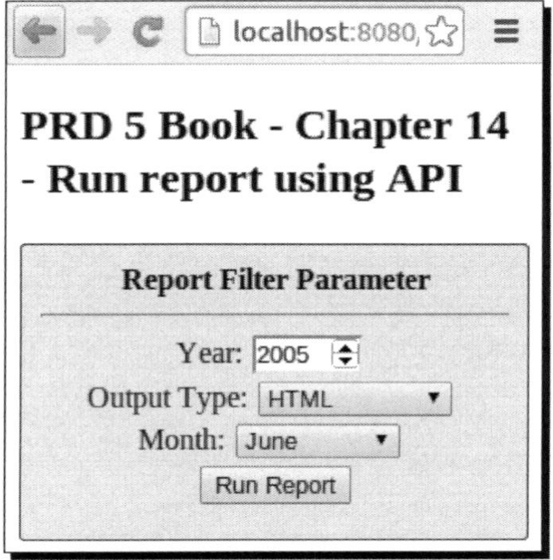

What just happened?

We created a web client so that the user has a friendly interface at his/her disposal when its time to select report Parameters. To do so, we created a JSP, gave it the name of `index.jsp`, and configured its code. Later on through the URL `http://localhost:8080/prdweb`, we accessed our application and were able to utilize the configured UI.

Time for action – creating a standalone application

We are going to package our project and then close Eclipse. We will manually configure the configuration files of Apache Tomcat to create a user who has access to the Manager App and increase the default size of the deployable applications. We will initiate Apache Tomcat and, through a web browser, start the Manager App. Within the Manager App, we will select the project we packaged earlier and deploy it so that we can execute our app in a standalone way. The steps to do this are as follows:

1. We will create a package for the distribution of our application. We will head to the **Project Explorer** panel, select the node named **prd5Ch14**, right-click on it, and go to **Export** | **WAR File**. We will be presented with a window on which we will configure the following:
    - For **Web project**, we will select our project (**prd5Ch14**).
    - For **Destination**, we will select a path, for example, `/home/user/prd5Ch14.war`.
    - Regarding **Target runtime**, we will check the option **Optimize for a specific server runtime** and select **Apache Tomcat v7.0**.
    - We will click on **Finish** to continue.

Web Application Archive (**WAR**) is a file format that contains every component of a web application (Servlets, JSPs, HTML files, and so on).

2. We are now done working with the IDE, so we will close Eclipse.
3. Before deploying our application, we need to make a few modifications to Tomcat's Manager App. The Manager App will allow us to deploy and administer our web applications.

    We will now create a user who can access the Manager App. To do so, we will edit the file `[TOMCAT_HOME]/conf/tomcat-users.xml`, delete its current contents, and copy the following code:

```
<?xml version='1.0' encoding='utf-8'?>
<tomcat-users>
  <role rolename="tomcat"/>
  <role rolename="manager-gui"/>
  <user username="tomcat" password="password"
  roles="tomcat,manager-gui"/>
</tomcat-users>
```

Here we are defining a user with a `username` called `tomcat` and a `password` with the value `password`, as well as giving him/her the roles `tomcat` and `manager-gui`; this last role is the one needed to access the Manager App.

We will save the changes to continue.

4. We will now increase the default size allowed for applications that can be deployed through the Manager App. We will open the file `web.xml` by going to `[TOMCAT_HOME]/webapps/manager/WEB-INF`, search for the section under the tag `<multipart-config>`, and edit it in the following way:

   ```
   <multipart-config>
     <!-- 150MB max -->
     <max-file-size>157286400</max-file-size>
     <max-request-size>157286400</max-request-size>
     <file-size-threshold>0</file-size-threshold>
   </multipart-config>
   ```

   By doing so, we will have established a maximum size of 150 MB (157,286,400 bytes). We will save the changes to continue.

5. We are now ready to start Apache Tomcat as explained in the beginning of this chapter.

   - On a Linux environment:

   1. Open a terminal and type:

      ```
      shell> cd [TOMCAT_HOME]/bin
      ```

   2. Start the service:

      ```
      shell> sh startup.sh
      ```

   - On a Windows environment:

   1. Open a terminal and type:

      ```
      shell> cd [TOMCAT_HOME]\bin
      ```

   2. Start the service:

      ```
      shell> startup.bat
      ```

6. Having initiated Apache Tomcat, we will direct our favorite browser to the URL `http://localhost:8080` and select the option **Manager App** as shown in the following screenshot:

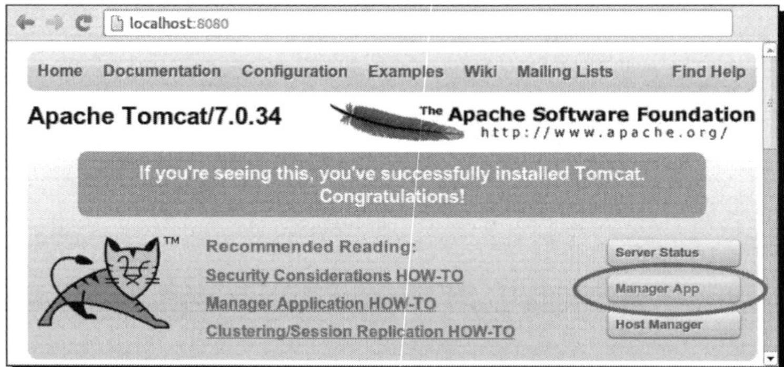

We will then log in using the previously defined user (username: `tomcat` and password: `password`).

7. We will be presented with a new web page on which we will scroll down and search for the section **Deploy**. Once there, we will use the option **Choose File** to search for the file `prd5Ch14.war` (which we created in step 1) and then click on the **Deploy** button as shown in the following screenshot:

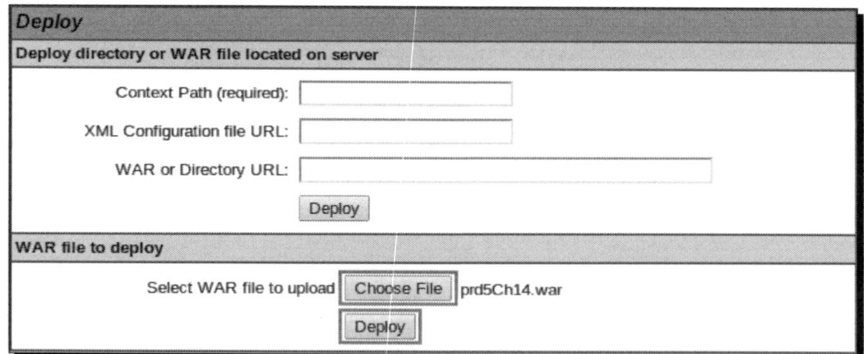

Once the deployment has finished, we will see that our application has now been added to the **Applications** section as shown in the following screenshot:

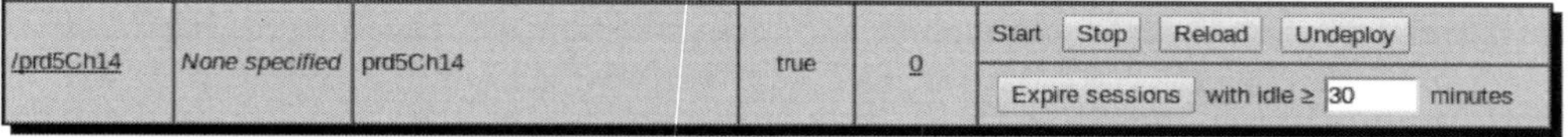

We are now ready to access our application through the following URL: `http://localhost:8080/prd5Ch14`.

What just happened?

We created the package `prd5Ch14.war` so that it contains our project and then closed Eclipse. We manually configured Apache Tomcat's `tomcat-users.xml` file and added the user `tomcat` with the necessary permissions to access the Manager App. We also configured the file `web.xml` to increase the maximum size of the applications that are deployed on Apache Tomcat; we set this value to 150 MB. After performing the said configurations, we initiated Apache Tomcat and used a web browser to access the URL `http://localhost:8080`; once there, we entered the Manager App and logged in using the user `tomcat`. We then headed to the **Deploy** section, selected the file `prd5Ch14.war`, and proceeded with the deployment of our application.

Have a go hero

Next, we will invite you to employ the knowledge you have acquired through this chapter to execute another PRD report in a standalone way.

The steps you should use are roughly the following:

1. Use Eclipse to create and configure a new dynamic web project.
2. Create and configure a Tomcat instance and all infrastructure components.
3. Add a report of your choice and modify it so that it connects through JNDI.
4. Create and configure code components (Listener and Servlet).
5. Package the project and deploy it on Apache Tomcat.

Pop quiz – graphics

Q1. Which of the following statements are true?

1. JEE is a programming language.
2. Servlets are software components executed on the client side.
3. JSPs are more oriented to UI.
4. Apache Tomcat is a multiplatform server written in Java.
5. Eclipse is an IDE.
6. We can extend Eclipse by adding new components through plugins.
7. In Eclipse, a Perspective is a combination of Views and Editors used for the modification of Java and HTML code.
8. Every time we wish to include a report within an Eclipse project, we need to set its connection type to JNDI.

Summary

We explained what Java Platform Enterprise Edition (JEE) is and its main components; among them, we discussed Servlets, JSP, EJB, and WS. We explained what Apache Tomcat is, and downloaded, configured, installed, and initiated it. We explained what Eclipse and WTP are. We downloaded Eclipse, configured its workspace, and installed and initiated it.

Within Eclipse, we created a new project of the type dynamic web and defined its runtime. In order to test our project, we created and configured an Apache Tomcat instance. We configured a JDBC/JNDI connection pool and copied MySQL's JDBC driver into our project. We also copied the required PRD libraries as well as the report `11_Adding_Charts.prpt`.

We created and configured a Listener for the initialization of PRD's API. To handle requests, processing, and routing, we created and configured a Servlet. We created a web client so that the user can interact with our application. Finally, we packaged our finished project.

Approaching the end of the chapter, we used Apache Tomcat to deploy our project so that it can be executed in a standalone way. As was done with the rest of the chapters, we proposed a practice exercise to strengthen the knowledge we obtained in this chapter.

Sakila DB Data Dictionary

In this section, we will show each table's data dictionary as well as a small sample of the data. We will divide the database model into three subdiagrams:

- Customer data
- Inventory
- Business

The Customer data database contains following tables.

The customer table

The `customer` table contains information about all customers described as follows:

Column	Description
`customer_id`	A primary key used to uniquely identify each customer in the table.
`store_id`	A foreign key identifying the customer's "home store". Customers are not limited to renting only from this store, but this is the store they generally shop at.
`first_name`	The customer's first name.
`last_name`	The customer's last name.
`email`	The customer's e-mail address.
`address_id`	A foreign key identifying the customer's address in the `address` table.
`active`	Indicates if the customer is an active customer. Setting this to `FALSE` serves as a logical deletion of the customer.
`create_date`	The date when the customer was added to the database.
`last_update`	The most recent row update. It has not been used in this book.

This information of all the customers is shown in a pictorial format in the following screenshot:

customer_id	store_id	first_name	last_name	email	address_id	active	create_date	last_update
1	1	MARY	SMITH	MARY.SMITH@sakilacustome	5	1	2006-02-14 22:04:36	2006-02-15 04:57:20
2	1	PATRICIA	JOHNSON	PATRICIA.JOHNSON@sakilac	6	1	2006-02-14 22:04:36	2006-02-15 04:57:20
3	1	LINDA	WILLIAMS	LINDA.WILLIAMS@sakilacust	7	1	2006-02-14 22:04:36	2006-02-15 04:57:20
4	2	BARBARA	JONES	BARBARA.JONES@sakilacust	8	1	2006-02-14 22:04:36	2006-02-15 04:57:20
5	1	ELIZABETH	BROWN	ELIZABETH.BROWN@sakilac	9	1	2006-02-14 22:04:36	2006-02-15 04:57:20
6	2	JENNIFER	DAVIS	JENNIFER.DAVIS@sakilacust	10	1	2006-02-14 22:04:36	2006-02-15 04:57:20
7	1	MARIA	MILLER	MARIA.MILLER@sakilacustor	11	1	2006-02-14 22:04:36	2006-02-15 04:57:20
8	2	SUSAN	WILSON	SUSAN.WILSON@sakilacusto	12	1	2006-02-14 22:04:36	2006-02-15 04:57:20
9	2	MARGARET	MOORE	MARGARET.MOORE@sakilac	13	1	2006-02-14 22:04:36	2006-02-15 04:57:20
10	1	DOROTHY	TAYLOR	DOROTHY.TAYLOR@sakilacu	14	1	2006-02-14 22:04:36	2006-02-15 04:57:20
11	2	LISA	ANDERSON	LISA.ANDERSON@sakilacust	15	1	2006-02-14 22:04:36	2006-02-15 04:57:20
12	1	NANCY	THOMAS	NANCY.THOMAS@sakilacust	16	1	2006-02-14 22:04:36	2006-02-15 04:57:20
13	2	KAREN	JACKSON	KAREN.JACKSON@sakilacust	17	1	2006-02-14 22:04:36	2006-02-15 04:57:20
14	2	BETTY	WHITE	BETTY.WHITE@sakilacustom	18	1	2006-02-14 22:04:36	2006-02-15 04:57:20
15	1	HELEN	HARRIS	HELEN.HARRIS@sakilacustor	19	1	2006-02-14 22:04:36	2006-02-15 04:57:20

The address table

The `address` table contains the address information of customers, staff, and stores described as follows:

Column	Description
`address_id`	A primary key used to uniquely identify each customer in the table.
`address`	A line of address information.
`address2`	Another line of address information that is used if the first line is not enough.
`district`	The region of an address; this may be a state, province, prefecture, and so on.
`city_id`	A foreign key identifying the city of the address in the city table.
`postal_code`	The postal code or zip code of the address.
`phone`	The phone number for the address.
`last_update`	The most recent row update. It has not been used in this book.

An example of the `address` table is shown in the following screenshot:

address_id	address	address2	district	city_id	postal_code	phone	last_update
1	47 MySakila Drive		Alberta	300			2006-02-15 04:45:30
2	28 MySQL Boulevard		QLD	576			2006-02-15 04:45:30
3	23 Workhaven Lane		Alberta	300		14033335568	2006-02-15 04:45:30
4	1411 Lillydale Drive		QLD	576		6172235589	2006-02-15 04:45:30
5	1913 Hanoi Way		Nagasaki	463	35200	28303384290	2006-02-15 04:45:30
6	1121 Loja Avenue		California	449	17886	838635286649	2006-02-15 04:45:30
7	692 Joliet Street		Attika	38	83579	448477190408	2006-02-15 04:45:30
8	1566 Inegl Manor		Mandalay	349	53561	705814003527	2006-02-15 04:45:30
9	53 Idfu Parkway		Nantou	361	42399	10655648674	2006-02-15 04:45:30
10	1795 Santiago de Com		Texas	295	18743	860452626434	2006-02-15 04:45:30
11	900 Santiago de Comp		Central Serbia	280	93896	716571220373	2006-02-15 04:45:30
12	478 Joliet Way		Hamilton	200	77948	657282285970	2006-02-15 04:45:30
13	613 Korolev Drive		Masqat	329	45844	380657522649	2006-02-15 04:45:30
14	1531 Sal Drive		Esfahan	162	53628	648856936185	2006-02-15 04:45:30
15	1542 Tarlac Parkway		Kanagawa	440	1027	635297277345	2006-02-15 04:45:30

The city table

The `city` table contains a list of cities described as follows:

Column	Description
`city_id`	A primary key used to uniquely identify each city in the table.
`city`	The name of the city.
`country_id`	A foreign key identifying the country the city belongs to in the `country` table.
`last_update`	The most recent row update. It has not been used in this book.

An example of the `city` table is shown in the following screenshot:

city_id	city	country_id	last_update
1	A Corua (La Corua)	87	2006-02-15 04:45:25
2	Abha	82	2006-02-15 04:45:25
3	Abu Dhabi	101	2006-02-15 04:45:25
4	Acua	60	2006-02-15 04:45:25
5	Adana	97	2006-02-15 04:45:25
6	Addis Abeba	31	2006-02-15 04:45:25
7	Aden	107	2006-02-15 04:45:25
8	Adoni	44	2006-02-15 04:45:25
9	Ahmadnagar	44	2006-02-15 04:45:25
10	Akishima	50	2006-02-15 04:45:25
11	Akron	103	2006-02-15 04:45:25
12	al-Ayn	101	2006-02-15 04:45:25
13	al-Hawiya	82	2006-02-15 04:45:25
14	al-Manama	11	2006-02-15 04:45:25
15	al-Qadarif	89	2006-02-15 04:45:25

The country table

The `country` table contains a list of countries described as follows:

Column	Description
`country_id`	A primary key used to uniquely identify each country in the table.
`country`	The name of the country.
`last_update`	The most recent row update. It has not been used in this book.

An example of the country table is shown in the following screenshot:

country_id	country	last_update
1	Afghanistan	2006-02-15 04:44:00
2	Algeria	2006-02-15 04:44:00
3	American Samoa	2006-02-15 04:44:00
4	Angola	2006-02-15 04:44:00
5	Anguilla	2006-02-15 04:44:00
6	Argentina	2006-02-15 04:44:00
7	Armenia	2006-02-15 04:44:00
8	Australia	2006-02-15 04:44:00
9	Austria	2006-02-15 04:44:00
10	Azerbaijan	2006-02-15 04:44:00
11	Bahrain	2006-02-15 04:44:00
12	Bangladesh	2006-02-15 04:44:00
13	Belarus	2006-02-15 04:44:00
14	Bolivia	2006-02-15 04:44:00
15	Brazil	2006-02-15 04:44:00

Inventory

The inventory database contains the following tables:

The film table

The film table contains a list of all films (logical information), not necessarily in stock. The stock information (physical copy) is in the table inventory described as follows:

Column	Description
film_id	A primary key used to uniquely identify each film in the table.
title	The title of the film.
description	A short description or plot summary of the film.
release_year	The year the film was released.
language_id	A foreign key pointing at the language table; it is used to identify the language of the film.
original_language_id	A foreign key pointing at the language table; it is used to identify the original language of the film. It is only used when a film has been dubbed into a new language.
rental_duration	The number of rental days.

Column	Description
`rental_rate`	The cost to rent the film for the period specified in the `rental_duration` column.
`length`	The length of the film in minutes.
`replacement_cost`	The amount due by a customer if the film has not been returned or if it is damaged.
`rating`	The rating assigned to the film. The possible values are G, PG, PG-13, R, or NC-17.
`special_features`	The lists in which common special features are included on the DVD. These features can be either `Trailers`, `Commentaries`, `Deleted Scenes`, `Behind the Scenes`, or nothing at all.
`last_update`	The most recent row update. It has not been used in this book.

An example of the `film` table is shown in the following screenshot:

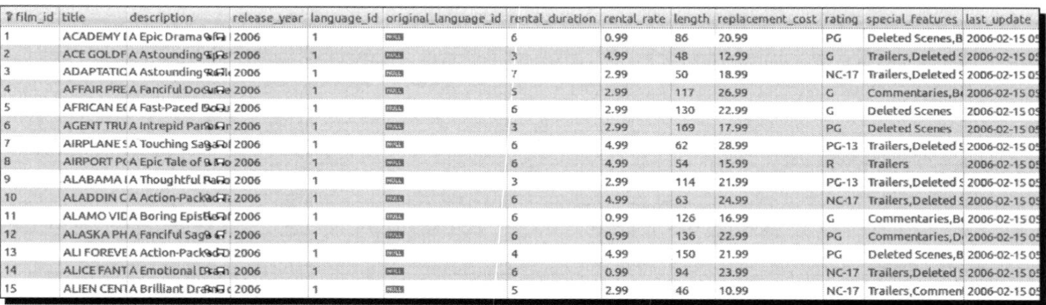

film_id	title	description	release_year	language_id	original_language_id	rental_duration	rental_rate	length	replacement_cost	rating	special_features	last_update
1	ACADEMY I	A Epic Drama of	2006	1	NULL	6	0.99	86	20.99	PG	Deleted Scenes,B	2006-02-15 05
2	ACE GOLDF	A Astounding	2006	1	NULL	3	4.99	48	12.99	G	Trailers,Deleted S	2006-02-15 05
3	ADAPTATIC	A Astounding	2006	1	NULL	7	2.99	50	18.99	NC-17	Trailers,Deleted S	2006-02-15 05
4	AFFAIR PRE	A Fanciful Doc	2006	1	NULL	5	2.99	117	26.99	G	Commentaries,Be	2006-02-15 05
5	AFRICAN EC	A Fast-Paced Do	2006	1	NULL	6	2.99	130	22.99	G	Deleted Scenes	2006-02-15 05
6	AGENT TRU	A Intrepid Pan	2006	1	NULL	3	2.99	169	17.99	PG	Deleted Scenes	2006-02-15 05
7	AIRPLANE S	A Touching Saga	2006	1	NULL	6	4.99	62	28.99	PG-13	Trailers,Deleted S	2006-02-15 05
8	AIRPORT PC	A Epic Tale of	2006	1	NULL	6	4.99	54	15.99	R	Trailers	2006-02-15 05
9	ALABAMA I	A Thoughtful Pa	2006	1	NULL	3	2.99	114	21.99	PG-13	Trailers,Deleted S	2006-02-15 05
10	ALADDIN C	A Action-Pack	2006	1	NULL	6	4.99	63	24.99	NC-17	Trailers,Deleted S	2006-02-15 05
11	ALAMO VIE	A Boring Epis	2006	1	NULL	6	0.99	126	16.99	G	Commentaries,Be	2006-02-15 05
12	ALASKA PH	A Fanciful Saga	2006	1	NULL	6	0.99	136	22.99	PG	Commentaries,D	2006-02-15 05
13	ALI FOREVE	A Action-Pack	2006	1	NULL	4	4.99	150	21.99	PG	Deleted Scenes,B	2006-02-15 05
14	ALICE FANT	A Emotional D	2006	1	NULL	6	0.99	94	23.99	NC-17	Trailers,Deleted S	2006-02-15 05
15	ALIEN CENT	A Brilliant Dra	2006	1	NULL	5	2.99	46	10.99	NC-17	Trailers,Commen	2006-02-15 05

The category table

The `category` table contains a list of all the categories that can be assigned to a film. More than one category can be assigned to a film. A many-to-many relationship is performed by the `film_category` table. The columns and values of the `category` table are as follows:

Column	Description
`category_id`	A primary key used to uniquely identify each category in the table.
`category`	The name of the category.
`last_update`	The most recent row update. It has not been used in this book.

The following screenshot shows the `category` table:

category_id	name	last_update
1	Action	2006-02-15 04:46:27
2	Animation	2006-02-15 04:46:27
3	Children	2006-02-15 04:46:27
4	Classics	2006-02-15 04:46:27
5	Comedy	2006-02-15 04:46:27
6	Documentary	2006-02-15 04:46:27
7	Drama	2006-02-15 04:46:27
8	Family	2006-02-15 04:46:27
9	Foreign	2006-02-15 04:46:27
10	Games	2006-02-15 04:46:27
11	Horror	2006-02-15 04:46:27
12	Music	2006-02-15 04:46:27
13	New	2006-02-15 04:46:27
14	Sci-Fi	2006-02-15 04:46:27
15	Sports	2006-02-15 04:46:27

The film_category table

The `film_category` table described as follows is used to support a many-to-many relationship between films and categories:

Column	Description
`film_id`	A foreign key identifying the film.
`category_id`	A foreign key identifying the category.
`last_update`	The most recent row update. It has not been used in this book.

The following screenshot shows the `film_category` table:

film_id	category_id	last_update
1	6	2006-02-15 05:07:09
2	11	2006-02-15 05:07:09
3	6	2006-02-15 05:07:09
4	11	2006-02-15 05:07:09
5	8	2006-02-15 05:07:09
6	9	2006-02-15 05:07:09
7	5	2006-02-15 05:07:09
8	11	2006-02-15 05:07:09
9	11	2006-02-15 05:07:09
10	15	2006-02-15 05:07:09
11	9	2006-02-15 05:07:09
12	12	2006-02-15 05:07:09
13	11	2006-02-15 05:07:09
14	4	2006-02-15 05:07:09
15	9	2006-02-15 05:07:09

The language table

The `language` table contains columns that may be used to identify the language ID and the original language of the film, described as follows:

Column	Description
`language_id`	A primary key used to uniquely identify each language in the table.
`language`	The English name of the language.
`last_update`	The most recent row update. It has not been used in this book.

The following screenshot shows the `language` table:

language_id	name	last_update
1	English	2006-02-15 05:02:19
2	Italian	2006-02-15 05:02:19
3	Japanese	2006-02-15 05:02:19
4	Mandarin	2006-02-15 05:02:19
5	French	2006-02-15 05:02:19
6	German	2006-02-15 05:02:19

The actor table

The actor table contains information about all the actors in the films. More than one actor can be assigned to a film. A many-to-many relationship is performed by the film_actor table described as follows:

Column	Description
actor_id	A primary key used to uniquely identify each actor in the table.
first_name	The actor's first name.
last_name	The actor's last name.
last_update	The most recent row update. It has not been used in this book.

The following screenshot shows the actor table:

actor_id	first_name	last_name	last_update
1	PENELOPE	GUINESS	2006-02-15 04:34:33
2	NICK	WAHLBERG	2006-02-15 04:34:33
3	ED	CHASE	2006-02-15 04:34:33
4	JENNIFER	DAVIS	2006-02-15 04:34:33
5	JOHNNY	LOLLOBRIGIDA	2006-02-15 04:34:33
6	BETTE	NICHOLSON	2006-02-15 04:34:33
7	GRACE	MOSTEL	2006-02-15 04:34:33
8	MATTHEW	JOHANSSON	2006-02-15 04:34:33
9	JOE	SWANK	2006-02-15 04:34:33
10	CHRISTIAN	GABLE	2006-02-15 04:34:33
11	ZERO	CAGE	2006-02-15 04:34:33
12	KARL	BERRY	2006-02-15 04:34:33
13	UMA	WOOD	2006-02-15 04:34:33
14	VIVIEN	BERGEN	2006-02-15 04:34:33
15	CUBA	OLIVIER	2006-02-15 04:34:33

The film_actor table

The film_actor table is used to support a many-to-many relationship between films and actors described as follows:

Column	Description
film_id	A foreign key identifying the film.
actor_id	A foreign key identifying the actor.
last_update	The most recent row update. It has not been used in this book.

The following screenshot shows the `film_actor` table:

actor_id	film_id	last_update
1	1	2006-02-15 05:05:03
1	23	2006-02-15 05:05:03
1	25	2006-02-15 05:05:03
1	106	2006-02-15 05:05:03
1	140	2006-02-15 05:05:03
1	166	2006-02-15 05:05:03
1	277	2006-02-15 05:05:03
1	361	2006-02-15 05:05:03
1	438	2006-02-15 05:05:03
1	499	2006-02-15 05:05:03
1	506	2006-02-15 05:05:03
1	509	2006-02-15 05:05:03
1	605	2006-02-15 05:05:03
1	635	2006-02-15 05:05:03
1	749	2006-02-15 05:05:03

The inventory table

Each row in the `inventory` table represents a physical copy of a film in a store, described as follows:

Column	Description
`inventory_id`	A primary key used to uniquely identify each item in the table.
`film_id`	A foreign key identifying the film.
`store_id`	A foreign key identifying the store that the physical copy of a film is in.
`last_update`	The most recent row update. It has not been used in this book.

The following screenshot shows the `inventory` table:

inventory_id	film_id	store_id	last_update
1	1	1	2006-02-15 05:09:17
2	1	1	2006-02-15 05:09:17
3	1	1	2006-02-15 05:09:17
4	1	1	2006-02-15 05:09:17
5	1	2	2006-02-15 05:09:17
6	1	2	2006-02-15 05:09:17
7	1	2	2006-02-15 05:09:17
8	1	2	2006-02-15 05:09:17
9	2	2	2006-02-15 05:09:17
10	2	2	2006-02-15 05:09:17
11	2	2	2006-02-15 05:09:17
12	3	2	2006-02-15 05:09:17
13	3	2	2006-02-15 05:09:17
14	3	2	2006-02-15 05:09:17
15	3	2	2006-02-15 05:09:17

The film_text table

The `film_text` table provides a detailed description of the films. This table is a summary of the `film` table. It is read only, as described:

Column	Description
`film_id`	A primary key used to uniquely identify each film summary in the table.
`title`	The title of the film.
`description`	A short description or plot summary of the film.

The following screenshot shows the `film_text` table:

film_id	title	description
1	ACADEMY DINOSAUR	A Epic Drama of a Feminist And a Mad Scientist who m
2	ACE GOLDFINGER	A Astounding Epistle of a Database Administrator And
3	ADAPTATION HOLES	A Astounding Reflection of a Lumberjack And a Car wh
4	AFFAIR PREJUDICE	A Fanciful Documentary of a Frisbee And a Lumberjack
5	AFRICAN EGG	A Fast-Paced Documentary of a Pastry Chef And a Dent
6	AGENT TRUMAN	A Intrepid Panorama of a Robot And a Boy who must E
7	AIRPLANE SIERRA	A Touching Saga of a Hunter And a Butler who must Dis
8	AIRPORT POLLOCK	A Epic Tale of a Moose And a Girl who must Confront a
9	ALABAMA DEVIL	A Thoughtful Panorama of a Database Administrator A
10	ALADDIN CALENDAR	A Action-Packed Tale of a Man And a Lumberjack who r
11	ALAMO VIDEOTAPE	A Boring Epistle of a Butler And a Cat who must Fight a
12	ALASKA PHANTOM	A Fanciful Saga of a Hunter And a Pastry Chef who mus
13	ALI FOREVER	A Action-Packed Drama of a Dentist And a Crocodile w
14	ALICE FANTASIA	A Emotional Drama of a A Shark And a Database Admi
15	ALIEN CENTER	A Brilliant Drama of a Cat And a Mad Scientist who mu

Business

The `business` database contains the following tables:

The staff table

The `staff` table contains information about all staff members described as follows:

Column	Description
`staff_id`	A primary key used to uniquely identify each staff member in the table.
`first_name`	The staff member's first name.
`last_name`	The staff member's last name.
`address_id`	A foreign key identifying the address of the staff member in the address table.
`picture`	A photograph of the employee.
`email`	The staff member's e-mail address.
`store_id`	The staff member's "home store". The employee can work at other stores but is generally assigned to the store that is listed.

Column	Description
`active`	Indicates whether the staff member is an active staff member. Setting this to `FALSE` serves as a logical deletion of the staff member.
`username`	The username used by the staff member to access the rental system.
`password`	The password used by the staff member to access the rental system.
`last_update`	The most recent row update. It has not been used in this book.

The following screenshot shows the `table_staff` table:

staff_id	first_name	last_name	address_id	picture	email	store_id	active	username	password
1	Mike	Hillyer	3	BLOB	Mike.Hillyer@sakil	1	1	Mike	8cb2237d0
2	Jon	Stephens	4	NULL	Jon.Stephens@sak	2	1	Jon	8cb2237d0

The store table

The `store` table contains information about all the stores described as follows:

Column	Description
`store_id`	A primary key used to uniquely identify each store in the table.
`manager_staff_id`	A foreign key identifying the manager of this store in the staff table.
`address_id`	A foreign key identifying the address of the store in the address table.
`last_update`	The most recent row update. It has not been used in this book.

The following screenshot shows the `store` table:

store_id	manager_staff_id	address_id	last_update
1	1	1	2006-02-15 04:57:12
2	2	2	2006-02-15 04:57:12

The rental table

The `rental` table contains information about each rental of each inventory item described as follows:

Column	Description
`rental_id`	A primary key used to uniquely identify each item in the table.
`rental_date`	The date and time at which the item was rented.
`inventory_id`	A foreign key identifying the physical film being rented in the inventory table.
`customer_id`	The customer who rents the film.
`return_date`	The date and time at which the film was returned.
`staff_id`	The staff member who processed the rental.
`last_update`	The most recent row update. It has not been used in this book.

The following screenshot shows the `rental` table:

rental_id	rental_date	inventory_id	customer_id	return_date	staff_id	last_update
1	2005-05-24 2	367	130	2005-05-26 2	1	2006-02-15 2
2	2005-05-24 2	1525	459	2005-05-28 1	1	2006-02-15 2
3	2005-05-24 2	1711	408	2005-06-01 2	1	2006-02-15 2
4	2005-05-24 2	2452	333	2005-06-03 0	2	2006-02-15 2
5	2005-05-24 2	2079	222	2005-06-02 0	1	2006-02-15 2
6	2005-05-24 2	2792	549	2005-05-27 0	1	2006-02-15 2
7	2005-05-24 2	3995	269	2005-05-29 2	2	2006-02-15 2
8	2005-05-24 2	2346	239	2005-05-27 2	2	2006-02-15 2
9	2005-05-25 0	2580	126	2005-05-28 0	1	2006-02-15 2
10	2005-05-25 0	1824	399	2005-05-31 2	2	2006-02-15 2
11	2005-05-25 0	4443	142	2005-06-02 2	2	2006-02-15 2
12	2005-05-25 0	1584	261	2005-05-30 0	2	2006-02-15 2
13	2005-05-25 0	2294	334	2005-05-30 0	1	2006-02-15 2
14	2005-05-25 0	2701	446	2005-05-26 0	1	2006-02-15 2
15	2005-05-25 0	3049	319	2005-06-03 0	1	2006-02-15 2

The payment table

The `payment` table contains information about each payment made by a customer, with information such as the amount and the rental being paid for (when applicable), described as follows:

Column	Description
`payment_id`	A primary key used to uniquely identify each payment in the table.
`customer_id`	A foreign key that identifies the customer making the payment in the `customer` table.
`staff_id`	A foreign key that identifies the staff member who processed the payment in the `staff` table.
`rental_id`	The rental that the payment is being applied to. This is optional because some payments are for outstanding fees and may not be directly related to a rental.
`amount`	The amount of the payment.
`payment_date`	The date on which the payment was processed.
`last_update`	The most recent row update. It has not been used in this book.

The following screenshot shows the `payment` table:

payment_id	customer_id	staff_id	rental_id	amount	payment_date	last_update
1	1	1	76	2.99	2005-05-25 11:3	2006-02-15 22:
2	1	1	573	0.99	2005-05-28 10:3	2006-02-15 22:
3	1	1	1185	5.99	2005-06-15 00:5	2006-02-15 22:
4	1	2	1422	0.99	2005-06-15 18:0	2006-02-15 22:
5	1	2	1476	9.99	2005-06-15 21:0	2006-02-15 22:
6	1	1	1725	4.99	2005-06-16 15:1	2006-02-15 22:
7	1	1	2308	4.99	2005-06-18 08:4	2006-02-15 22:
8	1	2	2363	0.99	2005-06-18 13:3	2006-02-15 22:
9	1	1	3284	3.99	2005-06-21 06:2	2006-02-15 22:
10	1	2	4526	5.99	2005-07-08 03:1	2006-02-15 22:
11	1	1	4611	5.99	2005-07-08 07:3	2006-02-15 22:
12	1	1	5244	4.99	2005-07-09 13:2	2006-02-15 22:
13	1	1	5326	4.99	2005-07-09 16:3	2006-02-15 22:
14	1	1	6163	7.99	2005-07-11 10:1	2006-02-15 22:
15	1	2	7273	2.99	2005-07-27 11:3	2006-02-15 22:

Pop Quiz Answers

Chapter 2, Installation and Configuration

Pop quiz – system requirements, JDBC driver, Sakila DB, and RAM

Q1	1. False 2. False 3. True 4. False 5. True

Chapter 3, Start PRD and the User Interface (UI) Layout

Pop quiz – layout of PRD

Q1	1. True 2. False 3. True 4. False 5. True 6. False 7. True 8. False

Chapter 4, Instant Gratification – creating your first report with PRD

Pop quiz – data sets, functions, and objects

Q1	1. False 2. True 3. False 4. False 5. True 6. False

Chapter 5, Adding a Relational Data Source

Pop quiz – JDBC, functions y encoding charset

Q1	1. False 2. False 3. False 4. False 5. True

Chapter 6, Adding Groups

Pop quiz – positioning hierarchy and gGroups

Q1	1. False 2. False 3. True 4. False

Chapter 7, Adding Parameters

Pop quiz – format y Parameters

Q1	1. True 2. True 3. False 4. False 5. False 6. True 7. False

Chapter 8, Using Formulas in Our Reports

Pop quiz – formulas

Q1	1. True 2. False 3. True 4. True 5. False 6. False

Chapter 9, Adding Charts

Pop quiz – charts

Q1	1. True 2. False 3. False 4. False 5. True 6. True 7. False

Chapter 10, Adding Subreports

Pop quiz – Subreports

Q1	1. False 2. True 3. False 4. True 5. False 6. False

Chapter 11, Publish and Run Reports in Pentaho BA Server

Pop quiz – Pentaho

Q1	1. False 2. True 3. True 4. True 5. False 6. True 7. False 8. True

Chapter 12, Making a Difference – Reports with Hyperlinks and Sparklines

Pop quiz – Hyperlinks and sparklines

Q1	1. False 2. True 3. False 4. False 5. True 6. False

Chapter 13, Environment, Stylesheets, and Crosstabs

Pop quiz – environment, stylesheets, and crosstabs

Q1	1. True 2. False 3. True 4. True 5. False 6. False

Chapter 14, PRD Reports Embedded in Web Applications

Pop quiz – graphics

Q1	1. False 2. False 3. True 4. True 5. True 6. True 7. False 8. False

Index

A

B

G

H

I

R

S

T

U

V

W

X

Thank you for buying
Pentaho 5.0 Reporting By Example Beginner's Guide

About Packt Publishing

Packt, pronounced 'packed', published its first book "*Mastering phpMyAdmin for Effective MySQL Management*" in April 2004 and subsequently continued to specialize in publishing highly focused books on specific technologies and solutions.

Our books and publications share the experiences of your fellow IT professionals in adapting and customizing today's systems, applications, and frameworks. Our solution based books give you the knowledge and power to customize the software and technologies you're using to get the job done. Packt books are more specific and less general than the IT books you have seen in the past. Our unique business model allows us to bring you more focused information, giving you more of what you need to know, and less of what you don't.

Packt is a modern, yet unique publishing company, which focuses on producing quality, cutting-edge books for communities of developers, administrators, and newbies alike. For more information, please visit our website: `www.packtpub.com`.

About Packt Open Source

In 2010, Packt launched two new brands, Packt Open Source and Packt Enterprise, in order to continue its focus on specialization. This book is part of the Packt Open Source brand, home to books published on software built around Open Source licences, and offering information to anybody from advanced developers to budding web designers. The Open Source brand also runs Packt's Open Source Royalty Scheme, by which Packt gives a royalty to each Open Source project about whose software a book is sold.

Writing for Packt

We welcome all inquiries from people who are interested in authoring. Book proposals should be sent to `author@packtpub.com`. If your book idea is still at an early stage and you would like to discuss it first before writing a formal book proposal, contact us; one of our commissioning editors will get in touch with you.

We're not just looking for published authors; if you have strong technical skills but no writing experience, our experienced editors can help you develop a writing career, or simply get some additional reward for your expertise.

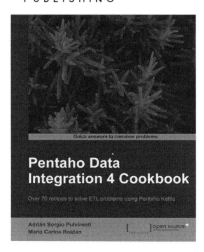

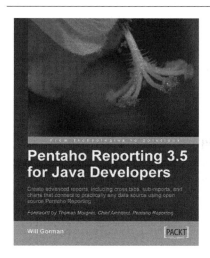

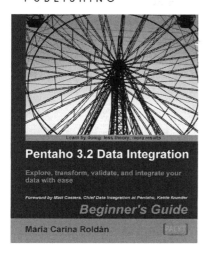

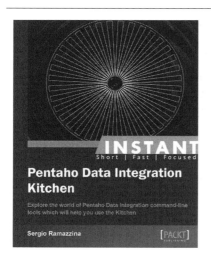

10197004R00193

Made in the USA
San Bernardino, CA
07 April 2014